TEXTBOOK OF PARASITOLOGY

TEXTBOOK OF PARASITOLOGY

By
Ashok Kumar
Dept. of Zoology
Bundelkhand University
Campus Department
Jhansi (India)

D P H

DISCOVERY PUBLISHING HOUSE PVT. LTD.
NEW DELHI-110 002

Published by:
Namit Wasan
DISCOVERY PUBLISHING HOUSE PVT. LTD.
4383/4B, Ansari Road, Darya Ganj
New Delhi-110 002 (India)
Phone : +91-11-23279245; 23253475; 43596065
E-mail : discoverybooksindia@gmail.com
discoverypublishinghouse@gmail.com
namitwasan9@gmail.com
web : www.discoverypublishinggroup.com

First Edition: **2010**

ISBN: 978-81-8356-555-4

Textbook of Parasitology

Printed at:
Infinity Imaging Systems
Delhi

Preface

Infections of humans caused by parasites number in the billions and range from relatively innocuous to fatal. The diseases caused by these parasites constitute major human health problems throughout the world. (For example, approximately 30 percent of the world's population is infected with the nematode Ascaris lumbricoides.) The incidence of many parasitic diseases (e.g., schistosomiasis, malaria) have increased rather than decreased in recent years. Other parasitic illnesses have increased in importance as a result of the AIDS epidemic (e.g., cryptosporidiosis, Pneumocystis carinii pneumonia, and strongyloidiasis). The migration of parasite-infected people, including refugees, from areas with high prevalence rates of parasitic infection also has added to the health problems of certain countries.

A misconception about parasitic infections is that they occur only in tropical areas. Although most parasitic infections are more prevalent in the tropics, many people in temperate and subtropical areas also become infected, and visitors to tropical countries may return with a parasite infection.

The unicellular parasites (protozoa) and multicellular parasites (helminths, arthropods) are antigenically and biochemically complex, as are their life histories and the pathogenesis of the diseases they cause. During their life, parasitic organisms typically go through several developmental stages that involve changes not only in structure but also in biochemical and antigenic composition. Some helminth larval stages have little resemblance to the adult stages (for example, those of tapeworms and flukes). Some parasitic protozoa also change greatly during their life history; for example, Toxoplasma gondii is an intestinal coccidian in cats but in humans takes on a different form and localizes in deep tissues. Some of these infections can convert from a well-tolerated or asymptomatic condition to life-threatening disease. Many parasitic infections are transmitted from animals to humans (zoonotic infections); the human disease may or may not resemble the disease caused in the lower animal host.

—Author

Contents

Preface

1. Introduction **1**

2. Parasitism **7**

Introduction
Types of Parasitism
Parasitoid
Types of Parasitoids
Parasitic Fungi
Parasitic Plants
Types of Parasitic Plants
Parasitic Protists

3. Parasitic Worm **30**

Introuction
Flatworm
Nematode
Nematode Systematics
Parasitic Species
Leech
Acanthocephala
Cestoda
Digenea

4. Parasitic Protozoa **64**

Introduction
Trypanosoma (T. Cruzi, T. Gambiense)
Leishmaniasis

Giardia
Balantidaisis
Cryptosporidium Parvum
Malaria

5. **Antimicrobial Chemotherapy** 73
Introduction
Biochemical Basis of Antimicrobial Action
Inhibition of Bacterial Cell Wall Synthesis
Bacterial Cytoplasmic Membranes
Resistance Due to Altered Receptors
Combinations of Antimicrobial Agents

6. **Free-living Amoebae** 97
Introduction
Free-living Amoebae, Acanthamoeba Sp.
Free-living Amoebae, Rhizopoda

7. **Protection from Malaria** 102
Introduction
Pathophysiology and Lifecycle of the Malarial Parasite
Anchoring of Infected Rbc's to the Vascular Endothelial Cells
Complications in Malarial Infections
Challenges in Formulating An Effective Malarial Vaccine
Parasitic Complexity

8. **Microbiology of the Genitourinary System** 130
Introduction
Infections
Pathogenesis
Clinical Presentation
Microbiologic Diagnosis

9. **Vector (Organisms)** 147
Introduction
Mosquito
Feeding Habits
Mosquitoes and Health

Flea
Tick
Triatominae

10. Tissue Nematodes **172**
Introduction
Tissue Nematodes, Trichinella Spiralis, Differential Diagnosis
Tissue Nematodes, Trichinella Spiralis, Therapy
Tissue Nematodes, Trichinella Spiralis, Prevention

11. Diffrerent Parasites **176**
Introduction
Mutualism
Life Cycles and Transmission of Parasites
Classifying Parasites
Major Classes of Parasites
Arachnid
Acarina

12. Parasitosis in Children **198**
Introduction
Study Groups and Methods
Results
Ascaris Lumbricoides

13. Parasitoid Wasp **210**
Introduction
Taxonomy and Systematics
Systematics
Arthropod
Molting

14. Human Intestinal Parasites Worms **222**
Introduction
Parasites, Some Different Varieties
Parasite Signs, Adults, Children
Prevent, Eliminate Parasites

Index *235*

1

Introduction

Parasitology traditionally has included the study of three major groups of animals: parasitic protozoa, parasitic helminths (worms), and those arthropods that directly cause disease or act as vectors of various pathogens. A parasite is a pathogen that simultaneously injures and derives sustenance from its host. Some organisms called parasites are actually commensals, in that they neither benefit nor harm their host (for example, *Entamoeba coli*). Although parasitology had its origins in the zoologic sciences, it is today an interdisciplinary field, greatly influenced by microbiology, immunology, biochemistry, and other life sciences.

Infections of humans caused by parasites number in the billions and range from relatively innocuous to fatal. The diseases caused by these parasites constitute major human health problems throughout the world. (For example, approximately 30 percent of the world's population is infected with the nematode *Ascaris lumbricoides*.) The incidence of many parasitic diseases (e.g., schistosomiasis, malaria) have increased rather than decreased in recent years. Other parasitic illnesses have increased in importance as a result of the AIDS epidemic (e.g., cryptosporidiosis, *Pneumocystis carinii* pneumonia, and strongyloidiasis). The migration of parasite-infected people, including refugees, from areas with high prevalence rates of parasitic infection also has added to the health problems of certain countries.

A misconception about parasitic infections is that they occur only in tropical areas. Although most parasitic infections are more prevalent in the tropics, many people in temperate and subtropical areas also become infected, and visitors to tropical countries may return with a parasite infection.

The unicellular parasites (protozoa) and multicellular parasites (helminths, arthropods) are antigenically and biochemically complex, as are their life histories and the pathogenesis of the diseases they cause. During their life, parasitic organisms typically go through several developmental stages that involve changes not only in structure but also in biochemical and antigenic composition. Some helminth larval stages have little resemblance to the adult stages (for example, those of tapeworms and flukes). Some parasitic protozoa also change greatly during their life history; for example, *Toxoplasma gondii* is an intestinal coccidian in cats but in humans takes on a different form and localizes in deep tissues. Some of these infections can convert from a well-tolerated or asymptomatic condition to life-threatening disease. Many parasitic infections are transmitted from animals to humans (zoonotic infections); the human disease may or may not resemble the disease caused in the lower animal host.

Thus, descriptions of the basic properties of the pathogens, the pathogenesis of the diseases they cause, host defenses, and epidemiology are highlighted. Practical information on clinical manifestations, diagnosis, and control has been included in the chapters on specific pathogens. Most chapters treat a group of related pathogens (for example, trematodes, cestodes).

This section gives the reader a broad, in-depth coverage of medically important parasites. Such coverage is essential to give students the awareness and understanding necessary for proper diagnosis, treatment, and prevention of the parasitic infections. The most important element in diagnosing a parasitic infection is often the physician's suspicion that a parasite may be involveda possibility that is too often overlooked. This kind of awareness requires a knowledge of the biology of the parasites. Diagnosis of parasitic infections requires laboratory support, since the signs and symptoms are often nonspecific. A variety of methods and specimens are used for diagnosis. Since the most common parasites are enteric, microscopic examination of fecal specimens is done more often than any other laboratory procedure in the diagnosis of parasitic disease. Culturing has little application in the diagnosis of most parasitic infections, although it has been employed, for example, for *Trichomonas vaginalis* and *Entamoeba histolytica* infections. Immunodiagnostic tests are useful in several infections, including extraintestinal amebiasis, visceral larva migrans, and trichinosis.

Because the laboratory is so important in diagnosis, its personnel must be well-trained. Continuing training and refresher courses should be encouraged and supported. In the United States, excellent short courses in diagnostic parasitology are available in various state and federal health laboratories and at the Centers for Disease Control (CDC) in Atlanta. These laboratories also offer a variety of diagnostic services in parasitology, including specialized serologic tests. Medical scientists in the United States should be aware of the Parasitic Disease Drug Service at CDC, from which they may obtain drug information and certain drugs not readily available. Announcements of regional workshops and continuing education programmes in parasitology can be found in various journals, for example the *American Society for Microbiology News*.

Parasitism is the most expensive disease in the sheep industry if one considers the cost of deworming and the decreased performance that is caused by parasites. Due to variation in climatic conditions, location, and sheep density, no single recommendation can be made that will be effective in flocks across the country. However, there are a few things to keep in mind when developing an internal parasite control programme.

Internal parasites can be considered in three broad groups: roundworms, tapeworms and flukes. Roundworms attach to the intestinal surface and suck blood or serum from the animal. The most serious of these parasites is Haemonchus contortus. These worms will drain enough blood that the sheep will become anemic, very unthrifty and may die from blood loss. Other parasites in this group are Ostertagia, Nematodirus and lungworms. Haemonchus is the most efficient at developing resistance to dewormers. Generally if the deworming programme can control Haemochus the other roundworm will be controlled as well. Young growing lambs are particularly susceptible to roundworms and should be dewormed when they are 3 to 4 months old Tapeworms do not do as much damage to sheep as roundworms. The greatest concern is that if large numbers of worms are present they can physically block the intestinal tractnd cause death Flukes invade and migrate through the liver. Sheep are very sensitive to flukes and even one fluke can cause enough damage to kill a sheep. The life cycle of flukes requires a snail intermediate host. Therefore fluke problems are found in areas of standing water. One species of fluke, Fasciola magna can also infect deer and is a serious problem in northern Minnesota and Wisconsin.

In developing a deworming programme always keep in mind the two populations of parasites: one population of adult wormers in the animal and one population of immature larvae on the pasture. If you deworm sheep and turn them out in an infected pasture they will be reinfected with worms in 30 days. Plan your deworming to coincide with pasture rotation. Nearly all infective larvae are killed by freezing temperature so late fall is an excellent time to deworm your ewes as you can keep them clean all winter. During the grazing period pasture rotation combined with deworming will give you the most comprehensive parasite control programme possible. A pasture should be empty as long as possible before sheep are reintroduced. Usually this results in rotation every 4-6 weeks. During this 4-6 weeks most of the infective larvae (immature forms of parasitic worms) will die and the pasture will be relatively clean when you turn dewormed sheep back in.

The best time for fall deworming is after the first killing frost. Deworming at this time will allow parasite free ewes until lambing. If a white wormer, such as Valbazen or Panacur is used in the summer, then Levasol (Tramisol) or lvomec are excellent choices for fall deworming. Remember to refrain from using Valbazen on early pregnant ewes as it has been shown to cause fetal defects in the first trimester of pregnancy.

Levasole and Tramisol contain the same drug and concentration of drug, they can be considered as equivalent. Valbazen is effective against flukes at 6ml/100# orally. Valbazen should not be used in pregnant ewes as the active ingredient, Albenazole, can cause developmental defects in the fetus. Cattle pour on formulations of avermectins have not been shown to be effective in sheep. Another management tool is to conduct occasional exams on random fecal samples to determine the level of parasitism in your flock. This can be done by any large animal veterinarian for a small fee. This will give you a rough idea of the amount of parasites in the sheep and indirectly the number of larvae in the pasture. Be sure the fecal samples are fresh when delivered to your veterinarian. Internal parasites can be cost-effectively controlled by the use of pasture rotation, freezing temperatures, strategic deworming and periodic fecal analysis by your veterinarian. Parasitic worms that infect sheep are species specific. They only affect ruminants and cannot be passed to humans or other monogastric animals. External parasite problems are far more infrequent than internal parasite problems, however they are responsible for sporadic wool loss and itching sheep. Mites, lice and keds are all seen occasionally as flock problems. We occasionally will see heel mites on the feet and legs of sheep. The mites are microscopic so they can not be visualized with the naked eye, but what can be seen is a scaly lesion on the lower leg that appears to irritate the sheep. We have seen the best response with dipping the feet in Taktic solution. Lice can be a serious problem in flocks in the winter months. Often the first sign is wool tags on gates, fences, and feeders. Often the shepherd notices sheep that are constantly itching and wool loss. The most cost effective method of controlling lice is to pour the sheep with Delice R pour on twice 14 days apart. Sheep keds, Melophagus ovinus, are often referred to as sheep tics. Actually this is incorrect as they are not ticks but are rather a wingless fly. These are easily seen with the naked eye but are often not noticed until shearing. Small or even moderate ked infestations are generally not noticeable as they only cause mild irritation to the skin. Because they are easily seen heavy infestation can be avoided by treating the entire flock when they are found. Again Delice R pour on is the most cost effective product on the market. While external parasite are far less common than internal parasites as a cause of sickness or death in sheep on an individual flock basis they can have an impact. Shepherds should be on the lookout for clinical signs of external parasitism, especially in winter when they are most evident and when we can prevent the infestation in the next lamb crop.

2

Parasitism

INTRODUCTION

Parasitism is a type of symbiotic relationship between two different organisms. The parasite benefits from a prolonged, close association with the host, which is harmed. In general, parasites are much smaller than their hosts, show a high degree of specialization for their mode of life and reproduce more quickly and in greater numbers than their hosts. Classic examples of parasitism include the interactions between vertebrate hosts and such diverse animals as the tapeworms, flukes, *Plasmodium* species and scabs.

The harm and benefit in parasitic interactions concern the biological fitness of the organisms involved. Parasites reduce host fitness in many ways, ranging from general or specialized pathology (such as castration), impairment of secondary sex characteristics, to the modification of host behaviour. Parasites increase their fitness by exploiting hosts for food, habitat and dispersal.

Although the concept of parasitism applies unambiguously to many cases in nature, it is best considered part of a continuum of types of interactions between species, rather than an exclusive category. Particular interactions between species may satisfy some but not all parts of the definition. In many cases, it is difficult to demonstrate that the host is harmed. In others, there may be no apparent specialization on the part of the parasite, or the interaction between the organisms may be short-lived. In medicine, only eukaryotic organisms are considered parasites, to the exclusion of bacteria and viruses. Some branches of biology, however, do regard members of these groups to be parasitic.

TYPES OF PARASITISM

Parasites are classified based on a variety of aspects of their interactions with their hosts and on their life cycles.

Those that live inside the host are called endoparasites (e.g., hookworms) and those that live on its surface are called ectoparasites (e.g., some mites).

An epiparasite is one that feeds on another parasite. This relationship is also sometimes referred to as "hyperparasitism".

Parasitoids are organisms whose larval development occurs within another organism's body, resulting in the death of the host. Thus, the interaction between the parasitoid and the host is fundamentally different than true parasites and their host, and shares some characteristics with predation. Social parasites take advantage of interactions between members of social organisms such as ants or termites. In kleptoparasitism, parasites appropriate food gathered by the host. An example is the brood parasitism practiced by many species of cuckoo. Many cuckoos use other bird species as "babysitters", depositing their eggs in the nest of the host species, which raise the cuckoo young as one of their own.

Parasitism can take the form of isolated cheating or exploitation among more generalized mutualistic interactions. For example, broad classes of plants and fungi exchange carbon and nutrients in common mutualistic mycorrhizal relationships; however, a few plants species (known as myco-heterotrophs) "cheat" by taking carbon from a fungus rather than donating it.

EVOLUTIONARY ASPECTS

Biotrophic parasitism is an extremely common mode of life that has arisen independently many times in the course of evolution. Depending on the definition used, as many as half of all animals have at least one parasitic phase in their life cycles, and it is also frequent in plants and fungi. Moreover, almost all free-living animals are host to one or more parasite taxa.

Parasites evolve in response to defense mechanisms of their hosts. Examples of host defenses include the toxins produced by plants to deter parasitic fungi and bacteria, the complex vertebrate immune system, which can target parasites through contact with bodily fluids, and behavioural defenses. An example of the latter is the avoidance by sheep of open pastures during spring, when roundworm eggs accumulated over the previous year hatch en masse. As a result of these and other host defenses, some parasites evolve adaptations that are specific to a particular host taxon and specialize to the point where they infect only a single species. Such narrow host specificity can be costly over evolutionary time, however, if the host species becomes extinct. Thus, many parasites are capable of infecting a variety of host species that are more or less closely related, with varying success.

Host defences also evolve in response to attacks by parasites. Theoretically, parasites may have an advantage in this evolutionary arms race because of their more rapid generation time. Hosts reproduce less quickly than parasites, and therefore have fewer chances to adapt than their parasites do over a given span of time.

In some cases, a parasite species may coevolve with its host taxa. In theory, long-term coevolution should lead to a relatively stable relationship tending to commensalism or mutualism, in that it is in the evolutionary interest of the parasite that its host thrives. A parasite may evolve to become less harmful for its host or a host may evolve to cope with the unavoidable presence of a parasite to the point that the parasite's absence causes the host harm. For example, although animals infected with parasitic worms are often clearly harmed, and therefore parasitized, such infections may also reduce the prevalence and effects of autoimmune disorders in animal hosts, including humans

The presumption of a shared evolutionary history between parasites and hosts can sometimes elucidate how host taxa are related. For instance, there has been dispute about whether flamingos are more closely related to the storks and their allies or to ducks, geese and their relatives. The fact that flamingos share parasites with ducks and geese is evidence these groups may be more closely related to each other than either is to storks.

Parasitism is part of one explanation for the evolution of secondary sex characteristics seen in breeding males throughout the animal world, such as the plumage of male peacocks and manes of male lions. According to this theory, female hosts select males for breeding based on such characteristics because they indicate resistance to parasites and other disease.

ECOLOGY

Quantitative Ecology

When considering the distribution of a single parasite species, one finds that parasite individuals exhibit an aggregated distribution among host individuals. This means that most hosts harbour a few or no parasites, while a few hosts carry the vast majority of parasite individuals. This poses considerable problems for students of parasite ecology: the use of parametric statistics should be avoided. Log-transformation of data before the application of parametric test, or the use of non-parametric statistics is recommended by several authors; however, these give rise to further problems. Therefore, modern day quantitative parasitology is based on more advanced biostatistical methods.

Diversity Ecology

Hosts represent discrete habitat patches that can be occupied by parasites. A hierarchical set of terminology has come into use to describe parasite assemblages at different host scales.

Infrapopulation

An infrapopulation is all the parasites of one species in a single individual host.

Metapopulation

A metapopulation is all the parasites of one species in a host population.

Infracommunity

An infracommunity is all the parasites of all species in a single individual host.

Component Community

A component community is all the parasites of all species in a host population.

Compound Community

A compound community is all the parasites of all species in all host species in an ecosystem.

The diversity ecology of parasites differs markedly from that of free-living organisms. That is, the determinants of species richness and relative abundance animals. For free-living organisms, diversity ecology features many strong conceptual frameworks including Macarthur and Wilson's theory of island biogeography, Diamond's assembly rules and, more recently, null models such as Hubbell's neutral theory of biodiversity and biogeography. Frameworks are not so well-developed for parasites and in many ways they do not fit the free-living models. For example, island biogeography is predicated on fixed spatial relationships between habitat patches ("sinks"), usually with reference to a mainland ("source"). Parasites inhabit hosts, which represent mobile habitat patches with dynamic spatial relationships. There is no true "mainland" other than the sum of hosts (host population); in this way, parasite component communities in host populations are metacommunities.

Nonetheless, different types of parasite assemblages have been recognised in host individuals and populations, and many of the patterns observed for free-living organisms are also pervasive among parasite assemblages. The most prominent of these is the interactive-isolationist continuum. This proposes that parasite assemblages occur along a cline from interactive communities, where niches are saturated and interspecific competition is high, to isolationist communities, where there are many vacant niches and interspecific interaction is not as important as stochastic factors in providing structure to the community. Whether this is so, or whether community patterns simply reflect the sum of underlying species distributions (no real "structure" to the community), has not yet been established.

Adaptation

Parasites infect hosts that exist within their same greographical area (sympatric) more effectively.This phenomenon is supported by the "Red Queen hypothesis - which states that interactions between species (such as host an parasites) lead to constant natural selection for adaptation and counter adaptation." The parasites track the locally common host genotypes which help them to adapt to their hosts. On the contrary, the parasites are less infective to allopatric (from different geographical region) hosts. Experiments published in 2002, discuss the analysis of two different snail populations from two different sources - Lake Lanthe and Lake Poerua in New Zealand, which were exposed to two pure parasites (digenetic trematode) taken from the same lakes. In the experiment, the snails were infected by their sympatric parasites, allopatric parasites and mixed sources of parasites. The results suggest that the parasites were more highly effective in infecting their sympatric snails than their allopatric snails. Though the allopatric snails were still infected by the parasites, the infectivity was on a much smaller scale when compared to the sympatric snails. Hence, the parasites were found to have adapted to infecting local populations of snail hosts.

Transmission

Parasites inhabit living organisms, and as a result face problems that free-living organisms do not. Hosts, the only habitats in which parasites can survive, actively try to avoid, repel and destroy parasites. Parasites employ numerous strategies for getting from one host to another, a process sometimes referred to as parasite transmission, or the colonization of new hosts.

Many endoparasites infect their host by penetrating its external surface, while others must be ingested by the host. Once inside the host, adult endoparasites need to shed offspring into the external environment in order to infect other hosts. Many adult endoparasites reside in the host's gastrointestinal tract, where offspring can be shed along with host excreta. Adult stages of tapeworms, thorny-headed worms and most flukes use this method.

Among protozoan endoparasites, such as the malarial parasites and trypanosomes, infective stages in the host's blood are transported to new hosts by biting-insects, or vectors.

Larval stages of endoparasites often infect sites in the host other than the blood or gastrointestinal tract. In many such cases, larval endoparasites require their host to be consumed by the next host in the parasite's life cycle in order to survive and reproduce. Alternatively, larval endoparasites may shed free-living transmission stages that migrate through the host's tissue into the external environment, where they actively search for or await ingestion by other hosts. The foregoing strategies are used, variously, by larval stages of tapeworms, thorny-headed worms, flukes and parasitic roundworms.

Many ectoparasites, such as monogenean worms, rely on direct contact between hosts to colonize new hosts, but other methods are also used. Ectoparasitic arthropods may rely on host-host contact (e.g. many lice) shed eggs that survive off the host (e.g. fleas) and/or wait in the external environment for an encounter with a host (e.g. ticks). Some aquatic leeches locate hosts by sensing movement and only attach when certain temperature and chemical cues are present.

Some parasites modify host behaviour to make transmission to other hosts more likely. For example, in California salt marshes, the fluke *Euhaplorchis californiensis* reduces the ability of its killifish host to avoid predators This parasite matures in egrets, which are more likely to feed on infected killifish than on uninfected fish. Another example is the protozoan *Toxoplasma gondii,* a parasite that matures in cats but can be carried by many other mammals. Uninfected rats avoid cat odours, but rats infected with *T. gondii* are drawn to this scent, a change which may increase transmission to feline hosts.

Roles in Ecosystems

Modifying the behaviour of infected hosts to make transmission to other hosts more likely is one way parasites can affect the structure of ecosystems. For example, in the case of *Euhaplorchis californiensis*,discussed above, it is plausible that the abundance of local predator and prey species would be different if this parasite were absent from the system.

Although parasites are often omitted in depictions of food webs, they usually occupy the top position. Parasites can function like keystone species, reducing the dominance of superior competitors and allowing competing species to co-exist.

Many parasites require multiple hosts of different species to complete their life cycles and rely on predator-prey or other stable ecological interactions to get from one host to another. In this sense, the parasites in an ecosystem reflect the "health" of that system.

PARASITOID

A parasitoid is an organism that spends a significant portion of its life history attached to or within a single host organism which it ultimately kills (and often consumes) in the process. Thus they are similar to typical parasites except in the certain fate of the host. In a typical parasitic relationship, the parasite and host live side by side without lethal damage to the host. Typically, the parasite takes enough nutrients to thrive without preventing the host from reproducing. In a parasitoid relationship, the host is killed, normally before it can produce offspring. When treated as a form of parasitism, the term necrotroph is sometimes (though rarely) used.

This type of relationship seems to occur only in organisms that have fast reproduction rates, such as insects, or (rarely) mites. Parasitoids are also often closely coevolved with their hosts. Most biologists use the term parasitoids to refer only to insects with this type of life history, but some argue the term should be used more embrasively to include parasitic nematodes, seed weevils, and certain bacteria and viruses (e.g. bacteriophages) all of which obligately destroy their host.

The term parasitoid was coined in 1913 by the German writer O. M. Reuter (and adopted in English by his reviewer, W.M. Wheeler) to describe the strategy in which during its development, the parasite lives in or on the body of a single host individual, eventually killing that host, the adult parasitoids being free-living.

Types of Parasitoids

Idiobiont parasitoids are those which prevent any further development of the host after initial parasitization, and this typically involves a host life stage which is immobile (e.g., an egg or pupa), and almost without exception they live outside the host. Koinobiont parasitoids allow the host to continue its development and often do not kill or consume the host until the host is about to either pupate or become an adult; this therefore typically involves living within an active, mobile host. Koinobionts can be further subdivided into endoparasitoids, which develop inside of the prey, and ectoparasitoids, which develop outside the host body, though they are frequently attached or embedded in the host's tissues.

It is not uncommon for a parasitoid itself to serve as the host for another parasitoid's offspring. The latter is commonly termed a hyperparasite but this term is slightly misleading, as both the host *and* the primary parasitoid are killed. A better term is secondary parasitoid, or hyperparasitoid; most such species known are in the insect order Hymenoptera.

Insects

About 10% of described insect species are parasitoids, but as many parasitoid groups are poorly known taxonomically the true figure is probably nearer 20%. There are four insect orders that are particularly renowned for this type of life history. By far the majority are in the order Hymenoptera. The largest and best known group comprises the so-called "Parasitica" within the Hymenopteran suborder Apocrita: the largest subgroups of these are the chalcidoid wasps (superfamily *Chalcidoidea*) and the ichneumon wasps (superfamily *Ichneumonoidea*), followed by the Proctotrupoidea and Platygastroidea. Outside of the Parasitica there are many other Hymenopteran lineages which include parasitoids, such as most of the Chrysidoidea and Vespoidea, and the rare Symphytan family *Orussidae*. The flies (order Diptera) include several families of parasitoids, the largest of which is the family Tachinidae, and also smaller families such as Pipunculidae, Conopidae, and others. The other two orders are the "twisted-wing parasites" (order *Strepsiptera*), which is a small group consisting entirely of parasitoids, and the beetles (order *Coleoptera*), which includes at least families, Ripiphoridae and Rhipiceridae, that are largely parasitoids, and rove beetles (family Staphylinidae) of the genus *Aleochara*. Occasional members of other orders can be parasitoids; one of the more remarkable is the moth family Epipyropidae, which are ectoparasitoids of planthoppers.

In Fiction

Many "parasites" portrayed in fiction are actually parasitoids; these include:

- The Xenomorphs from the *Alien* films.
- The X Parasites and Metroids from the *Metroid* series.
- Several of the symbiotes from the Spider-Man comics.
- The Flood from the *Halo* video game series.
- The Headcrabs from the game *Half-Life*.
- The "shit-weasels" from Stephen King's novel, *Dreamcatcher*.
- The Magog from the television series, *Gene Roddenberry's Andromeda*.
- The Black Oil alien virus from *The X-Files*.
- The Broodlings from the *Starcraft* games.
- The earwig from "The Caterpillar" episode of Night Gallery. Based on the old wives tale about the earwig.

PARASITIC FUNGI

The evolution of fungi is mainly dependent on the further development and spread of green plants. The majority of fungal species is saprophytic, some few are parasitic. The latter are at least in certain stages of their life cycle dependent on a particular supply of nutrients (vitamins, for example) that can only be provided by living cells. It is quite striking that fungal diseases are rather rare in nature due to the very effective defence mechanisms of plants that inhibit a spread of parasitic fungi. The solid cell wall including all its introsusceptions and appositions (the cuticle, for example) that inhibits the penetration of the tissues and cell lumina by fungi, bacteria, viruses, etc. is the first line of defence. Additionally, a wide spectrum of secondary defence compounds exists, many of which are fungicides and/or bactericides. These substances are often not produced until infection occurs (i.e. until their production is induced, example: phytoalexines).

It is remarkable that plant parasites (and this is equally true for fungi, bacteria, and viruses) are strictly host-specific. Some of them depend on an alternation of hosts, so that one stage of the parasite's development occurs in one host, the following in another that is phylogenetically not closely related to the first host. Parasites cause far larger damages in monocultures (agriculture) than in plant communities rich in species due to their high host specificity. The annual loss of foodstuff caused by them corresponds to an amount large enough to provide 300 million people.

Parasitic fungi have at least three strategies to get hold of plant ingredients:

- They produce enzymes for the breakdown of cell walls and cuticles.
- They produce toxins that do either reduce the activity of the host cells or inhibit it completely.
- They produce plant-specific substances (hormones, for example) thus meshing with the hormonal equilibrium of the plant cell and causing disruptions of the growth and differentiation of the cells and tissues. *Gibberella fujikuroi*, for example, secretes gibberellins that influence the growth of the host plant (rice). Studies of this fungus lead to the detection of the gibberellins (class of phytohormones).

The literature about parasitic fungi is very extensive. Many studies originate in economic considerations. The majority deals with the classification of the fungi, their life cycles, the symptoms of the plants and their diagnostic, the host range, and the search for the host's factors of resistance. The plants' molecular mechanism of action after infection with fungi has by now just been elucidated in a few cases, and these examples can only partially be generalized due to the variety of possible reactions.

The resistance of the hosts is not only based on the general and unspecific defence mechanisms mentioned above, but also on the production of specific, genetically determined substances directed against specific fungi. Genetic analyses showed that the resistance is on one hand caused by the existence of dominant alleles of the respective genes, and on the other hand by resistance genes that are inherited independently of each other.

Classification of Parasitic Fungi

It is distinguished between two types of parasitism:

- **Necrotrophic Parasitism**: the infection leads to a destroying of the tissue and thus to the death of the plant. The fungi are often only optionally parasitic, they can just as well proliferate in dead or withering plant material.
- **Biotrophic Parasitism**: In this case, parasite and host live together for longer periods of time. The parasite takes nutrients and growth-regulating substances from the plant, but does not kill it. Most biotrophic fungi are obligatory parasites. They survive only limited saprophytic phases; especially the development of a fruiting body is dependent on the presence of a host. The cultivation of single (vegetative) stages of these fungi in cell-free nutrient medium succeeded only in a few exceptions.

Parasitic fungi can be found in all classes of fungi, the hosts in all systematic groups of plants (and blue-green algae). The kingdom of fungi subdivides into myxomycetes or moulds (slime fungi) and eumycetes, the higher fungi.

One of the economically most important representatives of the parasitic myxomycetes is *Plasmodium brassicae*, the causative agent of clubroot, a disease whose symptoms can be seen in the roots of numerous species of cruciferes. The changed differentiation pattern of the infected host tissue is caused by a 50-100 fold increased auxine content, a 10-100 fold rise of the cytokinin content, and an increased degree of ploidy of the respective tissues' nuclei.

Spongospora subterraneae is the causative agent of the potato's powdery scab that can serve as a vector for the potato-mop-top-virus.

Eumycetes

Phytophthora species need among a few others Solanaceae (species of the potato family) as hosts. *Phytophthora infestans* is the causative agent of late blight of potato. The early destruction of the foliage and the reduction of the rate of photosynthesis caused by it leads to heavy crop failure. The host spectrum is - in contrast to some other *Phytophthora*-species (potato, tomato, and a few others) - very restricted. The fungus was the cause of a big famine in Ireland in the middle of the 19th century (1845-47). A huge migration into the USA was the consequence.

Ascomycetes. Numerous species like *Taphrina insititae* (host: plums and others), *T. betula* (birch), *T. cerasi* (cherry), *T. deformans* (peach) and others that cause leaf curls in different hosts belong to the ascomycetes. Most of these species develop haustoria (exception: *T. deformans*), i.e. processes into the inner of the host cell lumen. The most important precondition for the development of a haustorium is a local perforation of the plant cell wall. The growing haustorium widens into a vesicle-like structure after having penetrated the cell lumen. The host cell's plasmalemma is not penetrated. Haustoria do therefore not grow into the plasma of the host cells. Electron microscopic studies of different types of haustoria showed that the plasmalemma changed structurally, though. It folds up and a lot of electron-dense material is incorporated into the membrane. These observations point to an active defence reaction of the cells. Leaf curls are caused by an increased, but uneven growth of single leaf areas. Experimental data suggest that the leaves' content of cytokinins and IAA is increased.

The species causing witches' broom in numerous host trees belongs to the *Taphrina* family, too. The symptom is produced by an increased number of vegetative points that are the reason for an irregular, tuft-shaped branching pattern of the infected plant parts.

The order *Erysiphales* consists of the family Erysiphaceae (mildew). Mildew is the collective name for a variety of Erysiphacae-species that live parasitically on a number of angiosperms: *Erysiphe graminis* (corn mildew), *E. communis* (on pumpkin), and *E. polygoni* (on peas, clover, and other Leguminosae). The fungal mycelium spreads usually on the upper or the undersurface of the leaf. A few epidermal cells are penetrated by occasional haustoria.

Numerous subspecies of *Erysiphe graminis* have specialized on cereals. Some species, for example, grow on wheat but not on barley, while the opposite is true for others.

Ceratocystis ulmi and related species cause the Dutch elm disease. The disease was discovered in Britain in 1927, where 10% of all elms were infected between 1930 and 1940. In the dry summer of 1947, it spread epidemically in Germany, too.

Botrytis cinerea (grey mould) is a not much specialized parasite. It infects lettuce leaves as well as a variety of juicy fruits (tomatoes, strawberries, etc.) if the weather is humid enough.

Basidiomycetes. Two important orders of parasitic fungi belong to the basidiomycetes: Ustilaginales (smuts) and Uredinales (rusts). The order Agaricales consists mainly of the already discussed mycorrhizal fungi, only few species are parasitic (honey fungus, for example). More than 1000 species of Ustilaginales live parasitically on hosts of more than 75 angiosperm families. They produce dark, powder-like traces consisting of fruiting bodies strung together on leaves, shoots, flowers, and fruits. They develop usually no haustoria. Their extensive mycelium spreads through the intercellular spaces of the host plants. Uredinales include about 4,000 species in 100 genera. They are characterized by the red-brownish colour (rusts!) of their spores. Smuts develop haustoria and infect a range of angiosperms, gymnosperms, and pteridophytes. *Puccinia graminis* is the classic example of a fungus with an alteration of hosts. Its haploid (monocariontic) mycelium grows on *Berberis* (barberry), its dicariontic mycelium on different grasses. *P. graminis* is characterized by a complex alternation of generations. Up to five different types of spores can be generated during its course. *P. graminis* can live on grasses for an infinite time in its dicariontic state, if barberry is not present.

The preconditions for this change, however, are mild winters, since the dicariontic, asexual uredospores (summer spores) cannot survive long and cold winters. Wind can on the other hand disperse fungus spores thousands of kilometres so that a local extermination of barberry provides no lasting protection against *Puccinia*. This species consists of a number of subspecies, too. One has specialized on wheat, another on oat, a third on rye, etc. *Puccinia graminis* belongs to the few parasitic fungi that can be cultivated cell-free on agar (under addition of yeast extract).

Fungi imperfecti. This is the collective name for fungus species that do not develop fruiting bodies and that are therefore rather difficult to classify. Because of ultrastructural studies, it is assumed today that most of them belong to the ascomycetes. Several species have been used as test objects for studying molecular processes occurring during the infection of plants. We will therefore discuss them two subchapters later.

Parasitic aquatic fungi are rather unknown to the public, since they are of no economic importance. Only few scientists have studied them intensely.

More than 200 filamentous marine fungi have been described. Between a quarter or a third of them live parasitically on algae. Most of them belong to the ascomycetes. Brown, red, and green algae as well as diatoms serve as their hosts. *Lagenisma coscinodisca*, a diatom parasite, has been especially well documented with the help of the electron microscope.

Most parasites of freshwater algae belong to the chytrids that were discovered by A. BRAUN (Berlin) in 1856. He described them as follows:

> "The whole little plant consists of a simple, vesicle-like cell that does often penetrate the cells of the nutritive organism with a root-like excrescence."

Chytrids develop no hyphae, but a non-cellular and partially rather extensive system of rhizoids that seizes the host cells and can even enclose them. Nearly every known species of algae has its own specific parasite. The fungus infections should not be underestimated. Infections of nearly all algal cell-colonies have often been observed towards the end of a 'water bloom', i.e. the massive growth of an algal species.

Chytrids infect both blue-green algae (*Cyanophyceae*) and Volvocales, as well as Chlorococcales. These three groups of algae differ in the chemical composition of their cell walls so that the respective parasites have to have the most diverse enzyme systems at their disposal. The destruction of a cell occurs only after a cell-to-cell contact has been established, i.e. the fungus secretes no lytic substance into the adjacent medium that destroys all cells of a colony that are surrounded by a gelatinous coat.

Years of research into the population dynamics of diatom and cyanophycean parasites showed, that the fungus infection is able to reduce the number of individuals drastically, especially at the beginning of a population's growth, and to accelerate the decline of a population lastingly. The studies took place in South England's Lake District. A reduction in the number of individuals of an algal species is usually compensated by an increase in the population size of another species. Such quantitative analyses and a larger attention to the consequences of the fungus infection offer possible explanations for the fact that a species of algae is dominant in one year and does scarcely, or not at all occur in the following year.

The infection of algal colonies with chytrids is not the only reason for the disintegration of a water bloom. Other reasons, like the lack of nutrients (especially of phosphate) or weather-caused changes are often decisive, especially if the fungus infection is limited and only few cells of a colonyare destroyed.

PARASITIC PLANTS

Parasitism for plants is a relationship in which one organism uses the nutrients and water of another plant, the host.

A holoparasite is a relationship where parasitism is obligatory. A hemiparasite is exemplified by a plant that can live either as a parasite or on its own, hence this plant is a facultative parasite.

Parasitic plants belong to about 19 families of flowering plants. The many species of mistletoes, belonging to Viscaceae and Loranthaceae, comprise about three-quarters of all parasitic species. Several other families of parasitic flowering plants are also well-known, especially the broomrapes (Orobanchaceae) and dodders (Cuscutaceae).

Parasitism has evolved many times in dicotyledons, i.e., there has been convergence toward several types.

General Properties of Parasitic Plants

The following are some general properties of parasitic plants.

1. Nutrients and water are transported via a physiological bridge, called the haustorium.
2. A parasite connects its vascular system (at least one of the tissues) to that of the host plant.
3. The parasite may totally discard its own photosynthesis.
4. Parasites may be mostly exposed at the surface of the host (epiparasite) or mostly hidden within the host organ (endoparasite). The endoparasitic portion is composed of thread-like haustoria permeating the host tissue with a sinker, a single structure that becomes embedded in the host tissue.

Parasites become established via germination. Seeds land on the host tissue, for stem parasites especially in bird droppings, and germinate after reading a chemical stimulus from the host. A modified lateral root becomes an haustorium; this root is chemotrophic, i.e., responding to a chemical gradient, and contacts the host epidermis. The root then attaches by pushing against the plant and forming a disc, called a hapteron, and secretes a polysaccharide adhesive. The root tip then mechanically penetrates the host, apparently without enzymatic digestion, and establishes a vascular connection by attaching vessels and positioning phloem next to leaky host phloem.

Mistletoes were formerly alleged to receive no host carbohydrates, but substantial heterotropic carbon gain has been measured in mistletoes, even without phloem connections. Direct xylem-to-xylem continuity between host and parasite is not easy to demonstrate. Mistletoes often exhibit high transpiration rates during the day, through stomates and cracks in the epidermis. Losing substantial water from the leaves and stems of the parasite results in a steep water potential gradient, favorable to drawing water into the mistletoe plant. Nitrogen is supplied to the parasite in the xylem stream, and the high transpiration rates, hence, high water demands appear instead to represent a nitrogen-gathering mechanism for the mistletoe.

Typical thick, fleshy root parasites generally lack any adaptations to restrict water loss from their achlorophyllous stems and leaves, because they tend to lack the waxy coating, cuticle.

Dodder and mistletoes are serious problems for plants. Dodder is weedy and can cover woody plants and damage certain economically important crop plants. Mistletoe can become so abundant on a tree, that most of the foliage is of the parasite not the host. In general, experts generally state that parasitic plants rarely, perhaps never, kill the host plant, so that the host and parasite live unhappily together is some balance.

Types of Parasitic Plants

These are three families, all having opposite leaves, which in some species may be photosynthetic. In the temperate Northern Hemisphere, the three commonly seen genera of Viscaceae, which have nonshowy flowers but white or red fruits, are *Phoradendron*, *Viscum*, and the dwarf mistletoes of *Arceuthobium*. Loranthaceae is a tropical family with showy yellow, orange, or red tubular flowers, including *Nuytsia floribunda*, a tree of Australia that parasitizes roots of grasses. A remarkable endoparasitic loranth is *Tristerix aphylla*, which attacks a columnar cactus in Chile. Many species of mistletoes appear to have photosynthetic leaves, and thereby may be hemiparasites, but for most physiological studies of leaves have not been attempted.

- ***Root Parasites***

Root parasites belong to a number of families and are either nonphotosynthetic or photosynthetic. Broomrapes (either classified as family Orobanchaceae or subfamily Orobanchoideae of Scrophulariaceae) have nonphotosynthetic fleshy stems, e.g., the genera *Orobanche*, *Conopholis*, and *Boschniakia*. Other nonphotosynthetic root parasites are found in the families Lennoaceae, Hydnoraceae, Rafflesiaceae e.g., *Mitrostemon* and *Bdallophyton*), and Balanophoraceae. Parasitic species in Santalaceae (the sandalwood family) and Krameriaceae (the ratony family) have photosynthetic leaves.

- ***Nonphotosynthetic Vines***

In temperate and some tropical regions of the world are parasitic vines of the Cuscutaceae (or the morning glory family, Convolvulaceae) called dodder, *Cuscuta*. Stems of dodder are orange to yellow or white. In tropical regions is the vine genus *Cassytha* of the laurel family (Lauraceae).

- ***Nonphotosynthetic Stem Parasites***

These are often cryptic until they flower and fruit. Stem and root parasites occur in the family Rafflesiaceae. In California is the rare *Pilostyles thurberi*, which bursts from stems of *Psorothamnus*, a leguminous woody desert plant. In Borneo is the plant with the largest flower, *Rafflesia arnoldii*, an endoparasite which erupts through the bark of trees and lianas in the grape family (Vitaceae). The nonphotosynthetic vines technically are also stem parasites.

Hemiparasites

Especially in the family Scrophulariaceae are some common hemiparasites, such as Indian paintbrush and owl's clover (*Castilleja*), lousewort (*Pedicularis*), and bird's beak (*Cordylanthus*). These have green, photosynthetic leaves, but a substantial portion of the parasite's carbon is derived from the host plant, parasitized from the roots.

California Parasitic Plants

The most recent flora of California listed 45 species of parasitic dicotyledons that are native or introduced to the state, including the introduced European mistletoe, *Viscum album*. In Los Angeles County, species of two groups are most commonly seen: the twining vines of dodder (genus *Cuscuta*) and the woody mistletoes of the genus *Phoradendron*. In coniferous forests you may find the golden-colored dwarf mistletoes of the genus *Arceuthobium* (12 species). Much more difficult to find are the secretive root parasites of the Orobanchaceae and Lennoaceae, which are only rarely seen, and only botanists are ever likely, if persistent enough, to find *Pilostyles thurberi*, very uncommon stem parasite of a leguminous desert shrub. The flora also lists about 70 species of hemiparasites occurring in California, all but one species belonging to Family Scrophulariaceae. Of the hemiparasites, owl's clover and Indian paintbrush (*Castilleja*) are very common herbs. This combined list of parasites and hemiparasites comprises less than 2% of the total species in California, but collectively they provide a fascinating life style.

There are five species of *Phoradendron* that can be easily observed during casual walks and drives through Southern California.

1. Attacking the California sycamore (*Platanus racemosa*) on the UCLA campus and throughout the urban region and canyons is the big-leaf mistletoe, *Phoradendron macrophyllum*, but this species also occurs on many other deciduous trees, including alder (*Alnus*), cottonwood (*Populus*), and walnut (*Juglans*).

2. On woody stems of oaks (*Quercus*) of oak woodland can often be found oak mistletoe, *Phoradendron villosum*, which has green leaves approximately the same size as in the big-leaf mistletoe.

3. Much narrower leaves characterize fir mistletoe, *Phoradendron pauciflorum*, which occurs often around 2000 meters in yellow pine forest growing on white fir, *Abies concolor*.

4. On the eastern, desert-facing slope of our mountains occurs pinyon-juniper woodland and in neighboring Joshua tree woodland. Here the California juniper, *Juniperus californica*, is a dominant plant species, and often this gymnosperm is

heavily infested with juniper mistletoe, *Phoradendron juniperinum*. This stem parasite has shorter and narrow leaves, and from a distance may appear like the host plant, but the host has instead very tiny, scale-like leaves.

5. In the deserts of Southern California are tree legumes, notably the species of mesquite (*Prosopis*), palo verde (*Cercidium*), ironwood (*Olneya*), and catclaw acacia (*Acacia*), which can be infected by desert mistletoe, *Phoradendron californicum*. Desert mistletoe, like many desert species, has very much reduced, scale-like leaves on its reddish stems.

PARASITIC PROTISTS

Parasite - an organism that lives on or in a host organism and causes harm to that organism.

Vector - an organism that can carry a parasite, and is responsible for infecting other organisms (host) with that parasite. Vectors themselves are not harmful, but in the battle against human disease, controlling the vector can control the transmission of parasites.

Malaria

Protist: Plasmodium

Vector: Anopholes Mosquito

Statistics

- According to the World Health Organization, 300-500 million cases of malaria occur each year
- Malaria results in 1.5-2.7 million deaths per year (much more than AIDS)
- Most cases occur in Africa and South America
- Symptoms include fever, headache, vomitting and other flu-like symptoms
- The protist lives inside the bloodstrea, eventually clogging capillaries and destroying blood cells, which will lead to death if not treated.

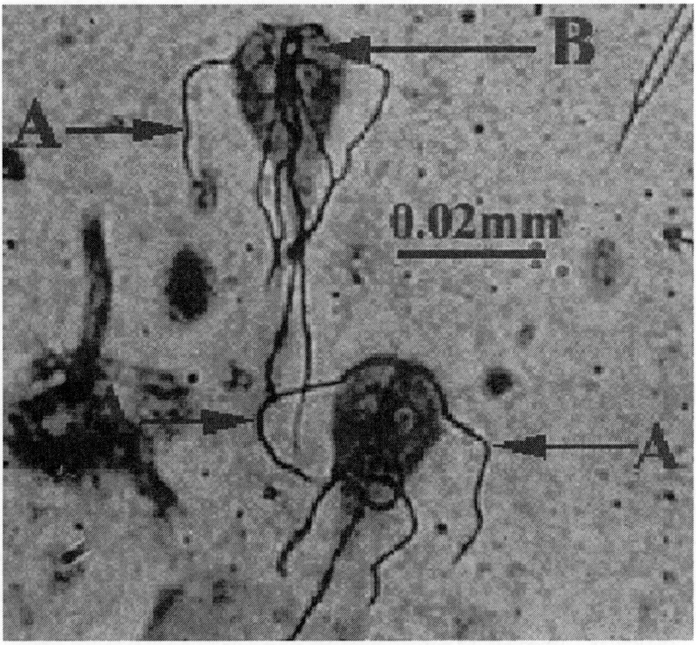

Fig. 2.1

B = Protist, Giardia A = flagella

African Sleeping Sickness (or Trypanosomiasis)

Protist: Trypanosoma

Vector: Tse Tse Fly

Statistics

- Occurs mostly in sub-saharan africa
- Symptoms include fever, headaches, pain in joints-followed by a phase when the parasite infects the central nervous system, causing confusion, lack of coordination, and uncontrolled sleepiness. Without treatment, the host will die.

Giardiasis

Protist: Giardia

Transmission: Drinking contaminated water (usually outdoor streams and other untreated water).

Symptoms: Severe diarrhea and vomitting, the protist takes up residence in the digestive tract.

Other Protist Parasites

Cryptsporidium - this protist was responsible for a major health crisis in detroit when the city's drinking water became contaminated.

Amebic Dysentery - also known as Montezuma's Revenge, travellers often contract this in other countries (causes diarrhea).

3

Parasitic Worm

INTRODUCTION

Parasitic worms or helminths are a division of eukaroytic parasites that, unlike external parasites such as lice and fleas, live inside their host They are worm-like organisms that live and feed off living hosts, receiving nourishment and protection while disrupting their hosts' nutrient absorption, causing weakness and disease. Those that live inside the digestive tract are called intestinal parasites. They can live inside humans as well as other animals.

Helminthology is the study of parasitic worms and their effect on their hosts.

Parasitic worms are categorized into three groups:

1. cestodes;
2. nematodes; and
3. Trematodes.

These are the principal morphologic differences of the different families of helminths.

Diseases caused in humans by helminth infection include ascariasis, dracunculiasis, elephantiasis, hookworm, lymphatic filariasis, onchocerciasis, schistosomiasis, and trichuriasis.

Reproduction

Parasitic worms are sequential hermaphrodites and reproduce depending on the species of worm, either with the presence of a male and female worm, joining sperm and eggs, producing fertile eggs, such as hookworms, or by breaking off segments that contain both male and female sex organs that are able to produce fertile eggs without the presence of a male or female. (e.g., tapeworms)

All worm offspring are passed on through poorly-cooked meat, especially pork, wild fish, and beef, contaminated water, feces and mosquitoes. However, it is estimated that 40 million Americans are infected with the most common roundworm, the pinworm.

Worm eggs or larvae or even adults enter the human body through the mouth, anus, nose, or skin, with most species attaching themselves to the intestinal tract. With the presence of digestive enzymes, worm egg shells are dissolved, releasing a brand-new worm; unlike its egg shell, the parasitic worm is protected from the body's powerful digestive enzymes by producing a protective keratin layer.

Immune Response

Response to worm infection in humans is a Th2 response in the majority of cases. This results in inflammation of the gut, and results in cyst-like structures forming around the egg deposits throughout the body. The host's lymphatic system is also heavily taxed the longer helminths propagate, which excrete toxins after feeding. These toxins are released into the intestines to be absorbed by the host's bloodstream. This phenomena makes the host susceptible to more common diseases such as seasonal viruses and bacterial infections.

FLATWORM

The flatworms (Phylum Platyhelminthes from the Greek *platy*, meaning "flat" *helminth-*, meaning worm) are a phylum of relatively simple soft-bodied invertebrate animals. With about 25,000 known species they are the largest phylum of acoelomates.

Flatworms are found in marine, freshwater, and even damp terrestrial environments. A troublesome terrestrial example is the New Zealand flatworm, *Arthurdendyus triangulatus*, which rapidly colonized large areas of Ireland and Scotland since its destroyed most of the indigenous earthworms. Most flatworms are free-living, but many are parasitic. There are four classes: Trematoda (flukes), Cestoda (tapeworms), Monogenea, and Turbellaria.

The flatworm's cephalized soft body is ribbon-shaped, flattened dorso-ventrally (from top to bottom), and bilaterally symmetric. Flatworms are the simplest triploblastic animals with organs. This means their organ systems form out of three germ layers: an outer ectoderm and an inner endoderm with a mesoderm between them. Turbellarians generally have a ciliated epidermis. There is also no true body cavity (coelom) except the gut; hence, flatworms are classified as acoelomates.The interior of the acoelomate body is filled with somewhat loosely spaced mesodermal tissue called parenchyma tissue.Flatworms have a hydrostatic skeleton, which consists of a water filled body cavity that is controlled by muscles.Flatworms exhibit an undulating form of locomotion.Depending on species and age, individuals can range in size from almost microscopic to over 20 m long. The longest ever recorded flatworm was a tapeworm over 90 ft (27 m) long.

Haptor

The haptor is a part of Platyhelminthes used to attach to its host. These differ between the prohaptor which is on the anterior end of the body and the opisthaptor, which is part of the posterior end of the body.The prohaptor has various adhesive and feeding structures. In some species, the prohaptor may have a number of cephalic or head glands that secrete a sticky adhesive substance, and shallow muscular suckers, all used for attachment. In other species there is an oral sucker, with various degrees of muscularisation that surrounds the mouth.The opisthaptor is primarily responsible for the attachment of the monogeneans to the host. The morphology of the opisthaptor is highly variable. It may have suckers in various degrees of development, large hooks called anchors (or hamuli), small hooks that are remnants from the larval stage, or complex clamps that may be either muscular or sclerotised.

Circulation and Nervous System

There is no true circulatory or respiratory system, but like all other animals, flatworms do take in oxygen. Extracellular body fluids (interstitial fluids) percolate between cells to help distribute nutrients, gases, and waste products.

Flatworms respire at their integument; gasses diffuse directly across their moist outer surface. This type of system is called *integumentary exchange*.

However, flatworms do have a bilateral nervous system; they are the simplest animals to have one. Two cordlike nerves branch repeatedly in an array resembling a ladder. The head end of some species even has a collection of ganglia acting as a rudimentary brain to integrate signals from sensory organs such as eyespots.

Feeding

Usually the digestive tract has one opening, so the animal can feed, digest, and eliminate undigested particles of food simultaneously, as most animals with tubular guts are able to do. This blind-ended gastrovascular cavity functions similarly to that of the Cnidaria. However, in a few particularly long flatworms or those with highly branched guts, there may be one or more anuses. A small group where the gut is absent or non-permanent, called acoel flatworms, appear to be unrelated to the other Platyhelminthes. They eat rarely, maybe a few times per year (once or twice). Their diet includes small bugs found in soils and other types of worms, smaller then itself. Despite the simplicity of the digestive chamber, they are significantly more complex than cnidarians in that they possess numerous organs, and are therefore said to show an organ level of organization. Mesoderm allows for the development of these organs, and true muscle. Major sense organs are concentrated in the front end of the animals for species who possess these organs.Muscular contraction in the gut causes a strong sucking force which allows flatworms to ingest food.

Reproduction

Flatworm reproduction is hermaphroditic, meaning each individual produces eggs and sperm. When two flatworms mate, they exchange sperm so both become fertilized. Some flatworms, such as *Pseudobiceros hancockanus* engage in penis fencing, in which two individuals fight, trying to pierce the skin of the other with their penises; the first to succeed inseminates the other, which must then carry and nourish the fertilized eggs. Flatworms usually do not fertilize their own eggs.

Turbellarians classified as planarians (usually freshwater, non-parasitic) can also reproduce asexually by transverse fission. The body constricts at the midsection, and the posterior end grips a substrate. After a few hours of tugging, the body rips apart at the constriction. Each half grows replacements of the missing pieces to form two whole flatworms. This also means that if one of these planarian flatworms is cut in half, each half will regenerate, forming two separate, fully-functioning flatworms.

Classes

Flatworms were formerly considered to be basal among the protostomes. Molecular evidence suggests that this is only true of the orders Acoela and Nemertodermatida, which are thus given their own phylum Acoelomorpha. These findings, however, are still not accepted by all biologists. The systematic position of Catenulida seems uncertain, although Donoghue and Cracraft would place it as a sister group to all other non-Acoelomorpha flatworms. Xenoturbella was at first believed to be a flatworm as well, but it is now obvious that it belongs in its own phyla. The remaining and true flatworms form a monophyletic group that developed from more complex ancestors, and grouped with several other phyla as the Platyzoa. The traditional classifications of flatworms is primarily based on differing degrees of parasitism and divided into three monophyletic classes:

- Trematoda - flukes, probably paraphyletic to Cestoda.
- Cestoda - tapeworms.
- Monogenea - ectoparasitic flukes with simpler life cycles than Trematode flukes. They live an exclusively parasitic existence.

The remaining flatworms are grouped together for convenience as the class Turbellaria, now comprising the following orders:

- Catenulida
- Macrostomida
- Lecithoepitheliata
- Rhabdocoela
- Prolecithophora
- Proseriata
- Tricladida
- Polycladida - Marine flatworms

Most of these groups include free-living forms. The flukes and tapeworms, though, are parasitic, and a few cause massive damage to humans and other animals.

Biochemical Memory Experiments

In 1955, Thompson and James V. McConnell conditioned planarian flatworms by pairing a bright light with an electric shock. After repeating this several times they took away the electric shock, and only exposed them to the bright light. The flatworms would react to the bright light as if they had been shocked. Thompson and McConnell found that if they cut the worm in two, and allowed both worms to regenerate each half would develop the light-shock reaction. In 1962, McConnell repeated the experiment, but instead of cutting the trained flatworms in two he ground them into small pieces and fed them to other flatworms. Incredibly these flatworms learned to associate the bright light with a shock much faster than flatworms who had not been fed trained worms.

This experiment intended to show that memory could perhaps be transferred chemically. The experiment was repeated with mice, fish, and rats, but it always failed to produce the same results. The perceived explanation was that rather than memory being transferred to the other animals, it was the hormones in the ingested ground animals that changed its behaviour. McConnell believed that this was evidence of a chemical basis for memory, which he identified as memory RNA. McConnell's results are now attributed to observer bias. No double-blind experiment has ever reproduced his results.

NEMATODE

The roundworms or nematodes (phylum Nematoda) are the most diverse phylum of pseudocoelomates, and one of the most diverse of all animals. Nematode species are very difficult to distinguish; over 80,000 have been described, of which over 15,000 are parasitic. It has been estimated that the total number of described and undescribed roundworms might be more than 500,000.

Nematodes have successfully adapted to nearly every ecological niche from marine to fresh water, from the polar regions to the tropics, as well as the highest to the lowest of elevations. They are ubiquitous in freshwater, marine, and terrestrial environments, where they often outnumber other animals in both individual and species counts, and are found in locations as diverse as Antarctica and oceanic trenches. They represent, for example, 90% of all life on the seafloor of the Earth]. The many parasitic forms include pathogens in most plants, animals, and also in humans. Some nematodes can undergo cryptobiosis. Hundreds of *Caenorhabditis elegans*, featured in a research project on mission STS-107, survived the Space Shuttle Columbia Disaster.

Taxonomy and Systematics

The name "Nematoda" means "the thread-like ones", from Ancient Greek *nema*, "thread" and *-ode*, "like". The group was originally established by Karl Rudolphi in 1808 under the name Nematoidea, but reclassified as family Nematodes by Burmeister in 1837. They were eventually renamed Nematoda by K. M. Diesing in 1861. Nathan Cobb in 1919 argued that they should be called Nemata or Nemates, and in English "nemas" rather than "nematodes", but Diesing's revision has stuck.

After some confusion which saw the nematodes placed – often together with the horsehair worms (Nematomorpha) – as a class or order (e.g. independently by Leuckar and von Siebold in 1848 in various groups such as the Aschelminthes, Ray Lankester in 1877 finally promoted them to the rank of phylum. This was done to acknowledge the fact that roundworms are not part of another group of "worms", but represent a unique and highly distinct lineage.

Phylogeny

The relationships of the nematodes and their close relatives among the protostomian Metazoa are unresolved. Traditionally, they were held to be a lineage of their own, but in the 1990s it was proposed that they form a clade together with moulting animals such as arthropods. This group has been named Ecdysozoa. However, the monophyly of the Ecdysozoa was never unequivocally accepted: while most researchers however consider at least the placement of arthropods as more distant relatives of annelids – with which they were formerly united – to be warranted, the presumed close relationships of the nematodes and relatives with the arthropods has been a major point of contention.

Even though the amount of data since accumulated in regard to this problem is staggering, the situation seems if anything less clear these days. DNA sequence data, initially strongly supporting the Ecdysozoa hypothesis, has become rather equivocal on ecdysozoan monophyly, and is simply unable to refute either a close or a more distant relationship between the arthropod and nematode lineages. That the roundworms have a large number of peculiar apomorphies and in many cases a parasitic lifestyle confounds morphological analyses. Genetic analyses of roundworms suggest that – as is also indicated by their unique morphological features – the group has been under intense selective pressure during its early radiation, resulting apparently in accelerated rates of both morphological and molecular evolution. Furthermore, no distinctive apomorphies of Ecdysozoa are known; even moulting has recently been confirmed to occur outside the presumed clade.

Conversely, the identity of the closest living relatives of the Nematoda has always been well-resolved. Morphological characters and molecular phylogenies agree with placement of the roundworms as sister taxon to the parasitic horsehair worms (Nematomorpha); together they make up the Nematoida. Together with the Scalidophora (formerly Cephalorhyncha), the Nematoida form the Introverta. It is entirely unclear whether the Introverta are, in turn, the closest living relatives of the enigmatic Gastrotricha; if so, they are considered a clade Cycloneuralia, but there is much disagreement both between and among the available morphological and molecular data. The Cycloneuralia or the Introverta – depending on the validity of the former – are often ranked as a superphylum

Nematode Systematics

Due to the lack of knowledge regarding many nematodes, their systematics is contentious. Traditionally, they are divided into two classes, the Adenophorea and the Secernentea; as it seems, the latter are indeed a natural group of closest relatives. But the "Adenophorea" appear to be a paraphyletic assemblage of roundworms simply retaining a good number of ancestral traits; the Enoplia do not seem to be monophyletic either but to contain two distinct lineages. The "Chromadoria" seem to be another paraphyletic assemblage, with the Monhysterida representing a very ancient minor group of nematodes. Among the Secernentea, the Diplogasteria may need to be united with the Rhabditia. while the Tylenchia might be paraphyletic with the Rhabditia

Thus, the current understanding of roundworm systematics and phylogeny can be expressed as follows:

Phylum Nematoda

- Basal order Monhysterida
- Basal subclass/Class Enoplia
- Basal subclass/Class Dorylaimia
- Class Secernentea:
    - Subclass Diplogasteria (disputed)

- Subclass Rhabditia (paraphyletic?)
- Subclass Spiruria
- Subclass Tylenchia (disputed)
- Chromadoria assemblage

Morphology

Roundworms are unsegmented, bilaterally symmetric and triploblastic protostomes with a complete digestive system. They have no circulatory or respiratory systems so they use diffusion to breathe.

Although they lack a circulatory system, nutrients are transported throughout the body via fluid in the pseudocoelom. They are thin and are round in cross section. Nematodes are one of the simplest animal groups to have a complete digestive system, with separate orifices for food intake and waste excretion, a pattern followed by all subsequent, more complex animals. The body cavity is a pseudocoelom (persistent blastula), which lacks the muscles of coelomate animals that protects the body from drying out, from digestive juices, or from other harsh environments. Although this cuticle allows movement and shape changes via a hydrostatic skeletal system, it is very inelastic so does not allow the volume of the worm to increase. Therefore, as the worm grows, it has to molt and form new cuticles. The cuticles don't allow volume to increase so as to keep hydrostatic pressure inside the organism very high. For this reason, the roundworms do not possess circular muscles (just longitudinal ones) as they're not required. This hydrostatic pressure is the reason the roundworms are round.

Nematodes have a simple nervous system, with a main ventral nerve cord and a smaller dorsal nerve cord Sensory structures at the anterior end are called amphids, while sensory structures at the posterior end are called phasmids. There are no circular muscles, so the body can only undulate from side to side. Contact with solid objects is necessary for locomotion; its thrashing motions vary from mostly to completely ineffective at swimming.

Most free-living nematodes are microscopic, though a few parasitic forms can grow to over a meter in length (typically as parasites of very large animals such as whales). The largest nematode species ever recorded, *Placentonema gigantissima*, was discovered parasitizing the placenta of a Sperm Whale (*Physeter catodon*). It was found to measure 8.5 m in length, with a diameter of 0.3 mm and containing 32 ovaries. Other large nematodes include the Giant Kidney Worm (*Dioctophyma renale*), a parasite most commonly found in minks (*Mustela* sp.), but also in dogs and humans, that can reach up to 103 cm in length.

Nematodes generally eat bacteria, fungi and protozoans, although some are filter feeders. Excretion happens through a separate excretory pore. Nematodes also contract bacterial infections within excretion pores.

Reproduction

Reproduction is usually sexual. Males are usually smaller than females (often much smaller) and often have a characteristically bent tail for holding the female for copulation. During copulation, one or more chitinized spicules move out of the cloaca and are inserted into genital pore of the female. Amoeboid sperm crawl along the spicule into the female worm. Nematode sperm is thought to be the only eukaryotic cell without the globular protein G-actin.

Eggs may be embryonated or unembryonated when passed by the female, meaning that their fertilized eggs may not yet be developed. In free-living roundworms, the eggs hatch into larva, which eventually grow into adults; in parasitic roundworms, the life cycle is often much more complicated.

Nematodes as a whole possess a wide range of modes of reproduction. Some nematodes, specifically *Heterorhabditis* sp., undergo a process called *endotokia matricida*: intrauterine birth causing maternal death Some nematodes, like other animals (for example segmented worms), are hermaphroditic. The hermaphroditic nematode keeps its self-fertilized eggs inside its uterus until they hatch. The juvenile nematodes will then ingest the parent nematode. This process is significantly promoted in environments with a low or reducing food supply . The nematode model species *Caenorhabditis elegans* and *C. briggsae* exhibit androdioecy, which is very rare amongst animals. The single genus *Meloidogyne* (root-knot nematodes) exhibit a range of reproductive modes including sexuality (amphimixis), facultative sexuality, meiotic parthenogenesis (automixis) and mitotic parthenogenesis (apomixis).

Free-living Species

In free-living species, development usually consists of four molts of the cuticle during growth. Different species feed on materials as varied as algae, fungi, small animals, fecal matter, dead organisms and living tissues. Free-living marine nematodes are important and abundant members of the meiobenthos. They play an important rôle in the decomposition process, aid in recycling of nutrients in marine environments and are sensitive to changes in the environment caused by pollution. One roundworm of note is *Caenorhabditis elegans*, which lives in the soil and has found much use as a model organism. *C. elegans* has had its entire genome sequenced, as well as the developmental fate of every cell determined, and every neuron mapped.

Parasitic Species

Nematodes commonly parasitic on humans include ascarids (*Ascaris*), filarids, hookworms, pinworms (*Enterobius*) and whipworms (*Trichuris trichiura*). The species *Trichinella spiralis*, commonly known as the trichina worm, occurs in rats, pigs, and humans, and is responsible for the disease trichinosis. *Baylisascaris* usually infests wild animals but can be deadly to humans as well. *Haemonchus contortus* is one of the most abundant infectious agents in sheep around the world, causing great economic damage to sheep farms. In contrast, entomopathogenic nematodes parasitize insects and are considered by humans to be beneficial.

One form of nematode is entirely dependent upon the wasps which are the sole source of fig fertilization. They prey upon the wasps, riding them from the ripe fig of the wasp's birth to the fig flower of its death, where they kill the wasp, and their offspring await the birth of the next generation of wasps as the fig ripens.

Plant parasitic nematodes include several groups causing severe crop losses. The most common genera are *Aphelenchoides* (foliar nematodes), *Ditylenchus*, *Globodera* (potato cyst nematodes), *Heterodera* (soybean cyst nematodes), *Longidorus*, *Meloidogyne* (root-knot nematodes), *Nacobbus*, *Pratylenchus* (lesion nematodes), *Trichodorus* and *Xiphinema* (dagger nematodes). Several phytoparasitic nematode species cause histological damages to roots, including the formation of visible galls (e.g. by root-knot nematodes) which are useful characters for their diagnostic in the field. Some nematode species transmit plant viruses through their feeding activity on roots. One of them is *Xiphinema index*, vector of GFLV (Grapevine Fanleaf Virus), an important disease of grapes.

Other nematodes attack bark and forest trees. The most important representative of this group is *Bursaphelenchus xylophilus*, the pine wood nematode, present in Asia and America and recently discovered in Europe.

Nematodes in Agriculture

Depending on the species, a nematode may be beneficial or detrimental to plant health.

From an agricultural perspective, there are two categories of nematode: predatory ones, which will kill garden pests like cutworms, and pest nematodes, like the root-knot nematode, which attack plants.

Predatory nematodes can be bred by soaking a specific recipe of leaves and other detritus in water, in a dark, cool place, and can even be purchased as an organic form of pest control.

Rotations of plants with nematode resistant species or varieties is one means of managing parasitic nematode infestations. Another is treatment with natural antagonists such as the fungus *Gliocladium roseum*.

LEECH

Leeches are annelids comprising the subclass Hirudinea. There are fresh water, terrestrial, and marine leeches. Like the Oligochaeta, they share the presence of a clitellum. Like earthworms, leeches are hermaphrodites.

The European Medical Leech (*Hirudo medicinalis*) and some congeners as well as some other species have been used for clinical bloodletting for thousands of years, although most leeches do not feed on human blood, but on small invertebrates, which they eat whole.

Haemophagic leeches attach to their hosts and remain there until they become full, at which point they fall off to digest. A leech's body is composed of 34 segments. They all have an anterior (oral) sucker formed from the first six segments of their body, which is used to connect to a host for feeding, and also release an anesthetic to prevent the host from feeling the leech. They use a combination of mucus and suction (caused by concentric muscles in those six segments) to stay attached and secrete an anti-clotting enzyme into the host's blood stream.

Some species of leech will nurture their young, while providing food, transport, and protection; which is unusual behavior in an invertebrate.

Systematics and Taxonomy

The leeches are presumed to have evolved from certain Oligochaeta, most of which feed on detritus. However, some species in the Lumbriculidae are predatory and have similar adaptations as found in leeches. Consequently, the systematics and taxonomy of leeches is in need of review. While leeches form a clade, the remaining oligochetes are not their sister taxon but a diverse paraphyletic group containing some lineages that are closely related to leeches, and others that are far more distant.

There is some dispute as to whether Hirudinea should be a class itself, or a subclass of the Clitellata. The resolution mainly depends on the eventual fate of the oligochaetes, which as noted above do not form a natural group as traditionally circumscribed. Another possibility would be to include the leeches in the taxon Oligochaeta, which would then be ranked as a class and contain most of the clitellates. The Branchiobdellida are leechlike clitellates which were formerly included in the Hirudinea but are apparently just rather close relatives.

The more primitive Acanthobdellidea are often included with the leeches, but some authors treat them as a separate clitellate group. True leeches, of the infraclass Euhirudinea, have both anterior and posterior suckers and are divided into two groups:

- Rhynchobdellida (or Rhynchobdellae): jawless leeches, armed with a muscular straw-like proboscis puncturing organ in a retractable sheath.
- Arhynchobdellida (or Arhynchobdellae): Leeches which lack a proboscis and which may or may not have jaws armed with teeth.

True leeches, of the subclass Euhirudine, with both anterior and posterior suckers, are divided into two groups:

- *Rhynchobdellae:* "Jawless" leeches, armed with a muscular straw-like proboscis puncturing organ in a retractable sheath. The Rhynchobdellae consist of two families: The Glossiphoniidae (flattened leeches wth a poorly defined anterior sucker) and the Piscicolidae (have cylindrical bodies and a usually well-marked, bell-shaped, anterior sucker). The Glossiphoniidae live in fresh-water habitats; the Pisciolidae are found in seawater habitats.
- *Arhynchobdellid:* Leeches which lack a proboscis and which may or may not have jaws armed with teeth. Arhynchobellids are divided into two orders Gnathobdellae and Pharyngobdellae.
- *Gnathobdelae:* In this order of "jawed" leeches, armed with teeth, is found the quintessential leech: the European medical (bloodsucking) leech, *Hirudo medicinalis*. It has a tripartite-jaw filled with hundreds of tiny sharp teeth. The incision mark left on the skin by the European medical leech is an inverted Y inside a circle. Its North American counterpart is *Macrobdela decora*, a much less efficient medical leech. Within this order, the family Hirudidae is characterized by aquatic leeches and the family Haemadipsidae by terrestrial leeches. In the latter are *Haemadipsa sylvestris*, the Indian leech and *Haemadipsa zeylanica* (Yamabiru), the Japanse Mountain or Land Leech.

- *Pharyngobdellae:* These so called worm-leeches consist of freshwater or amphibious leeches that have lost the ability to penetrate a host's tissue and suck blood. They are carnivorous and equipped with a relatively large, toothless, mouth to ingest worms or insect larvae, which are swallowed whole.

  The Pharyngobdella have six to eight pairs of eyes, as compared with five pairs in Gnathobdelliform leeches, and include three related families. The Erpobdellidae are some species from freshwater habitats.

Reproduction

Leeches are hermaphrodites, meaning they are organisms that have both female and male reproductive organs (ovaries and testes respectively). They reproduce by reciprocal fertilization and sperm transfer occurs during copulation. The leech exercising the role of the male will grow a sperm sack near the end of their tail, and the leech playing the female will bite it off, thus reproducing. Similarly to the earth worms, leeches also use a clitellum to hold their eggs and secrete the cocoon.

During reproduction leeches utilize hyperdermic injection of their sperm. They use a spermatophore which is a structure containing the sperm. Once next to another leech, the two will line up with their anterior side opposite the others posterior. The leech then shoots the spermatophore into the clitellur region of the opposing leech where its sperm will make its way to the female reproductive parts.

Nutrition of Leeches

Starting from the anterior sucker is the jaw, the pharynx which extends to the crop, which leads to the Intestinum, where it ends at the posterior sucker. The crop is a type of stomach that works like an expandable storage compartment. The crop allows a leech to store blood up to five times its body size; and because the leech produces an anti-coagulant, the stored blood remains in a liquid state ; because of this ability to hold blood without the blood decaying, due to bacteria living inside the crop, medicinal leeches only need to feed two times a year.

It was long thought that bacteria in the gut carried on digestion for the leech instead of endogenous enzymes which are very low or absent in the intestine. Relatively recently it has been discovered that all leeches and leech species studied do produce endogenous intestinal exopeptidases which can unlink free terminal-end amino acids, one amino acid monomer at a time, from a gradually unwinding and degrading protein polymer. However, unzipping of the protein can start from either the amino (tail) or carboxyl (head) terminal-end of the protein molecule. It just so happens that the leech exopeptidase (arylamidases), possibly aided by proteases from endosymbiotic bacteria in the intestine, starts from the tail or amino protein, free-end, slowly but progressively removing many hundreds of individual terminal amino acids for resynthesis into proteins that constitute the leech. Since leeches lack endopeptidases, the mechanism of protein digestion can not follow the same sequence as it would in all other animals where exopeptidases act sequentially on peptides produced by the action of endopeptidases. Exopeptidases are especially prominent in the common North American worm-leech *Erpobdella punctata*. This evolutionary choice of exopeptic digestion in Hirudinea distinguishes these carnivorous clitellates from Oligochaeta.

Deficiency of digestive enzymes (except exopeptidases) but more importantly deficiency of vitamins, B complex for example, in leeches is compensated for by enzymes and vitamins produced by endosymbiotic microflora. In *Hirudo medicinalis* these supplementary factors are produced by an obligatory symbiotic relationship with two bacterial species, *Aeromonas veronii* and a still uncharacterized *Rikenella* species. Non-bloodsucking leeches such as *Erpobdella punctata* are host to three bacterial symbionts, *Pseudomonas* sp., *Aeromonas* sp., and *Klebsiella* sp. (a slime producer). The bacteria are passed from parent to offspring in the cocoon as it is formed.

Though all species of leeches feed on blood, not all species can bite; 90% of them solely feed off decomposing bodies and open wounds of amphibians, reptiles, waterfowl, fish, and mammals (including, but not limited to, humans). A leech attaches itself when it bites, and it will stay attached until it has had its fill of blood. Due to an anticoagulant (hirudin) that leeches secrete, bites may bleed more than a normal wound after the leech is removed. The effect of the anticoagulant will wear off several hours after the leech is removed and the wound is cleaned.

Leeches normally carry parasites in their digestive tract which cannot survive in humans and do not pose a threat. However, bacteria, viruses, and parasites from previous blood sources can survive within a leech for months, and may be retransmitted to humans. A study found both HIV and hepatitis B in African leeches from Cameroon

Removal

One recommended method of removal is using a fingernail to break the seal of the oral sucker at the anterior end (the smaller, thinner end) of the leech, repeating with the posterior end, then flicking the leech away. As the fingernail is pushed along the person's skin against the leech, the suction of sucker's seal is broken, at which point the leech should detach its jaws.

A common but medically inadvisable technique to remove a leech is to apply a flame, a lit cigarette, salt, soap, or a caustic chemical such as alcohol, vinegar, lemon juice, insect repellent, heat rub, or certain carbonated drinks. These cause the leech to regurgitate its stomach contents into the wound and quickly detach. The vomit may carry disease and increases the risk of infection.

Simply pulling a leech off by grasping it can also cause regurgitation, and adds risks of further tearing the wound, and leaving parts of the leech's jaw in the wound, which can also increase the risk of infection.

An externally attached leech will detach and fall off on its own when it is satiated on blood, usually in about 20 minutes (but will stay there for as long as it can), while internal attachments, such as nasal passage or vaginal attachments, are more likely to require medical intervention.

Treatment

After removal or detachment, the wound should be cleaned with soap and water, and bandaged. Bleeding may continue for some time, due to the leech's anti-clotting enzyme. Applying pressure can reduce bleeding, although blood loss from a single bite is not dangerous. The wound normally itches as it heals, but should not be scratched as this may complicate healing and introduce other infections. An antihistamine can reduce itching, and applying a cold pack can reduce pain or swelling.

Some people suffer severe allergic or anaphylactic reactions from leech bites, and require urgent medical care. Symptoms include red blotches or an itchy rash over the body, swelling away from the bitten area (especially around the lips or eyes), feeling faint or dizzy, and difficulty breathing.

Prevention

There is no guaranteed method of preventing leech bites in leech-infested areas. The most reliable method is to cover exposed skin. The effect of insect repellents is disputed, but it is generally accepted that strong (maximum strength or tropical) insect repellents do help prevent bites.

Leech socks can be helpful in preventing bites when the full body will not be at risk of contact with leeches. Leech socks are pulled over the wearer's trousers to prevent leeches reaching the exposed skin of the legs and attaching there or climbing towards the torso. The socks are generally a light color that also makes it easier to spot leeches climbing up from the feet and looking for skin to attach to.

There are many home remedies to help prevent leech bites. Many people have a great deal of faith in these methods, but none of them has been proven effective. ome home remedies include: a dried residue of bath soap, tobacco leaves between the toes, pastes of salt or baking soda, citrus juice, and eucalyptus oil. Diluted calcium hydroxide may also be used as a repellent, but may be damaging or irritating to the skin.

ACANTHOCEPHALA

The Acanthocephala (Greek, *akanthos*, thorn + *kephale*, head) is a phylum of parasitic worms known as acanthocephales, thorny-headed worms, or spiny-headed worms, characterised by the presence of an evertable proboscis, armed with spines, which it uses to pierce and hold the gut wall of its host. Acanthocephalans typically have complex life cycles, involving a number of hosts, including invertebrates, fishes, amphibians, birds, and mammals. About 1150 species have been described.

Morphological Characteristics

There are several morphological characteristics that distinguish acanthocephalans from other phyla of parasitic worms.

Digestion

Acanthocephalans lack a mouth or alimentary canal. This is a feature they share with the cestoda (tapeworms), although the two groups are not related. Adult stages live in the intestines of their host and uptake nutrients which have been digested by the host, directly, through their body surface.

Proboscis

The most notable feature of the acanthocephala is the presence of an anterior, protrudible proboscis that is usually covered with spiny hooks (hence the common name: thorny headed worm). The proboscis bears rings of recurved hooks arranged in horizontal rows, and it is by means of these hooks that the animal attaches itself to the tissues of its host. The hooks may be of two or three shapes, usually, longer, more slender hooks are arranged along the length of the proboscis, with several rows of more sturdy, shorter nasal hooks around the base of the proboscis. The proboscis is used to pierce the gut wall of the final host, and hold the parasite fast while it completes its life cycle. Like the body, the proboscis is hollow, and its cavity is separated from the body cavity by a *septum* or *proboscis sheath*. Traversing the cavity of the proboscis are muscle-strands inserted into the tip of the proboscis at one end and into the septum at the other. Their contraction causes the proboscis to be invaginated into its cavity. The whole proboscis apparatus can also be, at least partially, withdrawn into the body cavity, and this is effected by two retractor muscles which run from the posterior aspect of the septum to the body wall.

Phylogenetic Relationships

Acanthocephalans are highly adapted to a parasitic mode of life, and have lost many organs and structures through evolutionary processes. This makes determining relationships with other higher taxa through morphological comparison problematic. Phylogenetic analysis of the 18S ribosomal gene has revealed that the Acanthocephala are most closely related to the rotifers, or may even belong in that phylum. The two are included among the Platyzoa.

Size

The size of the animals varies greatly, from forms a few millimetres in length to *Gigantorhynchus gigas*, which measures from 100 to 650 mm.

Skin

The body surface of the acanthocephala is peculiar. Externally, the skin has a thin cuticle covering the epidermis, which consists of a syncytium with no cell walls. The syncytium is traversed by a series of branching tubules containing fluid and is controlled by a few wandering, amoeboid nuclei. Inside the syncytium is an irregular layer of circular muscle fibres, and within this again some rather scattered longitudinal fibres; there is no endothelium. In their micro-structure the muscular fibres resemble those of nematodes.

Except for the absence of the longitudinal fibres the skin of the proboscis resembles that of the body, but the fluid-containing tubules of the proboscis are shut off from those of the body. The canals of the proboscis open into a circular vessel which runs round its base. From the circular canal two sac-like projections called the *lemnisci* run into the cavity of the body, alongside the proboscis cavity. Each consists of a prolongation of the syncytial material of the proboscis skin, penetrated by canals and sheathed with a muscular coat. They seem to act as reservoirs into which the fluid which is used to keep the proboscis "erect" can withdraw when it is retracted, and from which the fluid can be driven out when it is wished to expand the proboscis.

Nervous System

The central ganglion of the nervous system lies behind the proboscis sheath or septum. It innervates the proboscis and projects two stout trunks posteriorly which supply the body. Each of these trunks is surrounded by muscles, and this nerve-muscle complex is called a *retinaculum*. In the male at least there is also a genital ganglion. Some scattered papillae may possibly be sense-organs.

"Brain-jacking"

Thorny-headed worms begin their life cycle inside invertebrates that reside in lakes and rivers. *Gammarus lacustris*, a small crustacean that feeds near ponds and rivers, is one invertebrate that the thorny-headed worm may occupy. This crustacean is depredated by ducks and hides by avoiding light and staying away from the surface. However, when infected by a thorny-headed worm it becomes attracted toward light and surfaces itself. *Gammarus lacustris* will even go so far as to find a rock or a plant on the surface, clamp its mouth down, and latch on, making it easy prey for the duck.

It is thought that when *Gammarus lacustris* is infected with a thorny-headed worm, the parasite causes serotonin to be massively expressed. Serotonin is a neurotransmitter involved in emotions and mood. Researchers have found that during mating *Gammarus lacustris* expresses high levels of serotonin. Also during mating, the male *Gammarus lacustris* clamps down on the female and holds on for days. Researchers have additionally found that blocking serotonin releases clamping. Another experiment found that serotonin also reduces the photophobic behavior in *Gammarus lacustris*. Thus, it is thought that the thorny-headed worm physiologically changes the behavior of the *Gammarus lacustris* in order to enter its final host, the bird.

Sex

The Acanthocephala are dioecious. There is a structure called the *genital ligament* which runs from the posterior end of the proboscis sheath to the posterior end of the body. In the male, two testes lie on either side of this. Each opens in a vas deferens which bears three diverticula or *vesiculae seminales*. The male also possesses three pairs of cement glands, found behind the testes, which pour their secretions through a duct into the vasa deferentia. These unite and end in a penis which opens posteriorly.

In the female, the ovaries are found, like the testes, as rounded bodies along the ligament. From these masses of ova dehisce into the body cavity and float in its fluid. Here the eggs are fertilized and segment so that the young embryos are formed within their mother's body. The embryos escape into the uterus through the *uterine bell*, a funnel like opening continuous with the uterus. At the junction of the bell and the uterus there is a second small opening situated dorsally. The bell "swallows" the matured embryos and passes them on into the uterus, and from there, out of the body via the oviduct. Should the bell swallow any of the ova, or even one of the younger embryos, these are passed back into the body cavity through the second, dorsal, opening.

The embryo passes from the body of the female into the alimentary canal of the host and leaves this with the feces.

Other Features

A curious feature shared by both larva and adult is the large size of many of the cells, e.g. the nerve cells and cells forming the uterine bell. Polyploidy is common, with up to 343n having been recorded in some species. The acanthocephalans lack an excretory system, although some species have been shown to possess flame cells (protonephridia).

History

The earliest recognisable description of Acanthocephala - a worm with a proboscis armed with hooks - was made by Italian author Francesco Redi (1684). In 1771 Koelreuther proposed the name Acanthocephala. Muller independetly called them Echinorhynchus in 1776. Rudolphi in 1809 formally named them Acanthocephala.

Currently the phylum is divided into four classes - Palaeacanthocephala, Archiacanthocephala, Polyacanthocephala and Eoacanthocephala.

Life-cycle

General Patterns

Acanthocephalans have complex life cycles, involving a number of hosts, for both developmental and resting stages. Complete life cycles have been worked out for only 25 species. Having been expelled by the female, the acanthocephalan embryo is released along with the feces of the host. For development to occur, the embryo needs to be ingested by an invertebrate, almost always a crustacean (there is one known life cycle which uses a mollusc as a first intermediate host). Inside the intermediate host, the acanthocephalan penetrates the gut wall, moves into the body cavity, encysts, and begins transformation into the infective *cystacanth* stage. This form has all the organs of the adult save the reproductive ones. The parasite is released when the first intermediate host is ingested. This can be by a suitable final host, in which case the cystacanth develops into a mature adult, or by a paratenic host, in which the parasite again forms a cyst. When consumed by a suitable final host, the cycstacant *excysts*, everts its proboscis and pierces the gut wall. It then feeds, grows and develops its sexual organs. Adult worms then mate. The male uses the excretions of its *cement glands* to plug the vagina of the female, preventing subsequent matings from occurring. Embryos develop inside the female, and the life cycle repeats.

An Example - Polymorphus sp.

Polymorphus sp. are parasites of seabirds, particularly the Eider Duck (*Somateria mollissima*). Heavy infections of up to 750 parasites per bird are common, causing ulceration to the gut, disease and seasonal mortality. Recent research has suggested that there is no evidence of pathogenicity of *Polymorphus* spp. to intermediate crab hosts. The cystacanth stage is long lived and probably remains infective throughout the life of the crab.

The life cycle of *Polymorphus* sp. normally occurs between sea ducks (e.g. eiders and scoters) and small crabs. Infections found in commercial-sized lobsters in Canada were probably acquired from crabs that form an important dietary item of lobsters. Cystacanths occurring in lobsters can cause economic loss to fishermen. There are no known methods of prevention or control.

CESTODA

Cestoda is a class of parasitic flatworms, commonly called tapeworms, that live in the digestive tract of vertebrates as adults and often in the bodies of various animals as juveniles. *Taenia saginata*, the beef tapeworm, can grow up to 40 feet long (12 m); other species may grow to over 100 feet (30 m).

Craig and Ito describe the gut-dwelling worm as segmented and band-like in its adult stage. Its first stage in tissues and organs of vertebrates, including humans, is the growth of a cyst-like juvenile (or metacestode). The potential cause of illness and disease is due to a metacestode stage happening in human tissues, rather than an adult tapeworm.

The tegument is the body surface of the adult tapeworm. Tapeworms take the host's nutrients and do not attack the mucosa of the small intestine or remove blood. Infections, therefore, are benign. Most often hosts do not show any signs of illness. A carrier can notice the segments (*proglottides*) when using the bathroom, for instance, in the feces in a toilet bowl. Because tapeworms move around constantly, one may find them in undergarments.

Anatomy

Scolex

The worm's *scolex* ("head") attaches to the intestine of the definitive host. In some species, the scolex is dominated by bothria, which are sometimes called "sucking grooves", and function like suction cups. Other species have hooks and suckers that aid in attachment. Cyclophyllid cestodes can be identified by the presence of four suckers on their scolex, though they may have other structures.

While the scolex is often the most distinctive part of an adult tapeworm, it is often unnoticed in a clinical setting as it is inside the patient. Thus, identifying eggs and proglottids in feces is important.

Mascular System

The main nerve center of a cestode is in its scolex. Motor and sensory innervation depends on the number and complexity of the scolex. Smaller nerves emanate from the commissures to supply the general body muscular and sensory ending. The cirrus and vagina are innervated and sensory endings around the genital pore are more plentiful than other areas. Sensory function includes both tactoreception and chemoreception.

Proglottids

The body is composed of successive segments (*proglottids*). The sum of the proglottids is called a strobila, which is thin, resembling a strip of tape, and is the source of the common name "tapeworm". Like some other flatworms, cestodes use flame cells (protonephridia) for excretion, which are located in the proglottids.

Mature or gravid proglottids are released from the tapeworm and leave the host in its feces.

Because each proglottid contains the male and female reproductive structures, they can reproduce independently. It has been suggested by some biologists[*who?*] that each should be considered a single organism, and that the tapeworm is actually a colony of proglottids.

The layout of proglottids comes in two forms, craspedote, meaning proglottids are overlapped by the previous proglottid, and acraspedote which indicates a non-overlapping conjoined proglottid.

DIGENEA

Digenea (Gr. *Dis* - double, *Genos* - race) is a subclass within the Platyhelminthes consisting of parasitic flatworms with a syncytial tegument and, usually, two suckers, one ventral and one oral. Adults are particularly common in the digestive tract, but occur throughout the organ systems of all classes of vertebrates. Once thought to be related to the Monogenea, it is now recognised that they are closest to the Aspidogastrea and that the Monogenea are more closely allied with the Cestoda. Around 6,000 species have been described to date.

Morphology

Key Features

Characteristic features of the digenea include a syncitial tegument; that is, a tegument where the junctions between cells are broken down and a single continuous cytoplasm surrounds the entire animal. A similar tegument is found in other members of the Neodermata; a group of platyhelminths comprising the Digenea, Aspidogastrea, Monogenea and Cestoda. Digeneans possess a vermiform, unsegmented body-plan and have a solid parenchyma with no body cavity, as in all platyhelminths.

There are typically two suckers, an anterior oral sucker surrounding the mouth, and a ventral sucker sometimes termed the *acetabulum*, on the ventral surface. The oral sucker surrounds the mouth, while the ventral sucker is a blind muscular organ with no connection to any internal structure.

Monostome is a term used to describe worms with one sucker (oral). Flukes with an oral sucker and an acetabulum at the posterior end of the body are called *Amphistomes*. *Distomes* are flukes with an oral sucker and a ventral sucker, but the ventral sucker if somewhere other than posterior. These terms are common in older literature, when they were thought to reflect systematic relationships within the groups. They have fallen out of use in modern digenean taxonomy.

Reproductive System

The vast majority of digeneans is hermaphroditic. This is likely to be an adaptation to low abundance within hosts, allowing the life cycle to continue when only one individual successfully infects the final host. Fertilisation is internal, with sperm being transferred via the cirrus to the Laurer's Canal or genital aperture. A key group of digeneans which are dioecious are the schistosomes. Asexual reproduction in the first larval stage is ubiquitous.

While the sexual formation of the digenean eggs and asexual reproduction in the first larval stage (miracidium) is widely reported, the developmental biology of the asexual stages remains a problem. Electron microscopic studies have shown that the light microscopically visible germ balls consist of mitotically dividing cells which give rise to embryos and to a line of new germ cells that become included in these embryonic stages. Since the absence of meiotic processes is not proven, the exact definition remains doubtful.

Male Organs

Protandry is the general rule among the Digenea. Usually two testes are present, but some flukes can have more than 100. Also present are vasa efferentia, a vas deferens, seminal vesicle, ejaculatory duct and a cirrus (analogous to a penis) usually (but not always) enclosed in a cirrus sac. The cirrus may or may not be covered in proteinaceous spines. The exact conformation of these organs within the male terminal genitalia is taxonomically important at the familial and generic levels.

Female Organs

Usually there is a single ovary with an oviduct, a seminal receptacle, a pair of vitelline glands (involved in yolk and egg-shell production) with ducts, the ootype (a chamber where eggs are formed), a complex collection of glands cells called *Mehlis' gland*, which is believed to lubricate the uterus for egg passage.

In addition, some digeneans possess a canal called Laurer's Canal, which leads from the oviduct to the dorsal surface of the body. The function of this canal is debated, but it may be used for insemination in some species or for disposal of waste products from reproduction in other species. Most trematodes possess an ovicapt, an enlarged portion of the oviduct where it joins the ovary. It probably controls the release of ova and spaces out their descent down the uterus.

The uterus typically opens into a common genital atrium that also received the distal male copulatory organ (cirrus) before immediately opening onto the outer surface of the worm. The distal part of the uterus may be expanded into a metraterm, set off from the proximal uterus by a muscular sphincter, or it may be lined with spines, as in the Monorchiidae and some other families.

Digestive System

As adults, most digeneans possess a terminal or subterminal mouth, a muscular pharynx that provides the force for ingesting food, and a forked, blind digestive system consisting of two tubular sacs called caeca (sing. caecum). In some species the two gut caeca join posteriorly to make a ring-shaped gut or cyclocoel. In others the caeca may fuse with the body wall posteriorly to make one or more anuses, or with the excretory vesicle to form a uroproct. Digeneans are also capable of direct nutrient uptake through the tegument by pinocytosis and phagocytosis by the syncitium. Most adult digeneans occur in the vertebrate alimentary canal or its associated organs, where they most often graze on contents of the lumen (e.g., food ingested by the host, bile, mucus), but they may also feed across the mucosal wall (e.g., submucosa, host blood). The blood flukes, such as schistosomes, spirorchiids and sanguinicolids, feed exclusively on blood. Asexual stages in mollusc intermediate hosts feed mostly by direct absorption, although the redia stage found in some groups does have a mouth, pharynx and simple gut and may actively consume host tissue or even other parasites. Encysted metacercarial stages and free-living cercarial stages do not feed.

Nervous System

Paired ganglia at the anterior end of the body serve as the brain. From this nerves extend anteriorly and posteriorly. Sensory receptors are, for the most part, lacking among the adults, although they do have tangoreceptor cells. Larval stages have many kinds of sensory receptors, including light receptors and chemoreceptors. Chemoreception plays an important role in the free-living miracidial larva recognising and locating its host.

Life Cycles

There is a bewildering array of variation on the complex digenean life cycle, and plasticity in this trait is probably a key to the group's success. In general, the life cycles may have two, three, or four obligate (necessary) hosts, sometimes with transport or paratenic hosts in between. The three-host life cycle is probably the most common. In almost all species, the first host in the life cycle is a mollusc. This has led to the inference that the ancestral digenean was a mollusc parasite and that vertebrate hosts were added subsequently.

The alternation of sexual and asexual generations is an important feature of digeneans. This phenomenon involves the presence of several discrete generations in one life-cycle.

A typical digenean trematode life cycle is as follows. Eggs leave the vertebrate host in faeces and use various strategies to infect the first intermediate host, in which sexual reproduction does not occur. Digeneans may infect the first intermediate host (usually a snail) by either passive or active means. The eggs of some digeneans, for example, are (passively) eaten by snails (or, rarely, by an annelid worm), in which they proceed to hatch. Alternatively, eggs may hatch in water to release an actively swimming, ciliated larva, the miracidium, which must locate and penetrate the body wall of the snail host.

After post-ingestion hatching or penetration of the snail, the miracidium metamorphoses into a simple, sac-like *mother sporocyst*. The mother sporocyst undergoes a round of internal asexual reproduction, giving rise to either *rediae* (sing. redia) or *daughter sporocysts*. The second generation is thus the daughter parthenita sequence. These in turn undergo further asexual reproduction, ultimately yielding large numbers of the second free-living stage, the *cercaria* (pl. cercariae).

Free-swimming cercariae leave the snail host and move through the aquatic or marine environment, often using a whip-like tail, though a tremendous diversity of tail morphology is seen. Cercariae are infective to the second host in the life cycle, and infection may occur passively (e.g., a fish consumes a cercaria) or actively (the cercaria penetrates the fish).

The life-cycles of some digeneans include only two hosts, the second being a vertebrate. In these groups, sexual maturity occurs after the cercaria penetrates the second host, which is in this case also the definitive host. Two host life-cycles can be primary (there never was a third host) as in the Bivesiculidae, or secondary (there was at one time in evolutionary history a third host but it has been lost).

In three-host life-cycles, cercariae develop in the second intermediate host into a resting stage, the *metacercaria*, which is usually encysted in a cyst of host and parasite origin, or encapsulated in a layer of tissue derived from the host only. This stage is infective to the definitive host. Transmission occurs when the definitive host preys upon an infected second intermediate host. Metacercariae excyst in the definitive host's gut in response to a variety of physical and chemical signals, such as gut pH levels, digestive enzymes, temperature, etc. Once excysted, adult digeneans migrate to more or less specific sites in the definitive host and the life cycle repeats.

Evolution

The evolutionary origins of the Digenea have been debated for some time, but there appears general agreement that the proto-digenean was a parasite of a mollusc, possibly of the mantle cavity. Evidence for this comes from the ubiquity of molluscs as first intermediate hosts for digeneans, and the fact that most aspidogastreans (the sister group to the Digenea) also have mollusc associations. It is thought that the early trematodes (the collective name for digeneans and aspidogastreans) likely evolved from rhabdocoel turbellarians that colonised the open mantle cavity of early molluscs.

It is likely that more complex life cycles evolved through a process of terminal addition, whereby digeneans survived predation of their mollusc host, probably by a fish. Other hosts were added by until the modern bewildering diversity of life cycle patterns developed.

There are some digenean families that are either basal to or *incertae sedis* among the orders listed above:

- Acanthocollaritrematidae
- Echinoporidae
- Gekkonotrematidae
- Gyliauchenidae
- Jubilariidae
- Meristocotylidae
- Mesotretidae

Human Digenean Infections

Only about 12 of the 6000 known species are infectious to humans, but some of these species are important diseases afflicting over 200 million people. The species that infect humans can be divided into groups, the schistosomes and the non-schistosomes.

Schistosomes

The Schistosomes occur in the circulatory system of the definitive host. Humans become infected after free-swimming cercaria liberated from infected snails penetrate the skin. These dioecious worms are long and thin, ranging in size from 10 to 30 mm in length to 0.2 to 1.0 mm in diameter. Adult males are shorter and thicker than females, and have a long groove along one side of the body in which the female is clasped. Females reach sexual maturity after they have been united with a male. After mating the two remain locked together for the rest of their lives. They can live for several years and produce many thousands of eggs.

The four species of schistosomes that infect humans are members of the genus *Schistosoma.*

Non-schistosomes

There seven major species of non-schistosomes that infect humans. People become infected after ingesting metacercarial cysts on plants or in undercooked animal flesh. Most species inhabit the human gastrontestinal tract, where they shed eggs along with host feces. *Paragonimus westermani,* which colonizes the lungs, can also pass its eggs in saliva. These flukes generally cause mild pathology in humans, but more serious effects may also occur.

MONOGENEA

Monogenea (adj. monogenean) are a group of largely ectoparasitic members of the flatworm phylum Platyhelminthes, class Monogenea.

Characteristics

Monogenea are small parasitic flatworms mainly found on skin or gills of fish. They are rarely longer than about 2cm. A few species infecting certain marine fish are larger and marine forms are generally larger than those found on fresh water hosts. Monogeneans lack respiratory, skeletal and circulatory systems and have no or weakly-developed oral suckers. . Monogenea attach to hosts using hooks, clamps and a variety of other specialized structures. They are often capable of dramatically elongating and shortening as they move. Biologists need to ensure that specimens are completely relaxed before measurements are taken.

Like all ectoparasites monogeneans have well developed attachment structures. The anterior structures are collectively termed the prohaptor, while the posterior ones are collectively termed the opisthaptor. The posterior opishaptor with its hooks, anchors, clamps etc. is typically the major attachment organ.

Like other flatworms, Monogenea have no true body cavity (coelom). They have a simple digestive system consisting of a mouth opening with a muscular pharynx and an intestine with no terminal opening (anus). Generally, they also are [hermaphroditic] with functional reproductive organs of both sexes occurring in one individual. Most species are oviparous but a few are vivarous. Monogenea are Platyhelminthes and therefore are among the lowest invertebrates to possess three embryonic germ layers—endoderm, mesoderm, and ectoderm. In addition, they have a head region that contains concentrated sense organs and nervous tissue (brain).

Systematics and Evolution

The ancestors of Monogenea were probably free-living flatworms similar to modern Turbellaria. According to the more widely accepted view, "rhabdocoel turbellarians gave rise to monogeneans; these, in turn, gave rise to digeneans, from which the cestodes were derived. Another view is that the rhabdocoel ancestor gave rise to two lines; one gave rise to monogeneans, who gave rise to digeneans, and the other line gave rise to cestodes".

There are about 50 families and thousands of described species.

Some parasitologists divide Monogenea into two (or three) subclasses based on the complexity of their haptor: Monopisthocotylea have one main part to the haptor, often with hooks or a large attachment disc, whereas Polyopisthocotylea have multiple parts to the haptor, typically clamps. These groups are also known as Polyonchoinea and Heteronchoinea, respectively. Polyopisthocotyleans are almost exclusively gill-dwelling blood feeders, whereas Monopisthocotyleans may live on the gills, skin and fins.

Monopistocotylea include:

- Genus *Gyrodactylus,* which has no eyespots and is viviparous.
- Genus *Dactylogyrus,* which has four eyespots and is oviparous. This is one of the largest metazoan genera, with at least 970 species.
- Genus *Neobenedenia,* which is much larger and lives on the skin of many tropical marine species, causing problematic infections in marine aquaria.

All of which can cause epizootics in freshwater fish when raised in aquaculture.

Polyopisthocotylea include:

- Genus *Diclidophora,* which is primarily found in marine fish and primitive freshwater fish like sturgeons and paddlefish.

Ecology and Life-cycle

Monogeneans pocess the simplest life cycle among the parasitic platyhelminths. They have no intermediate hosts and are ectoparasitic on fish (seldom in the urinary bladder and rectum of cold-blooded vertebrates). Although they are hermaphrodites, the male reproductive system becomes functional before the female part. The eggs hatch releasing a heavily ciliated larval stage known as an *oncomiracidium.* The *oncomiracidium* has numerous posterior hooks and is generally the life stage responsible for transmission from host to host.

No known monogeneans infect birds, but one (*Oculotrema hippopotami*) infects mammals, parasitizing the eye of the hippopotamus.

4

Parasitic Protozoa

INTRODUCTION

Protozoa are single-celled organisms. They are the cause of more sickness, death, mutilation, and debilitation in the world than any other group of disease-causing organisms. As eukayotes, protozoa have a membrane-bound nucleus with well-defined chromosomes. They also have other cellular organelles that are characteristic of eukaryotes.

TRICHOMONAS VAGINALIS

This is a flagellate venereal disease that is found worldwide. Males carry the infection, but are usually asymptomatic. Females are also often asymptomatic. However, vaginal infections may cause inflammation, discomfort, and discharge. Secondary bacterial infections may occur along with trichomonas vaginalis.

The *Trichomonas vaginalis* organism feeds on bacteria and white blood cells. It can live outside the body in bath water, on toilet seats, or on washcloths. Diagnosis is by finding the parasite in discharges or by culture. The drug of choice for treating this condition is metronidazole.

TRYPANOSOMA (T. cruzi, T. gambiense)

These organisms are transmitted by an animal vector. They parasitize (they live in) insects and have secondary vertebrate hosts, such as cattle and humans. Most trypanosomes live in the blood and tissue fluids. Some important species, such as *T. cruzi*, live inside cells. Most are transmitted by blood-feeding invertebrates, such as flies.

African sleeping sickness is transmitted by the tsetse fly and is caused by *T. rhodesiense or T. gambiense*. These flies live in the heart of Africa, between 15 N and 20 S latitude. In some regions up to 30% of the populace is infected with trypanosomes.

In the vertebrate host, these organisms live in the blood, lymph nodes, spleen, and cerebrospinal fluid. The trypanosomes do not actually invade or live in cells. Instead, they inhabit spaces in connective tissue in various organs.

During an infection, the lymph nodes become swollen and congested, especially in the neck, groin and legs. Periods of fever accompany early stages of the infection.

Successive parasite populations change immunologically. This means that they disguise themselves to avoid being attacked and destroyed by the immune system. These successive populations cause increased swelling, pain, headaches, weakness, and cramps.

When the central nervous system becomes involved, the classic symptoms of sleeping-sickness are induced. Apathy, mental dullness, disturbances in coordination, tremors, paralysis, and convulsions usually follow.

As the infection progresses, sleepiness increases. People often fall asleep while eating or standing. Finally, coma and death occur.

Arsenical drugs are used in treatment, but toxicity is common. Serious complications can involve the nervous system, liver and heart. The trypanosomes can also become tolerant to these types of drugs. Suramin, pentamidine, and Berenil have been used successfully in early stages of the disease.

There is no vaccine because the parasites periodically change surface antigens—the markers that identify them as foreign to the immune system.

Chagas Disease

Chagas disease is common in Mexico and South America. It is thought that Charles Darwin suffered from chronic Chagus disease following his trip to South America. It is caused by *T. cruzi*, and is characterized by an acute phase in which several symptoms occur: anemia, loss of strength, nervous disorders, chills, muscle and bone pain, and varying degrees of heart failure. Death may occur 3-4 weeks after infection.

A chronic form of Chagas disease is seen usually in adults. The chronic form is characterized by dysfunctions in the central and peripheral nervous system. Many patients die of heart failure due to an enlargement of the heart and subsequent lack of cardiac muscle tone. Others suffer heart damage because the parasite damages the nervous supply to the heart. The heart muscle then atrophies (the muscle shrinks). The atrophy leads to congestive heart failure, because the muscle cannot pump blood efficiently. The intestine may also become immobile and enlarged due to the degradation of the nervous supply to that organ.

Nifurtimox, available in the US, kills the parasite when it is in the blood. However, there is no known treatment for the intracellular stages of the parasite. Treatment of parasite-induced heart failure is an attempt to control the symptoms. Intestinal problems usually require surgical repair.

LEISHMANIASIS

Leishmaniasis is caused by *Leishmania donovani* and is transmitted by sand flies. Leishmaniasis has a wide distribution that extends from the Mediterranean to Middle Asia, to southern Russia and China. It is also known as *kala-azar* (black fever) or Assam fever.

The disease usually begins slowly with a low-grade fever and malaise. This is followed by progressive wasting and anemia, protrusion of the abdomen from an enlarged liver and spleen, and finally by death in 2-3 years. In some forms, the parasite attacks the skin. In these cases, the parasite causes severe lesions that may persist in some forms or spontaneously heal in others.

Diagnosis is by finding the parasite in smears from skin lesions or in bone marrow, spleen, liver, or blood smears. Treatment consists of an injection of antimonial compounds, good nursing care, and nutritional supplementation.

GIARDIA

Giardia lamblia is the most common flagellate in the human digestive system. It is highly contagious and can be found almost anywhere that people are also found. It occurs in the highest concentrations in warm climates. Epidemics occur sporadically, and waterborne outbreaks have been reported in the US. In some geographic locations, giardiasis has become a traveler's diarrhea like ammoebic dystentery. Children are especially susceptible to infection.

The disease occurs when cysts are ingested, usually by drinking contaminated water. The protozoans attach to the surface of the intestine and feed on the mucous secretions of the intestine. A heavy infection can hinder the body's ability to take up nutrients. Symptoms usually appear two weeks after exposure and include: diarrhea, dehydration, stomach cramps, gas, and weight loss.

Prevention of giardiasis depends on good sanitation. Standard concentrations of chlorine for water treatment do not kill the infective form of giardia. In emergencies, the parasite can be killed by using 2-4 drops of household bleach in one litre of water, then by letting the water sit for one hour before drinking.

The disease is diagnosed by finding cysts in fecal smears. Treatment is typically with metronidazole (Flagyl®) and usually produces a cure within a few days. Alternatives include furazolidone, paromomycin, or bacitracin.

Amoebic Dysentery

Amoebic dysentery has been a great debilitator in times of war throughout the ages. Modern tourists often find they have picked up amoebic dysentery (popularly called "Montezuma's Revenge") along with their souvenirs. It is found throughout the world, and is caused by the protozoan *Entamoeba histolytica.*

The protozoan is transmitted by fecal cysts in contaminated food or water. Once ingested, the organism secretes enzymes (special chemicals) that digest in the intestinal lining. This leads to a perforated colon and peritonitis, which is an inflammation of the lining of the abdominal wall. These complications can be fatal. The liver and the lungs may also become hosts to the parasites.

Host responses vary, so symptoms also vary. Factors that affect the host's response include the physical and emotional condition of the host when his or her immune system is challenged. Usually, the disease develops slowly, with intermittent diarrhea, cramps, vomiting, and a general bad feeling. In severe cases, dehydration and anemia result from the loss of fluids and blood.

Diagnosis is made by finding the organism in stool samples. Treatment is a two-fold attack. Antibiotics are used to kill the organism in the body, and an agent is used to kill the microorganisms throughout the intestine. Several antibiotics are used, including metronidazole (the drug of choice), tetracycline, and chloroquine.

Amoebic meningoencephalitis

Amoebic meningoencephalitis is caused primarily by *Naegleria fowleri*. This is normally a free-living ameoba. The parasite gains entry into its host via the nasal passages when the person swims in infected waters. It colonizes the nasal epithelium, then travels down nerve tracts to the brain. Once in the brain, the infection causes headaches, fever, stiff neck, nausea, drowsiness, convulsions, and coma. Death occurs within 10 days, usually on the 5th or 6th day. The incubation period is 2-3 days to two weeks. No person-to-person transmission has been reported.

Balantidaisis

Balantidaisis is a form of dysentery. It is caused by the only ciliated protozoan parasite of humans (*Balantidium coli*). This parasite is found worldwide. There is a slight correlation between the incidence of the disease and the presence of hogs.

The balantidaisis organisms feed on epithelium and red blood cells in the colon and can cause ulcers. Diagnosis is by finding the parasite in feces.

Toxoplasmosis

Toxoplasmosis is caused by ingesting infective cysts of the parasite *Toxoplasma gondii*. The intestine is affected first, followed by the lymph nodes, which swell and become painful. Other symptoms include fever, headache, muscle pain, and anemia. Toxoplasmosis may also infect the eye, causing blindness.

In congenital toxoplasmosis, a mother infected at the time of conception or during pregnancy, transmits the infection to the developing fetus. The parasite infects the fetus by crossing the placental barrier. Most neo-natal infections are without symptoms. Some cause fetal death or birth defects. Fetal infection may result in spontaneous abortion or stillbirth.

Toxoplasmosis is acquired by eating raw or undercooked meat, and through contact with an infected feline, such as the household cat. Any cat, no matter how protected, well-fed, or well-cared for may pass the infective organism in excrement unless they are kept from hunting and eating the kill. Even strictly kept house cats may become infected through cockroach or fly hunting as these are transport hosts. Cats pass the organism for several days after becoming infected.

A woman who might be or is pregnant should not clean cat litter boxes or handle intestinal messes (vomit, hairballs, etc). Infection may also be acquired from gardening or ingesting unwashed, contaminated fruits and vegetables. Children's sandboxes should be covered to prevent contact with excretions from infected cats.

Diagnosis of toxoplasmosis is by demonstration of the organism in biopsy. More commonly, diagnosis is by demonstration of a specific antibody (protein marker in your blood) for the organism.

Treatment is usually with a combination of pyrimethamine and sulfonamides. Possible side effects of these drugs include low numbers of platelets and or white blood cells. These side effects can be avoided by taking supplements, particularly of folic acid.

Cryptosporidium Parvum

This protozoan is present in most surface water and is an obligate intracellular parasite of many species. Those species from mammals are generally infective for other mammals. *C. parvum* seems to lack strict host specificity and is thought to transmit from calves to mice in nature. Humans become infected usually via the ingestion of infected organisms in drinking water.

The infective stage of the organism, the oocyst, is about 3 μm in diameter. Through contamination of the environment, food, or water, a suitable host ingests oocysts. In the gastrointestinal or respiratory tracts of the host, sporozoites exit from the oocyst and parasitize epithelial cells. The infectious dose is thought to be less than 10 organisms and presumably one organism can initiate an infection. Watery diarrhea, cramps, and headache characterize Cryprosporidiosis in its most frequent intestinal form. The lungs and trachea can be affected as well, producing low-grade fever and coughing.

It is most dangerous to children and immunocompromised patients, such as AIDS patients, and people undergoing cancer chemotherapy. Healthy individuals normally have shorter duration of symptoms (<20 days) and spontaneous complete recovery. Immunodeficient individuals, especially AIDS patients, may have the disease for life, with diarrhea and pulmonary symptoms contributing to death.

There are no vaccines available for prevention of cryptosporidiosis in either animals or humans. Human infections have been reported on six continents, in developed and less developed countries and in urban and rural areas. In the U.S., large outbreaks have been associated with contaminated water supplies. Some experts estimate that 10 million cases of cryptosporidiosis occur per year. Several large waterborne outbreaks in municipal water sources have occurred since 1987 in Georgia, Texas, Oregon and Wisconsin.

MALARIA

Malaria, the world's most prevalent vector-borne disease, is caused by the *Plasmodium* species and has been known since the time of the Egyptians. Historical records show that descriptions of an intermittant fever are reported following the flooding of the Nile. In early American history, people living in coastal marsh areas would have separate inland living quarters for the summer season, if they were fortunate. Today some 1,000 cases of malaria are reported annually in the US while 500 million people are infected worldwide each year and 2-3 million die.

The parasite requires two hosts: a mosquito and a vertebrate. When a mosquito feeds on a human, the parasites are injected into the bite wound. The parasite undergoes some development prior to infecting red blood cells. In red blood cells, the parasite digests hemoglobin (the protein that carries oxygen in the blood), and leaves behind indigestible portions and waste materials in the blood cell. When the blood cell ruptures, the released waste causes some of the symptoms associated with malaria.

Malaria symptoms occur in cycles. Symptoms include chills, fever, and anemia. A typical attack is characterized by severe chills, followed by fever. The teeth chatter, and the victim may shiver intensely. Nausea and vomiting are common. Nausea and/ or vomiting is followed by an intense feeling of heat and mild delirium. The victim may sleep after an episode and until the next cycle.

Host defences are critical in limiting the infection. Exposure to the parasite may allow some hosts to develop some protective immunity. Relapses are possible, even years after the initial infection.

Uncomplicated attacks of malaria can be treated with chloroquine. One chloroquine-resistant strain of malaria is treated with mefloquine and quinine. The resistant strain is more likely to be found in select areas, but most malaria is responsive to chloroquine. Travellers heading for endemic areas must take prophylactive chloroquine or some other preventative medication.

A new and hopeful development is the clinical testing of a multi-gene DNA vaccine intended to prevent infection by the malaria parasite *Plasmodium falciparum* (Pf). The vaccine incorporates five genes that are designed to cause production of Pf immunogens and trigger an immune response against the malaria parasite in the sporozoite and liver stages of its life cycle. The vaccine has been mildly successful (50-65% efficacy) in field trials, but the protection doesn't last longer than two months. Numerous other approaches to a malaria vaccine are under investigation by various research groups.

SICKLE-CELL ANEMIA

Sickle cell anemia results from an alteration in the gene for hemoglobin that is protective against malaria. When an individual has two copies of the gene (homozygous) the gene is deadly.

However, in the heterozygous condition (one copy) the gene is protective. In this case, the mutation of some of the hemoglobin interferes with the normal growth and development of the parasite within the red blood cell. People with the gene for sickle-cell anemia have a lower incidence of malaria and less-severe cases of malaria than other members of the population.

5

Antimicrobial Chemotherapy

INTRODUCTION

Various antimicrobial agents act by interfering with: (1) cell wall synthesis; (2) plasma membrane integrity; (3) nucleic acid synthesis; (4) ribosomal function; and (5) folate synthesis.

Cell wall synthesis is inhibited by ß-lactams, such as penicillins and cephalosporins, which inhibit peptidoglycan polymerization, and by vancomycin, which combines with cell wall substrates. Polymyxins disrupt the plasma membrane, causing leakage. The plasma membrane sterols of fungi are attacked by polyenes (amphotericin) and imidazoles. Quinolones bind to a bacterial complex of DNA and DNA gyrase, blocking DNA replication. Nitroimidazoles damage DNA. Rifampin blocks RNA synthesis by binding to DNA directed RNA polymerase. Aminoglycosides, tetracycline, chloramphenicol, erythromycin, and clindamycin all interfere with ribosome function. Sulfonamides and trimethoprim block the synthesis of the folate needed for DNA replication.

Bacteria can evolve resistance to antibiotics. Resistance factors can be encoded on plasmids or on the chromosome. Resistance may involve decreased entry of the drug, changes in the receptor (target) of the drug, or metabolic inactivation of the drug.

Combinations of antibiotics may act synergistically-producing an effect stronger than the sum of the effects of the two drugs alone or antagonistically, if one agent inhibits the effect of the other.

Adverse Effects of Antimicrobial Agents

Many antibiotics are toxic to the host. Alterations of the normal intestinal flora caused by antibiotics may result in diarrhea or in superinfection with opportunistic pathogens.

The earliest evidence of successful chemotherapy is from ancient Peru, where the Indians used bark from the cinchona tree to treat malaria. Other substances were used in ancient China, and we now know that many of the poultices used by primitive peoples contained antibacterial and antifungal substances. Modern chemotherapy has been dated to the work of Paul Ehrlich in Germany, who sought systematically to discover effective agents to treat trypanosomiasis and syphilis. He discovered p-rosaniline, which has antitrypanosomal effects, and arsphenamine, which is effective against syphilis. Ehrlich postulated that it would be possible to find chemicals that were selectively toxic for parasites but not toxic to humans. This idea has been called the "magic bullet" concept. It had little success until the 1930s, when Gerhard Domagk discovered the protective effects of prontosil, the forerunner of sulfonamide. Ironically, penicillin G was discovered fortuitously in 1929 by Fleming, who did not initially appreciate the magnitude of his discovery. In 1939 Florey and colleagues at Oxford University again isolated penicillin. In 1944 Waksman isolated streptomycin and subsequently found agents such as chloramphenicol, tetracyclines, and erythromycin in soil samples. By the 1960s, improvements in fermentation techniques and advances in medicinal chemistry permitted the synthesis of many new chemotherapeutic agents by molecular modification of existing compounds. Progress in the development of novel antibacterial agents has been great, but the development of effective, nontoxic antifungal and antiviral agents has been slow. Amphotericin B, isolated in the 1950s, remains an effective antifungal agent, although newer agents such as fluconazole are now widely used. Nucleoside analogs such as acyclovir have proved effective in the chemotherapy of selected viral infections.

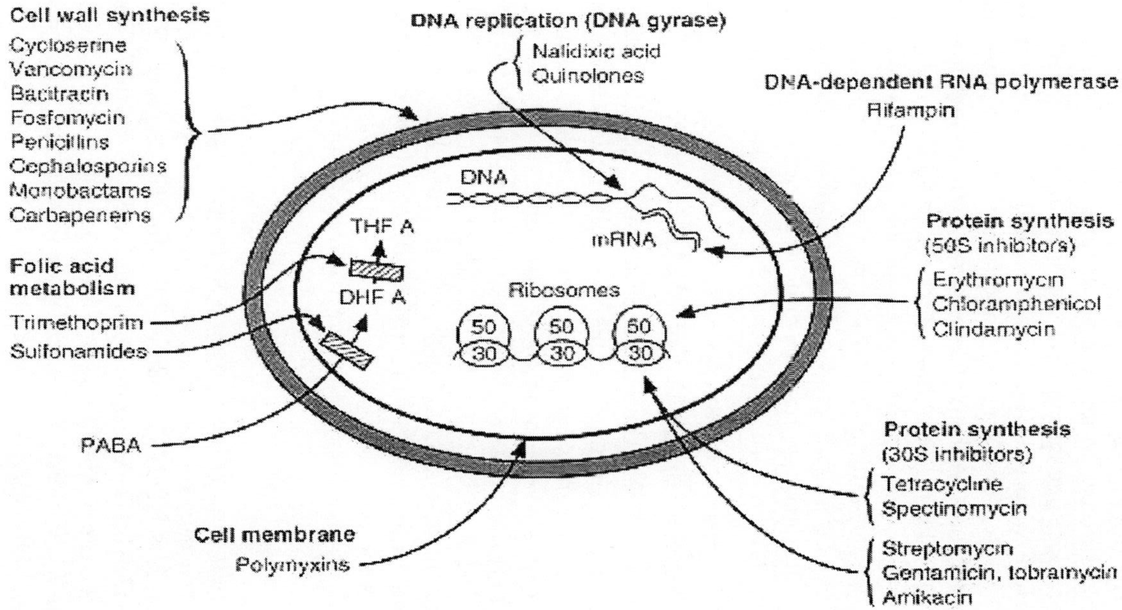

Fig. 5.1: Sites of action of different antimicrobial agent ABA, paraminobenzoic acid; DHFA, dihydrofolic acid; T, tetrahydrofolic acid.

BIOCHEMICAL BASIS OF ANTIMICROBIAL ACTION

Bacterial cells grow and divide, replicating repeatedly to reach the large numbers present during an infection or on the surfaces of the body. To grow and divide, organisms must synthesize or take up many types of biomolecules. Antimicrobial agents interfere with specific processes that are essential for growth and/or division . They can be separated into groups such as inhibitors of bacterial and fungal cell walls, inhibitors of cytoplasmic membranes, inhibitors of nucleic acid synthesis, and inhibitors of ribosome function. Antimicrobial agents may be either bactericidal, killing the target bacterium or fungus, or bacteriostatic, inhibiting its growth. Bactericidal agents are more effective, but bacteriostatic agents can be extremely beneficial since they permit the normal defenses of the host to destroy the microorganisms.

INHIBITION OF BACTERIAL CELL WALL SYNTHESIS

As noted in earlier chapters, bacteria are classified as Gram-positive and Gram-negative organisms on the basis of staining characteristics. Gram-positive bacterial cell walls contain peptidoglycan and teichoic or teichuronic acid, and the bacterium may or may not be surrounded by a protein or polysaccharide envelope. Gram-negative bacterial cell walls contain peptidoglycan, lipopolysaccharide, lipoprotein, phospholipid, and protein. The critical attack site of anti-cell-wall agents is the peptidoglycan layer. This layer is essential for the survival of bacteria in hypotonic environments; loss or damage of this layer destroys the rigidity of the bacterial cell wall, resulting in death.

Peptidoglycan synthesis occurs in three stages. The first stage takes place in the cytoplasm, where the low-molecular-weight precursors UDP-GlcAc and UDP-MurNAc-L-Ala-D-Glu-meso-Dap-D-Ala-D-Ala are synthesized. A number of antimicrobial agents interfere with these early steps in cell wall biosynthesis. UTP and N-acetylglucosamine alpha-1-P are converted to UDP-N-acetylglucosamine, which is subsequently converted by the enzyme phosphoenolpyruvate: UDP-GIcNAc-3-enol-pyruvyltransferase. Fosfomycins block this transfer by a direct nucleophilic attack on the enzyme. Because mammalian enzymes such as enolase, pyruvate kinase, carboxykinases, and the shikimate enlaces are not inhibited by these compounds, fosfomycins have no effect on the host. Three amino acids are added to the muramyl peptide to yield a tripeptide to which two more amino acids will be linked. The dipeptide D-alanyl-D-alanine is synthesized from two molecules of D-alanine by the enzyme D-alanyl-D-alanine synthetase. D-Alanine is produced from L-alanine by an alanine racemase. Cycloserine inhibits both alanine racemase and D-alanyl-D-alanine synthetase owing to the structural similarity of cycloserine and D-alanine and to the fact that cycloserine actually binds to the enzymes better than the D-alanine.

The second stage of cell wall synthesis is catalyzed by membrane-bound enzymes. The non-nucleotide portion of the precursor molecules previously made are transferred sequentially to a carrier in the cytoplasmic membrane. This carrier is a phosphorylated undecaprenyl alcohol. The lipid carrier functions as a point of attachment to the membrane for the precursors and allows for transport of the subunits across the hydrophobic interior of the cytoplasmic membrane to the outside surface. Bacitracin is a peptide antibiotic that specifically interacts with the pyrophosphate derivate of the undecaprenyl alcohol, preventing further transfer of the muramylpentapeptide from the precursor nucleotide to the nascent peptidoglycan.

The third stage of cell wall synthesis involves polymerization of the subunits and the attachment of nascent peptidoglycan to the cell wall. Polymerization occurs by transfer of the new peptidoglycan chain from its carrier in the membrane to the nonreducing N-acetylglucosamine of the new saccharide-peptide that is attached to the membrane. The new peptidoglycan is attached to preexisting cell wall peptidoglycan by a transpeptidase reaction that involves peptide chains in both polymers, one of which must possess a D-alanyl-D-alanine terminus. It is believed that the transpeptidase enzyme cleaves the peptide bond between two D-alanyl residues in the pentapeptide and become acylated via the carbonyl group of the penultimate D-alanine residue. This final reaction is inhibited by ß-lactam antibiotics. These antibiotics contain a critical four-membered ring, which undergoes an acylation reaction with the transpeptidases that cross-link the polymers mentioned above. The ß-lactam antibiotics are the penicillins (penams), cephalosporins (including oxacephems and cephamycins), penems, thienamycins (carbapenems), and aztreonam (monobactams). The enzymes involved in this final process of cell wall formation are called penicillin-binding proteins since they were discovered by labeling with radioactive penicillin G. The enzymes are different in Gram-positive and Gram-negative bacteria and in anaerobic species. Differences in the penicillin-binding proteins explain, to some extent, differences in antibacterial activity of the ß-lactam antibiotics. The penicillin-binding protein, to which a particular ß-lactam antibiotic binds, affects the morphologic response of the bacterium to the agent. For example, some antibiotics bind to a penicillin-binding protein that is involved in forming the septum between dividing cells; as a result, the bacteria continue to grow into long filaments, which eventually die. Binding to another penicillin-binding protein results in rapid lysis of a bacterium because the wall bulges and the bacterium bursts. ß-Lactams such as mecillinam (an amidino penicillin) do not bind to the penicillin-binding proteins of Gram-positive bacteria and therefore do not affect these bacteria. Aztreonam binds only to Gram-negative penicillin-binding proteins and does not inhibit Gram-positive or anaerobic species.

Vancomycin interrupts cell wall synthesis by forming a complex with the C-terminal D-alanine residues of peptidoglycan precursors. Complex formation at the outer surface of the cytoplasmic membrane prevents the transfer of the precursors from a lipid carrier to the growing peptidoglycan wall by transglycosidases. Biochemical reactions in the cell wall catalyzed by transpeptidases and D,D-carboxypeptidases are also inhibited by vancomycin and other glycopeptide antimicrobials. Because of its large size and complex structure vancomycin does not penetrate the outer membrane of gram-negative organisms. With resistance to beta-lactams increasing in frequency among staphylococci and enterococci, glycopeptides such as vancomycin remain important therapeutic agents against such bacteria.

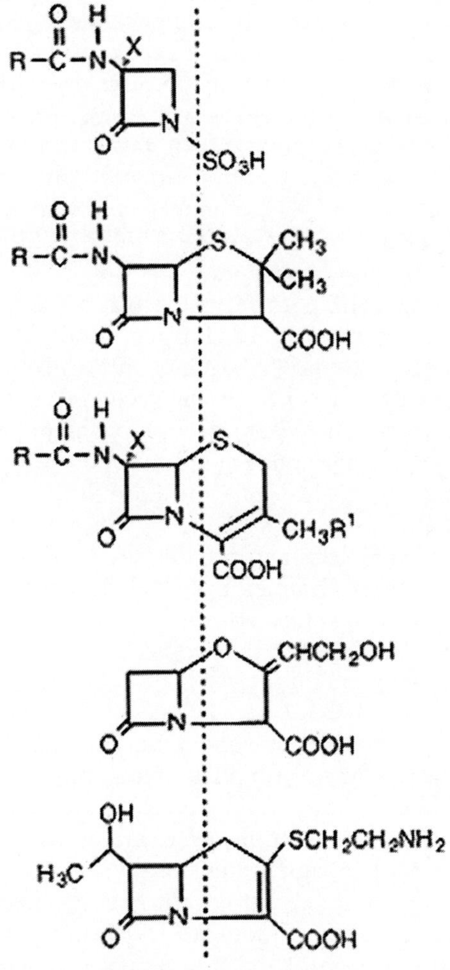

Monobactam

Penicillin

Cephalosporin
Cephamycin

Clavulanic acid

Thienamycin

Fig. 5.2: Basic structures of ß-lactam antibiotics. Penicillins and cephalosporins/cephamycins are widely used to inhibit both Gram-positive and Gram-negative bacilli. Monobactams inhibit only aerobic Gram-negative bacilli, clavulanic acid acts as a ß-lactamase inhibitor, and thienamycin inhibits a wide range of aerobic.

BACTERIAL CYTOPLASMIC MEMBRANES

Biologic membranes are composed basically of lipid, protein, and lipoprotein. The cytoplasmic membrane acts as a diffusion barrier for water, ions, nutrients, and transport systems. Most workers now believe that membranes are a lipid matrix with globular proteins randomly distributed to penetrate through the lipid bilayer. A number of antimicrobial agents can cause disorganization of the membrane. These agents can be divided into cationic, anionic, and neutral agents. The best-known compounds are polymyxin B and colistemethate (polymyxin E). These high-molecular-weight octapeptides inhibit Gram-negative bacteria that have negatively charged lipids at the surface. Since the activity of the polymyxins is antagonized by Mg^{2+} and Ca^{2+}, they probably competitively displace Mg^{2+} or Ca^{2+} from the negatively charged phosphate groups on membrane lipids. Basically, polymyxins disorganize membrane permeability so that nucleic acids and cations leak out and the cell dies. The polymyxins are of virtually no use as systemic agents since they bind to various ligands in body tissues and are potent toxins for the kidney and nervous system. Gramicidins are also membrane-active antibiotics that appear to act by producing aqueous pores in the membranes. They also are used only topically.

Fungal Membranes

Fungal membranes contain sterols, whereas bacterial membranes do not. The polyene antibiotics, which apparently act by binding to membrane sterols, contain a rigid hydrophobic center and a flexible hydrophilic section. Structurally, polyenes are tightly packed rods held in rigid extension by the polyene portion. They interact with fungal cells to produce a membrane-polyene complex that alters the membrane permeability, resulting in internal acidification of the fungus with exchange of $K+$ and sugars; loss of phosphate esters, organic acids, nucleotides; and eventual leakage of cell protein. In effect, the polyene makes a pore in the fungal membrane and the contents of the fungus leak out. Prokaryotic cells neither bind to nor are inhibited by polyenes. Although numerous polyene antibiotics have been isolated, only amphotericin B is used systemically. Nystatin is used as a topical agent and primaricin as an ophthalmic preparation.

A number of other agents interfere with the synthesis of fungal lipid membranes. These agents belong to a class of compounds referred to as imidazoles: miconazole, ketoconazole, clotrimazole, and fluconazole. These compounds inhibit the incorporation of subunits into ergosterol and may also directly damage the membrane.

Antibiotics that Inhibit Nucleic Acid Synthesis

Antimicrobial agents can interfere with nucleic acid synthesis at several different levels. They can inhibit nucleotide synthesis or interconversion; they can prevent DNA from functioning as a proper template; and they can interfere with the polymerases involved in the replication and transcription of DNA.

Interference with Nucleotide Synthesis

A large number of agents interfere with purine and pyrimidine synthesis or with the interconversion or utilization of nucleotides. Other agents act as nucleotide analogs that are incorporated into polynucleotides.

Flucytosine (5-fluorocytosine) is an antifungal agent that inhibits yeast species. It is converted in the fungal cell to 5-fluorouracfl, which inhibits thymidylate synthetase resulting in a deficit of thymine nucleotides and impaired DNA synthesis. Adenosine arabinoside inhibits viruses. It is phosphorylated in virus-infected cells and acts as a competitive analog of DATP, inhibiting the incorporation of DATP into DNA. Acyclovir is a nucleoside analog that, after being converted to a triphosphate, inhibits the thymidine kinase and DNA polymerase of herpes viruses. Zidovudine (AZT) inhibits human immunodeficiency virus (HM replication by interfering with viral RNA-dependent DNA polymerase (reverse transcriptase).

Agents that Impair the Template Function of DNA

A number of substances bind to DNA by intercalation. None of them is useful as an antibacterial agent; however, chloroquine and miracil D (lucanthone) inhibit plasmodia and schistosomes, respectively. These agents are thought to intercalate into the DNA and thereby to inhibit further nucleic acid synthesis. Acridine dyes such as proflavine act by this intercalation mechanism, but because they are toxic and carcinogenic in mammals they cannot be used as antibacterial agents.

Inhibition of DNA-Directed DNA Polymerase

Rifamycins are a class of antibiotics that inhibit DNA-directed RNA polymerase. Polypeptide chains in RNA polymerase attach to a factor that confers specificity for the recognition of promoter sites that initiate transcription of the DNA. Rifampin binds noncovalently but strongly to a subunit of RNA polymerase and interferes specifically with the initiation process. However, it has no effect once polymerization has begun.

Inhibition of DNA Replication

DNA gyrase and topoisomerase I act in concert to maintain an optimum supercoiling state of DNA in the cell. In this capacity, DNA gyrase is essential for relieving torsional strain during replication of circular chromosomes in bacteria. The enzyme is a tetrameric protein composed of two A and two B subunits. A transient, covalent bond between the A subunit and DNA occurs during the double strand passage reaction catalyzed by gyrase. Quinolones such as nalidixic acid bind to the cleavage complex composed of DNA and gyrase during this strand passage. This interaction of quinolone acts to stabilize the cleavage intermediate which has a detrimental effect on the normal DNA replication process. The effects of this inhibition result in the death of the bacterial cell. The newer fluoroquinolones such as ciprofloxacin, norfloxacin, and ofloxacin also interact with DNA gyrase and possess a broad spectrum of antimicrobial activity.

Nitroimidazoles such as metronidazole inhibit anaerobic bacteria and protozoa. The nitro group of the nitrosohydroxyl amino moiety is reduced by an electron transport protein in anaerobic bacteria The reduced drug causes strand breaks in the DNA. Mammalian cells are unharmed because they lack enzymes to reduce the nitro group of these agents.

Antimicrobial Inhibitors of Ribosome Function

A number of antibacterial agents act by inhibiting ribosome function. Bacterial ribosomes contain two subunits, the 50S and

30S subunits, and it is possible to localize the action of antibiotics to one or both subunits. It is also possible to isolate the specific ribosomal proteins to which an agent binds and to isolate bacterial mutants that lack a specific ribosomal protein and therefore show resistance to a particular agent.

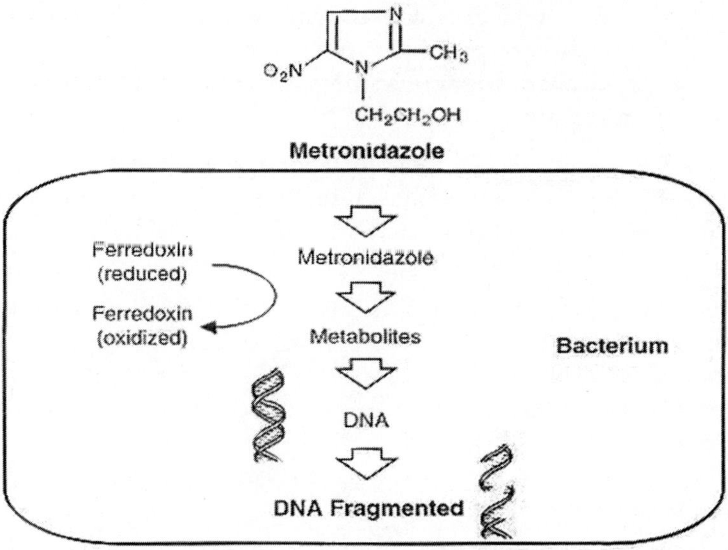

Fig. 5.3

Aminoglycosides act by binding to specific ribosomal subunits. Aminoglycosides are complex sugars connected in glycosidic linkage . They differ both in the molecular nucleus, which can be streptidine or 2-deoxystreptidine, and in the aminohexoses linked to the nucleus. Essential to the activity of these agents are free NH, and OH groups by which aminoglycosides bind to specific ribosomal proteins. Streptomycin, the first aminoglycoside studied, was a useful too] in elucidating protein synthesis. However, it is rarely used clinically today except to treat tuberculosis, and its mode of action differs to some extent from that of the other clinically useful aminoglycosides, which are 2-deoxystreptidine derivatives such as gentamicin, tobramycin, and amikacin. Streptomycin binds to a specific S12 protein in the 30S ribosomal subunit and causes the ribosome to misread the genetic code. Other aminoglycosides bind not only to the S12 protein of the 30S ribosome, but also to some extent to the L6 protein of the 50S ribosome. This latter binding is quite important in terms of the resistance of bacteria to aminoglycosides. Indeed, the aminoglycoside-type drugs can combine with other binding sites on 30S ribosomes, and they kill bacteria by inducing the formation of aberrant, nonfunctional complexes as well as by causing misreading.

Spectinomycin is an aminocylitol antibiotic that is closely related to the aminoglycosides. It binds to a different protein in the ribosome and is bacteriostatic but not bactericidal. It is used to treat penicillin-resistant gonorrhea.

Other agents that bind to 30S ribosomes are the tetracyclines. These agents appear to inhibit the binding of aminoacyl-tRNA into the A site of the bacteria] ribosome. Tetracycline binding is transient, so these agents are bacteriostatic. Nonetheless, they inhibit a wide variety of bacteria, chlamydias, and mycoplasmas and are extremely useful antibiotics.

There are three important classes of drugs that inhibit the 50S ribosomal subunit. Chloramphenicol is a bacteriostatic agent that inhibits both Gram-positive and Gram-negative bacteria. It inhibits peptide bond formation by binding to a peptidyl-transferase enzyme on the 50S ribosome. Macrolides are large lactone ring compounds that bind to 50S ribosomes and appear to impair a peptidyltransferase reaction or translocation, or both. The most important macrolide is erythromycin, which inhibits Gram-positive species and a few Gram-negative species such as *Haemophilus, Mycoplasma, Chlamydia,* and *Legionella.*

New molecules such as azithromycin and clarithromycin have greater activity than erythromycin against many of these pathogens. Lincinoids, of which the most important is clindamycin, have a similar site of activity. Both macrolides and lincinoids are generally bacteriostatic. inhibiting only the formation of new peptide chains.

Drugs that Inhibit Other Biochemical Targets

Both trimethoprim and the sulfonamides interfere with folate metabolism in the bacterial cell by competitively blocking the biosynthesis of tetrahydrofolate, which acts as a carrier of one-carbon fragments and is necessary for the ultimate synthesis of DNA, RNA and bacterial cell wall proteins . Unlike mammals, bacteria and protozoan parasites usually lack a transport system to take up preformed folic acid from their environment. Most of these organisms must synthesize folates, although some are capable of using exogenous thymidine, circumventing the need for folate metabolism.

Sulfonamides competitively block the conversion of pteridine and p-aminobenzoic acid (PABA) to dihydrofolic acid by the enzyme pteridine synthetase. Sulfonamides have a greater affinity than p-aminobenzoic acid for pteridine synthetase. Trimethoprim has a tremendous affinity for bacterial dihydrofolate reductase (10,000 to 100,000 times higher than for the mammalian enzyme); when bound to this enzyme, it inhibits the synthesis of tetrahydrofolate.

Antibacterial Agents that Affect Mvcobacteria

Isoniazid is a nicotinamide derivative that inhibits mycobacteria. Its precise mode of action is not known, but it affects the synthesis of lipids, nucleic acids, and the mycolic acid of the cell walls of these species. Ethambutol is also an antimycobacterial agent whose mechanism of action is unknown. It is mycostatic, whereas isoniazid is mycocidal. The other antituberculosis drugs, rifampin and streptomycin, affect mycobacteria in the same manner that they inhibit bacteria. Pyrazinamide is a synthetic analog of nicotinamide. It is bactericidal, but its exact mechanism is unknown.

Bacterial Resistance

Bacteria have proved adept at developing resistance to new antimicrobial agents. There are a number of ways in which bacteria can become resistant Most of the early studies of bacterial resistance focused on single-step mutational events of chromosomal origin. Resistance to the early sulfonamides, for example, was the result of a single amino acid change in the enzyme pteridine synthetase that caused sulfonamides to bind less well than p-aminobenzoic acid. Similarly, a single step mutation that altered a ribosomal protein conferred resistance to streptomycin. In the late 1950s, Japanese workers found that enteric bacteria such as Shigella dysenteriae had become resistant not only to sulfonamides but also to the tetracyclines and chloramphenicol. This resistance was due not to a chromosomal change, but rather to the presence of extrachromosomal DNA that was transmissible. This type of resistance is called plasmid-mediated resistance.

Bacteria also contain transposons, which can insert into plasmids and also into the chromosome Transposon-mediated resistance to most of the major antibiotics has been found in the past few years.

Antimicrobial agents exert a strong selective pressure on the development of both chromosomal and plasmid-mediated resistance, as discussed below. Administration of an antibiotic destroys the susceptible bacteria in a population, but may permit resistant ones to proliferate. From an epidemiologic viewpoint, plasmid-mediated resistance is the most important type, since it is transmissible, is usually highly stable, confers resistance to many different classes of antibiotics simultaneously, and often is associated with other characteristics that enable a microorganism to colonize and invade a susceptible host.

Mechanisms of Resistance

The basic mechanisms by which a microorganism can resist an antimicrobial agent are: (1) to alter the receptor for the drug (the molecule on which it exerts its effect); (2) to decrease the amount of drug that reaches the receptor by altering entry or increasing removal of the drug; (3) to destroy or inactivate the drug; and (4) to develop resistant metabolic pathways. Bacteria can possess one or all of these mechanisms simultaneously.

RESISTANCE DUE TO ALTERED RECEPTORS

ß-Lactam Resistance. The ability to analyze changes in receptors for ß-lactams by competition experiments in which penicillin is inhibited from binding to penicillin-binding proteins has explained a number of cases of bacterial resistance to penicillins and cephalosporins. In 1977, *Streptococcus pneumoniae* strains resistant to penicillin G were encountered in South Africa. Plasmids were not the cause of the resistance. Penicillin-resistant *S. pneumoniae* cells have altered penicillin-binding proteins, which bind penicillin less well. Resistance of *S pneumoniae* to penicillin has been increasing, and there are now relatively resistant isolates (minimal inhibitory concentration [MIC], 0.1 to 1 mg/ml) in many parts of the world.

Altered penicillin-binding proteins also explain the resistance of some *Staphylococcus aureus* strains to ß-lactamase-stable penicillins (the so-called methicillin-resistant strains). The ß-lactams induce synthesis of a new penicillin-binding protein, PBP2a, which does not bind any ß-lactam. The ß-lactam resistance of coagulase-negative staphylococci is also the result of altered penicillin-binding proteins. Staphylococcal organisms resistant to methicillin are resistant to all penicillins, cephalosporins, and carbapenems.

The resistance of group D streptococci to ß-lactam antibiotics appears to be the result of lower affinity of the penicillin-binding proteins for the penicillins. Enterococci are resistant to all cephalosporins because of failure to bind to the penicillin-binding proteins. One Gram-negative species for which resistance to ß-lactam antibiotics can be correlated with diminished affinity of the target enzymes is *N gonorrhoeae.*

Vancomycin Resistance. Certain transposable genetic elements encode special cell wall-synthesizing enzymes which change the structure of the normal D-Ala-D-Ala side chain in the peptidoglycan assembly pathway. The altered side chain (D-Ala-D-Lac) does not bind vancomycin and allows normal peptidoglycan polymerization to occur in the presence of the drug. Depending upon the nature of the vancomycin resistance gene, high-level resistance can occur to glycopeptides. Thus far, this type of resistance has been found in enterococci but not in multi-resistant isolates of *Staphylococcus aureus.*

Macrolide-lincomycin Resistance. Macrolide-lincomycin resistance in clinical isolates of staphylococci and streptococci has been recognized for several decades. The resistance is due to methylation of two adenine nucleotides in the 23S component of 50S RNA. This resistance is plasmid mediated, and the resistance is encoded on transposons. Resistance results from induction of an enzyme that is normally repressed. The methylated RNA binds macrolidelincomycin-type drugs less well than unmethylated RNA does. Induction of resistance varies by species, and in most Gram-positive species erythromycin is a more effective inducer of resistance than is clindamycin. The plasmids that mediate macrolide-lincomycin resistance in streptococci and staphylococci have extensive structural similarity, indicating that these plasmids readily pass between these species.

Rifampin Resistance. The resistance of bacteria to rifampin is caused by an alternation of one amino acid in DNA-directed RNA polymerase, which results in reduced binding of rifampin. The degree of resistance is related to the degree to which the enzyme is changed, but does not correlate strictly with enzyme inhibition. This form of resistance occurs at a low level in any population of bacteria so that resistance develops by natural selection during a course of therapy. Naturally resistant organisms are more common among members of the Enterobacteriaceae, explaining why agents of urinary tract infections rapidly became resistant to rifampin. The resistance of *Neisseria meningitides* to rifampin appeared in closed military settings in which rifampin has been used for prophylaxis.

Sulfonamide-trimethoprim Resistance. Sulfonamide can be rendered ineffective by altered or new dihydropteroic synthetase that has poor affinity for sulfonamides and preferentially binds p-aminobenzoic acid. Sulfonamide resistance of this type can result from a point mutation or from acquisition of a plasmid that causes synthesis of the new enzyme. A most serious resistance problem is an increase in resistance to trimethoprim. This plasmid- and transposon-mediated resistance is due to production of an altered dihydrofolate reductase that has markedly reduced affinity for trimethoprim.

Quinolone Resistance. Resistance to quinolones can be caused by mutations in DNA gyrase subunits A or B, reduced outer membrane permeability in gram-negative cells, or to active efflux transporters found in many bacteria. The highest level of resistance to the newer fluoroquinolones is most frequently associated with chromosomal mutations, causing amino acid substitutions in a highly conserved region in the A subunit of DNA gyrase. Multiple-mechanisms of resistance can occur in a single isolate of bacteria, leading to a higher level of resistance to many fluoroauinolones.

Resistance Due to Decreased Entry of a Drug

Tetracycline Resistance. The uptake of tetracycline by members of the Enterobacteriaceae is biphasic. In an initial energy-independent rapid phase, tetracycline binds to cell surface layers and passes by diffusion through the outer layers of the cell. In the second, energy-dependent phase, tetracycline crosses the cytoplasmic membrane, probably by means of a proton-motive force. The precise transport system has not been identified.

Tetracycline resistance is common in both Gram-positive and Gram-negative bacteria. In most cases it is plasmid encoded and inducible; however, chromosomal, constitutive resistance is found in some organisms such as *Proteus* species. Many plasmid-encoded specified tetracycline resistance determinants have been found in enteric bacteria. The most common of these determinants, TetB, is also present in *H influenzae.* Tetracycline resistance in *Staphylococcus aureus* is due primarily to small multicopy plasmids; chromosomal resistance is rare. Tetracycline resistance is found on nonconjugative plasmids in *Streptococcus faecalis* and on the chromosome of *S. pneumoniae, S. agalactiae* (group B streptococci), and oral streptococci. *Clostridium* species such as *C. difficile* harbor chromosomal genes for tetracycline resistance.

Basically, tetracycline resistance is due to a decrease in the levels of drug accumulation. Decreased uptake and increased efflux both probably participate. Resistant bacteria bind less tetracycline, and the tetracycline they do accumulate is lost by an energy-dependent process when they are in a drug-free milieu.

Plasmid-mediated resistance to tetracyclines can be partially overcome in Gram-positive species by modifying the tetracycline nucleus. Hence, achievable concentrations of minocycline and doxycycline, in particular, will inhibit some tetracycline-resistant streptococci such as *S pneumoniae,* and some *S aureus* strains. Molecular modification has not been successful in overcoming the tetracycline resistance of members of the Enterobacteriaceae or *Pseudomonas* or most *Bacteroides* species.

Tetracycline resistance is a major concern because it is located on plasmids near insertion sites, and these plasmids readily acquire other genetic information to enlarge the spectrum of resistance. The widespread use of tetracycline in animal feeds may be a factor in the extensive, worldwide resistance of members of the Enterobacteriaceae, particularly enteric species such as *Salmonella,* to tetracyclines and subsequently to many other drugs. Not only can tetracycline resistance move among members of the Enterobacteriaceae on plasmids, but plasmids mediating tetracycline resistance have moved between *S. aureus, S. epidermidis, S. pyogenes, S. pneumoniae* and *S, faecalis.*

Fosfomycin Resistance. Fosfomycin and fosmidomycin, which inhibit cell wall synthesis, enter bacteria by means of a glycerol-phosphate or glucose-6-phosphate transport system. Gram-positive bacteria in which the glucose-6-phosphate transport system is poorly developed do not take up these drugs in concentrations adequate to inhibit the cell wall synthesis. This resistance usually is chromosomal. The resistance of Gram-negative bacteria to these agents is related primarily to the presence in the population of some bacteria that can function without the transport system. Plasmids and transposons that transfer resistance to fosfomycin have been found in bacteria such as *Serratia marcescens.*

Aminoglycoside Resistance. In the most important form of aminoglycoside resistance, the compound is modified outside the cell and resistance is due partly to poor uptake of the altered compound. Also, all aminoglycosides have free amino and hydroxy groups that are essential for binding to ribosomal proteins. A number of enzymes can acetylate the amino groups and phosphorylate or adenylate the hydroxyl groups. Other forms of resistance, such as altered binding site on 30S ribosomes, are much less common.

In members of the Enterobacteriaceae and in *Pseudomonas* species, the aminoglycosides pass through the cell wall via channels designed to admit cationic molecules to the periplasmic space. These channels, called porin channels, are lined by the porin protein. Aminoglycosides are then translocated across the cell membrane by an energy-dependent proton-motive force and, in the cytoplasm, bind to ribosomes located just below the membrane. Aminoglycosides bind only to ribosomes actively engaged in protein synthesis. Binding to the ribosomes induces a protein involved in the uptake of the aminoglycosides.

Bacteria may contain in the periplasmic space enzymes that acetylate, phosphorylate, or adenylate aminoglycosides to various degrees. It is not clear whether the enzymes are free in the periplasmic space or bound to the cytoplasmic membrane. The modified aminoglycosides do not bind well to ribosomes, and hence uptake is poor or absent.

Aminoglycoside-modifying enzymes have been found in Gram-positive species such as *S. aureus, S. faecalis, S. pyogenes,* and enzymes are particularly prevalent in members of the Enterobacteriaceae and *P. aeruginosa. S. pneumoniae.* These Many of the genes for aminoglycoside-modifying enzymes are carried on transposons.

Anaerobic organisms such as *Bacteroides* species are resistant to aminoglycosides because they lack an oxygen-dependent transport system to move the drugs across the cytoplasmic membrane. Although most resistance of *S. aureus* to aminoglycosides is due to aminoglycoside-modifying enzymes, small-colony variants of staphylococci also show resistance, which may be due to a defect in adenylate cyclase or in cyclic adenosine 5'-monophosphate (cAMP)binding proteins such that cells with a reduced growth rate do not transport aminoglycosides into the cytoplasm. Some members of the Enterobacteriaceae and *P. aeruginosa* appear to be resistant because of altered porin channels, since these bacteria do not take up any drug and do not have aminoglycoside-inactivating enzymes.

Resistance Due to Destruction or Inactivation of a Drug

Chloramphenicol Resistance. Many Gram-positive and Gram-negative bacteria, including some recently discovered *H. influenzae* strains, are resistant to chloramphenicol because they possess the enzyme chloramphenicol transacetylate, which acetylates hydroxyl groups on the chloramphenicol structure. This enzyme, unlike the aminoglycoside-inactivating enzymes and ß-lactamases, is an intracellular enzyme of higher molecular weight and subunit structure. Acetylated chloramphenicol binds less well to the 50S ribosome.

ß-Lactam Resistance. The best-known mechanism of bacterial resistance is the resistance to ß-lactams, which is mediated by penicillinase enzymes. Resistance of *E. coli* to penicillin was recognized in 1940, before sufficient penicillin was made to be clinically useful. In the 1940s, resistance of staphylococci was shown to be due to a penicillinase. As these enzymes also attack other ß-lactam compounds such as cephalosporins, carbapenems, and monobactams, they would be more appropriately designated ß-lactamases. The most important activity of these enzymes is alteration of the ß-lactam nucleus (ß-lactamases are widely distributed in nature and are usually classified on the basis of the principal compounds they destroy (e.g., as penicillinases or cephalosporinases) ß-Lactamases may be chromosomally or plasmid mediated, and they may be constitutive or inducible.

In Gram-positive species, ß-lactamases are primarily exoenzymes; that is, they are excreted into the milieu around the bacteria. Virtually all hospital isolates of staphylococci, both *S. aureus* and *S. epidermidis*, have ß-lactamases, and 50 to 80 percent of community-acquired staphylococcal isolates produce ß-lactamases. In Gram-negative species, both aerobic and anaerobic, ß-lactamases are contained in the periplasmic space, thus effectively protecting the penicillin-binding proteins.

Resistance of staphylococci to ß-lactams was soon overcome with the antistaphylococcal penicillins and the cephalosporins.

Some strains of *S. aureus* produce more ß-lactamase constitutively and can destroy some of the cephalosporins.

In 1974, *H. influenzae* was shown to possess a plasmid mediated ß-lactamase. At present 10 to 35 percent of *H. influenzae* strains in the United States produce ß-lactamases. The TnA transposon has become more widespread, and the resistance of *Haemophilus* species to penicillin G and ampicillin seems to be increasing yearly. The *Haemophilus* ß-lactamase is the same structurally as the enzyme found in *E. coli, Salmonella, Shigella,* and *N gonorrhoeae*. The enzyme has generally been called the TEM enzyme after the initials of the Greek girl from whom an *E coli* strain containing a plasmid ß-lactamase was first isolated. These enzymes are also called Richmond-Sykes class IIIa enzymes from a classification proposed by Richmond and Sykes in 1973. By far the most common plasmid ß-lactamase found in nature is TEM-1, which accounts for 75 to 80 percent of plasmid-mediated ß-lactamase resistance worldwide. Recently new ß-lactamases have been found that hydrolyze compounds such as inomethoxy cephalosporin, which were not destroyed by other plasmid-encoded ß-lactamases. The new ß-lactamases have an altered amino acid composition, which permits binding to the cephalosporin and subsequent hydrolysis. How common these new enzymes will become is unknown.

Chromosomally mediated ß-lactamases are present in many *Enterobacter, Citrobacter, Proteus-Providencia,* and *Pseudomonas* species. All *Klebsiella* species possess a ß-lactamase, which acts primarily as a penicillinase and is chromosomally mediated. Constitutively produced ß-lactamases are also present in many anaerobic species.

Synthesis of Resistant Metabolic Pathway

No synthesis of a new type of cell wall resistant to ß-lactams has occurred, but some bacteria, particularly some streptococci, lack the hydrolytic enzymes necessary for forming a new cell wall, and so ß-lactams do not lyse these bacteria. An altered hydrolytic system thus converts a bactericidal antibiotic into a bacteriostatic agent. Whether such resistance occurs in Gram-negative species is not clear.

Some thymidine-requiring streptococci are not inhibited by trimethoprim and sulfonamides and so are not killed by these agents. These organisms are a rare cause of urinary tract infections. Other bacteria produce adequate deoxyribosylthymine 5'-monophosphate (DTMP) by alternative methods and, as a result. survive exposure to these folate inhibitors.

Certain *Candida* or *Cryptococcus* yeasts are resistant to flucytosine because they cannot convert it to its active component, fluorouracil. Other fungi can resist the polyenes and imidazoles because they synthesize membrane components by different metabolic mechanisms.

COMBINATIONS OF ANTIMICROBIAL AGENTS

Antibiotics are frequently used in combination for the following reasons: (1) to treat a life-threatening infection; (2) to prevent emergence of bacterial resistance; (3) to treat mixed infections of aerobic and anaerobic bacteria; (4) to enhance antibacterial activity (synergy); and (5) to use lower doses of a toxic drug. Combined treatment is reasonable when the precise agents of a serious infection are unknown. Use of two or more drugs to prevent the emergence of resistance is effective for tuberculosis and for therapy of some chronic infections. The use of combinations to achieve synergy is more complicated. Synergy occurs when a combination of two drugs causes inhibition or killing when used at a fourfold-lower concentration than that of either component drug used separately However, indifference or antagonism may occur instead. Indifference means that the combined action is the same as with either component; antagonism refers to a reduction in the activity of one or both components in the presence of the other

Important examples of bacterial synergy include: (1) combinations of anti-cell wall agents with aminoglycosides; (2) use of ß-lactamase inhibitors with ß-lactamase-susceptible antibiotics; and (3) combinations of drugs that act on sequential steps in bacterial metabolic or synthetic pathways. Examples of synergy that have proved clinically important are the combination of penicillin and streptomycin to treat *Enterococcus faecalis* endocarditis and the combination of carbenicillin and gentamicin to treat P aeruginosa infections. Recently the ß-lactamase inhibitor clavulanic acid or sulbactam has been combined with amino penicillins to inhibit *S aureus, Klebsiella pneumoniae, H influenzae*, and anaerobic organisms such as *Bacteroides* species, all of which are resistant to amoxicillin or ampicillin when they contain ß-lactamases. The combination of sulfamethoxazole and trimethoprim attacks two parts of the folic acid cycle and synergistically inhibits many bacteria. Finally, combinations of two penicillins that affect different stages of cell wall synthesis in Gram-negative bacteria are synergistic. This is true for the combination of mecillinam (amdinocillin), which binds to PBP2 of bacteria, and penicillins or cephalosporins, which bind to PBP lb or 3.

Antagonism can occur when a bacteriostatic agent is combined with a bactericidal agent. The classic example has been the combination of chlortetracycline and penicillin in treatment of pneumococcal meningitis. This effect has not been explained from a molecular standpoint, and tetracyclines and penicillins or cephalosporins are used to treat mixed infections such as pelvic inflammatory disease due to *N gonorrhoeae* and *Chlamydia.* Some ß-lactam antibiotics can induce ß-lactamases that inactivate other ß-lactams, and antagonism can be shown in the test tube, but the relevance for clinical infections is not established.

Toxicology of Antimicrobial Agents

Antimicrobial agents can be directly toxic, can interact with other drugs to increase their toxicity, or can alter microbial flora to cause infection by organisms that are normally saprophytic. Allergic reactions can be caused by an agent, but penicillins can produce either immediate, IgE-mediated, or delayed hypersensitivity reactions. Cutaneous reactions have been reported with every class of antimicrobial agent. Hematologic reactions can range from the life-threatening blood dyscrasia that occurs in 1 in 60,000 individuals who receive chloramphenicol to hemolytic anemia due to sulfonamides in individuals who lack the enzyme glucose-6-phosphate dehydrogenase. Depression of blood platelet activity has occurred with many agents. By altering the gastrointestinal flora, almost all antibiotics can cause overgrowth of *Clostridium difficile,* which produces a toxin that causes diarrhea and even pseudomembranous colitis. Alteration of intestinal flora by antibiotics can also result in overgrowth of *Candida* in the mouth, vagina, or gastrointestinal tract. Since a number of antibiotics are metabolized in the liver, damage to the liver can occur. This has been of particular concern with isoniazid, which is used to treat tuberculosis. Damage to the kidneys can follow the use of aminoglycosides. Neurologic toxicity is fortunately fairly uncommon, but the aminoglycosides can damage the auditory or vestibular apparatus if the dosage is not closely monitored.

Bacteria continue to evolve new mechanisms of resistance to old and to new antimicrobial agents. Some bacteria such as *P aeruginosa* are particularly adept at utilizing a number of different mechanisms simultaneously to become resistant to agents in virtually every class and those with such diverse sites of action as cell wall, protein biosynthesis, or DNA and RNA synthesis. Progress in medicine will keep patients alive who have nosocomial infections with resistant pathogens.

Mechanism to Reduce Bacterial Resistance

Proper selection of new antibiotics will be a major force in slowing the development of antimicrobial resistance. Proper hygiene practices will reduce plasmid transfer and the establishment of multiple drug-resistant bacteria in the hospital and will delay the appearance of such species in the community.

6

Free-living Amoebae

INTRODUCTION

Saprophytic amoebae from water, silt and wet soil which belong to the genera *Naegleria* and *Acanthamoeba* are cosmopolitan and potentially pathogenic. They seldom cause infection. In industrialised countries with a moderate climate these amoebae prefer fresh water with a temperature higher than average, such as public swimming pools and warm waste water from factories or power stations. This suggests that these amoebae must be widely distributed in a tropical environment. The protozoa can be cultured on agar on which bacteria such as *Escherichia coli* or *Enterobacter aerogenes* are growing. Species identification is the work of a specialist. Free-living amoeba have been shown to be a reservoir of pathogens such as certain *Legionella* species, *Burkhorlderia picketti* and even *Cryptococcus neoformans*. The pathogenic role -if any- of certain other amoeba-associated bacteria remains to be established (e.g. *Bosea massiliensis, Legionella anisa, Parachlamydia* sp., Rasbo bacterium, *Bradyrhizobium* sp.).

Infection with *Naegleria fowleri* is the consequence of bathing in contaminated fresh water at quite high temperatures. The infection follows penetration of water into the nasal cavities. From there the lamina cribriforma of the ethmoid bone is penetrated. Via the first cranial nerve, the infection spreads to the lowermost part of the frontal cerebral lobes. The amoebae reproduce rapidly in the cerebrospinal fluid. There is virtually no inflammatory reaction. Haemorrhagic necrosis of the base of the brain develops.

The infection leads to a fulminant meningo-encephalitis with fever, headache, vomiting and disturbances of smell and taste. The incubation time is 2 to 15 days. A history of bathing in surface water during the previous two weeks is significant. Sometimes the meningeal signs are preceded by rhinopharyngitis. A lumbar puncture produces cloudy or haemorrhagic liquor. The albumin content is elevated. There will be pleiocytosis, but the glycorrhachia is low. A varying number of red blood cells is found in the cerebrospinal fluid. *Naegleria* is most easily recognised by its motility in a fresh preparation. It is a small amoeba (trophozoite measures 10-35 m m) with smooth hemispherical pseudopodia. The parasite also has a stage during which flagella are formed. The cysts are spherical and may be found in tissues (unlike *E. histolytica* infections). The disease evolves fatally in less than 3 days. Very rare cases have survived by early treatment with amphotericin B (Fungizone), administered IV and intrathecally, possibly in combination with rifampicin. The only prevention consists of avoiding bathing in suspect water.

Another free-living amoeba, *Balamuthia mandrillaris* (Leptomyxiidae), may cause peri-orbital swelling and ulceration, followed by symptoms of granulomatous meningo-encephalitis, in both immunocompetent and immunocompromised persons. Other tissues can also be infected. Monkeys can also be infected with this organism. Previously this protozoon was regarded as harmless, living in soil. The cyst has a three-layered structure: endocyst, mesocyst and ectocyst. Treatment is based on prolonged administration of itraconazole 400 mg/day (adults). It is not clear how humans get infected, but transmission via swimming in contaminated surface water is one possibility.

FREE-LIVING AMOEBAE, *ACANTHAMOEBA* SP.

Several species of these free-living amoebae have been described: *Acanthamoeba castellanii, A. culbertsoni, A. polyphaga,*

A. astronyxis, A. hatchetti, A. rhysodes. The trophozoite measures 15-45 m m and exhibits fine thorn-like protrusions, acanthapodia. The name of the genus is derived from this feature (Gr. acanth = thorn). The cysts have a double wall. The outermost wall is wrinkled. The protozoa occur in numerous places (water, dust, waste). Unlike with *Naegleria*, infection of the central nervous system progresses slowly and occurs where there is immune suppression or in the course of a severe general illness. Generally it presents as a subacute granulomatous meningo-encephalitis with signs of a brain abscess, and develops in two to three weeks. Abscesses in other locations, and granulomatous skin lesions in which histological investigations show amoebae, have also been observed. Treatment is very difficult. Rifampicin has been used With pentamidine, cure can be achieved in systemic infections with *Acanthamoeba rhysodes*.

Keratitis is more common than cerebral inflammation. This was first described in 1974. These amoebae may infect small wounds of the cornea and then trigger a dangerous ulcerative keratitis which may develop into panophthalmitis. Initially this diagnosis is often missed and the lesion is considered to be a herpetic or fungal keratitis. *Acanthamoeba* infection may follow upon a herpetic keratitis. The amoebae are often scarce in corneal smears, culture is possible but often not available and sometimes the diagnosis is made purely on anatomopathological grounds, e.g. during a cornea transplantation. The number of cases has grown in recent years as the result of increased use of contact lenses and the practice of rinsing these with tap water. Possibly bacteria in the biofilm on dirty contact lenses constitute a good source of nutrition for the amoebae. If there is a superficial epithelial defect, whether or not caused by the contact lens, the amoebae may become invasive in the corneal stroma.

Treatment of *Acanthamoeba* keratitis is difficult. Sometimes a combination of propamidine isethionate eye drops (Brolene), topical neomycin, polyhexamethylene biguanide eye drops (Lavasept) and/or topical chlorhexidine (Hibitane) is given. Brolene, available in Great Britain, is an antiseptic which is moderately toxic for the corneal epithelium. The use of topical steroids is controversial but probably beneficial. Oral itraconazole is probably also active. Topical miconazole is sometimes also used. Pentamidine (a diamidine related to propamidine) is being evaluated.

Free-living Amoebae and Endo-amoebic Bacteria

Many amoebae feed on bacteria. Sometimes, the bacteria are killed and digested by the amoebae, sometimes the bacteria kill the amoebae, and sometimes, a kind of more or less stable symbiotic relationship is achieved. This can be temperature-dependent, e.g. certain *Parachlamydia* bacteria are endosymbiotic in amoebae at 30°C and lytic at 37°C. This suggests that bacteria present in amoebae in the cooler upper respiratory tract (nose) might be libeterated in the warmer lower tract, for example during an aspiration event. Co-culture of amoebae (e.g. *Acantamoeba polyphaga*) with bacteria recovered from different places (mouth, nose swabs,) could become an interesting tool for new discoveries in this field.

FREE-LIVING AMOEBAE, RHIZOPODA

The amoebae belong to the Rhizopoda (Gr. rhizo = root). These animals are related to a number of other protozoa, including the Actinopoda (Gr. actis = ray) and Foraminifera (L. foramen = opening). The taxonomic classification varies greatly from author to author. Some are being studied for their unique genetics. The genome of *Amoeba dubia* (syn. *Polychaos dubia*) contains over 600 Gigabase pairs, which is 200 times more DNA than in humans. *Acanthamoeba castellanii* contains mitochondria in which a special form of transfer-RNA editing takes place. This forms a subject of intensive research.

The class of Lobosea includes the orders of naked amoebae (e.g. *Entamoeba* and *Naegleria*) and the armoured amoebae (Arcellinida, amoebae with an armour of grains of sand or excreted silicate). This class contains protozoa which are pathogenic for humans.

The class of Actinopoda contains almost exclusively sea plankton. The organism have no direct medical importance but include some of the most beautiful micro-organisms observed.

The Actinopoda are also known as Radiolaria (radiating creatures) and Heliozoa (sun creatures). They often have an exoskeleton of opal ($SiO_2\ x\ nH_2O$) and have radial or bilateral symmetry. The cytoplasm forms radiating pseudopodia (axopodia) which penetrate through small holes in the exoskeleton, and which give this group its name. The accumulation of countless silica skeletons from dead Radiolaria has lead to geological sediments. In this respect they are similar to diatoms which are algae belonging to a completely different taxonomic group. (Diatoms have a siliceous skeleton consisting of two parts, like a pill box; see also "amnesiac shellfish poisoning"). The Acantaria are radially symmetrical Actinopoda with a skeleton of strontium sulphate. This dissolves relatively quickly in sea water after death.

The Foraminifera are also exclusively marine protozoa. At present the majority are benthic (living at the bottom of the sea), and some species belong to the plankton. Their exoskeleton consists of crystallised calcium carbonate (calcite or the rather more dense aragonite, sometimes even dolomite, i.e. $Mg/CaCO_3$). They have the shape of linear vessels or complex spiral chambers. Some Foraminifera are large (up to a few cm) and are then called nummulites (Lat. nummus = coin). The cytoplasm penetrates through pores in the skeleton and forms pseudopodia which may anastomose (reticulopodia). In the course of time the exoskeletons from the small dead animals accumulate in thick layers on the seabed provided the water is no more than 3700-4400 m deep. Below this depth they dissolve because the deep cold water can contain more CO_2 than warmer water. These may later be converted into chalk cliffs, which can also contain dead coral, the shells of molluscs and the microscopically small calcium shells of a certain group of very small algae (Haptophyta, Prymnesiophyta or Coccolithophoridae). The Egyptian pyramids, for example, were built of this material.

Previously the Xenophyophyta were counted as Rhizopoda but recently they have been reclassified in their own Phylum. Some of these unicellular deep-sea organisms may grow to 10-25 cm.

7

Protection from Malaria

INTRODUCTION

Malaria, unlike many diseases, has evolved as a result of millions of years of interactions at various levels with the mammalian system and hence has found ways to gather resistance to drugs and insensitivity to other treatment modalities. Co-evolution and co-adaptation of the parasite, recrudescence, recurrence, drug resistance, and the complex pathophysiology of the infection process complicate treatment regimens, most of which are ineffective. This brings us to the conclusion that vaccination is the ultimate eradicative strategy. This paper's core idea is to give an extensive overview on the latest developments of anti-malarial vaccine technology. Malaria, being a multifocal disease, is very complex on many grounds. In order to elicit proper and effective immune responses which are good enough to prevent mortality and morbidity, the parasite's multi stage pathology has been decoded, which in turn gives us a hint that many antigens are involved in establishing infection. Modern malarial vaccines, as against conventional ones, incorporate many antigens from various stages of the parasite's life cycle, so that the immune response is multi-gated. The main reason for this approach is that exposure to the whole parasite elicits a more potent, protective immune response than do the subunit vaccines tested thus far. It is more likely that immunization with only a few parasite proteins cannot duplicate the immunity elicited by exposure to a parasite that has thousands of proteins. Modern vaccines rely on the fact that if natural immunity could be mimicked, then vaccination would prevent severe malaria and malaria-related deaths. In the case of naturally acquired immunity, the complexity would be expanded by exposure to many polymorphic strains of *P. falciparum*. If this is the case, then the malaria genome and SNP projects may provide the essential foundation for duplicating this whole-organism immunity. Analysis of the sequence of the *P. falciparum* genome has dramatically expanded our knowledge regarding the paralogous expansion in the genome of parasite proteins expressed on the erythrocyte surface. In this article, we would like to address the latest research and developments on the integration of new technologies like reverse vaccinology, vaccinomics, microarrays, along with providing a better understanding of the pathogenesis of the malarial infection and the 'omics' revolution to herald the profiling of new candidate antigens responsible for engendering naturally acquired immunity, which will enable the formulation of protective vaccines.

Malaria has been one of the most prominent and ancient diseases which has been profiled and studied. It has been one of the greatest burdens to mankind, with a mortality rate that is unmatched by any other modern disease other than tuberculosis. This dreadful disease, caused by four different agents (*Plasmodium falciparum, Plasmodium vivax,* Plasmodium malariae and Plasmodium ovale) of the same genus, is a major health problem in most of the countries in the Tropics. Malaria affects more than 2400 million people, over 40% of the world's population, in more than 100 countries in the tropics from South America to the Indian peninsula. The tropics provide ideal breeding and living conditions for the anopheles mosquito, and hence this distribution. Over the years, as per statistical records, it has been estimated that there may be three hundred to five hundred million new infections and one to three million infection related deaths annually caused by malaria, and it has also been found that more than 90% of these deaths occur in the regions in and around Sub-Saharan Africa. Malaria kills in one year what

AIDS killed in 15 years. In 15 years, if 5 million have died of AIDS, 50 million have died of malaria. It accounts for 2.6 per cent of the total disease burden of the world. It is responsible for the loss of more than 35 million disability-adjusted life-years each year. Estimated worldwide expenditure on malaria research comes down to US$ 58 million, one thousandth of the US$ 56 billion spent globally on health research annually. Even with this overwhelming fatality and infection rates, epidemiological analyses in recent times have shown that the medical impact of Malaria may have been significantly underestimated. Inspite of all this, the enormous economic impact of Malaria has never been adequately considered. Malaria imposes a huge burden on human resources of a nation and in consequence, the Gross Domestic Product of the country gets reduced by as much as 1.3%.

Yet, in this age of tremendous technological and medical advancements, it is a big surprise that human knowledge power has not been able to control this disease, if not eradicate it. The intolerable impact of malaria has been sometimes fully or partially attributed to the increasing resistance of the Plasmodium parasite to chemoprophylactic and chemotherapeutic agents, and the resistance of the Anopheles sp. mosquito vector to insecticides, including the pyrethroids used in insecticide-impregnated bednets. Adding to these is the inability of the health, public and civic work departments of the affected countries in mobilizing and sustaining the resources required for malarial control. The economic status of a vulnerable country plays another role in determining the equippedness and control measures in case of epidemics and endemics. For example, there has been a resurgence of malaria in areas formerly free of the disease. These complications make the disease an even more tightly knit puzzle to solve. The World Health Organization (WHO) has forecast an annual growth of 16% in malarial cases. Considering these predictions as well as the current situation at hand, it is the duty of the scientific community to focus on the prospects and possibilities of developing a vaccine for malaria. In our review, we would like to outline the recent multidimensional efforts aimed at adopting suitable methods by which natural immunity like responses can be generated by a malarial vaccine. The pith of this work is to give a precise description on the various parasitic and host factors which are taken into consideration in modern malarial accinology.

PATHOPHYSIOLOGY AND LIFECYCLE OF THE MALARIAL PARASITE

The life cycle of the malarial parasite is very complex . *P. falciparum* and, to a much lesser extent, *P. vivax* are the main causes of disease and death due to malaria. Mosquitoes inject parasites in the form of sporozoites into the subcutaneous tissue and less frequently, directly into the bloodstream and from there, they travel to the liver. Recent evidence indicates that sporozoites pass through several hepatocytes before invasion is followed by parasite development. The co-receptor on sporozoites for invasion involves, in part, the thrombospondin domains on the circumsporozoite protein and on thrombospondin-related adhesive protein (TRAP). These domains bind specifically to heparin sulfate proteoglycans on hepatocytes in the region in apposition to sinusoidal endothelium and Kuppfer cells (Frevert et al 1993). Within the hepatocyte, each sporozoite develops into tens of thousands of merozoites, each able to invade a Red Blood Cell (RBC) on release from the liver. Disease begins only once the asexual parasite multiplies within the RBC. This is the only gateway to disease. *P. falciparum* and *P. vivax* within the RBC develop over 48 hours, producing around 20 merozoites from a mature parasite, each able to invade other RBCs. A small proportion of asexual parasites converts to gametocytes that are critical for the transmission of the infection to others through female anopheline mosquitoes but cause no disease. Here the strategy of *P. vivax* differs from that of *P. falciparum*. *P. vivax* develops into gametocytes soon after release of merozoites from the liver, whereas *P. falciparum* gametocytes develop much later. Early treatment of clinical malaria attacks by anti-bloodstage chemotherapy for *P. falciparum* also kills the developing gametocytes and in the case of *P. vivax*, it transmits before the symptomatic stage of the disease. The outcome of the infection differs from person to person and this is another manifestation of the highly variant factors involved in malarial infection and disease.

The sequence of invasion is probably similar for all *Plasmodium* sp. The parasite must engage receptors on RBCs for binding and undergo apical reorientation junction formation and signaling. The parasite then induces a vacuole derived from the RBC plasma membrane and enters the vacuole by a moving junction. Three organelles on the invasive or apical end of parasites (rhoptries, micronemes, and dense granules) define the phylum Apicomplexa. Receptors for invasion of RBC by merozoites and for invasion of liver by sporozoites are found in micronemes, on the cell surface, and in rhoptries. The distribution of these receptors within an organelle may protect the parasite from antibody-mediated neutralization, as the release after contact with the RBC may limit their exposure to antibody. A critical question in parasite biology remains the identification of the signaling pathways to release organellar contents in contact with a host RBC. Malarial parasites have intracellular signaling pathways through phosphoinositide, cyclic AMP (cAMP), and calcium-dependent pathways. What remains completely unknown is which merozoite surface molecules recognize the RBC surface and signal for the invasion process. These events include release of critical molecules from apical organelles and the initiation of the actin-myosin moving junction that brings the parasite within the vacuole that forms in the RBC. The TRAP protein interacts with skeletal proteins in malarial sporozoites and in *Toxoplasma gondii*, both *P. falciparum* and *P. vivax* can cause severe anemia, but only *P. falciparum* causes the multiple complications of cerebral malaria, hypoglycemia, metabolic acidosis, and respiratory distress. Certain differences in the biology of the two parasites partially explain the differences in patterns of disease. First, *P. falciparum* can invade a large percentage of the RBCs, whereas *P. vivax* is limited to reticulocytes. Similar differences are found between virulent and avirulent *P. yoelii*. Both invade reticulocytes preferentially, but once the reticulocytes are consumed, virulent *P. yoelii* can invade all RBCs, leading to higher parasitemia and death. A recent study by Chotivanich of severe malaria compared to uncomplicated falciparum malaria suggested a similar pattern, with the virulent *P. falciparum* invading all RBCs and the avirulent parasites invading only a subpopulation. A second difference is the surprising redundancy of invasion pathways in *P. falciparum*, lacking in *P. vivax*. *P. vivax* invades only Duffy blood group-positive RBCs (Miller et al 1976) and is largely limited to reticulocytes. In West Africa, where the Duffy blood group is missing on the RBCs, *P. vivax* essentially disappeared. The Duffy negative blood group has also occurred independently in Papua New Guinea, an area of high endemicity of *P. vivax*. The limitations in invasion of *P. vivax* have led to the discovery of two families of parasite receptors: (i) the parasite molecule that binds to the Duffy blood group system and Duffy binding-like (DBL) homologous proteins of *P. falciparum* and *P. knowlesi*; and (ii) the parasite reticulocyte-binding proteins of *P. vivax* and reticulocyte binding-like (RBL) homologous proteins of *P. falciparum* and *P. yoelii*. The various members of the DBL and RBL families may recognize different RBC receptors than the Duffy blood group or the receptor on reticulocytes. The receptor grouping into DBL and RBL refers to the family of homologous parasite proteins, not the specificity on the RBCs for binding.

There is a large family of RBL genes in *P. yoelii*. Each of the merozoites within a single infected RBC can express a different member of the RBL family. If each has a different RBC-binding specificity, then the parasite has a greater chance for survival. Thus, although the full details for the DBL and RBL families are unknown, they clearly determine much of the flexibility for invasion by the various *Plasmodium* sp. This flexibility, in turn, determines the maximum parasitemia and disease caused by the various parasites.

P. falciparum can use its multiple redundant alternative pathways to invade RBCs lacking a particular receptor such as sialic acid at equal or reduced efficiency. Three sialoglycoprotein-dependent pathways involving RBC and parasite co-receptors have been identified: (i) glycophorin A and the parasite DBL protein, EBA-175; (ii) glycophorin C/D and the DBL parasite protein, BAEBL; and (iii) a trypsin-resistant pathway involving a *P. falciparum* RBL protein. A fourth may involve sialic acid on glycophorin B. Despite markedly reduced invasion of glycophorin A-negative RBC, only glycophorin B mutations occur in Africa. Gerbich RBCs fail to express glycophorin D and express an altered glycophorin C and have reduced binding to the parasite molecule, BAEBL. Gerbich RBCs are rare in most parts of the world except in the falciparum-endemic regions of Papua New Guinea, where the allele frequency approaches 50%. Such redundancy and alternative pathways are a major advantage to the survival of *P. falciparum* in response to changes in host genetics. The parasite, however, may become less virulent as it adapts to survival in these deficient RBCs.

Studying the DBL and RBL families has begun to yield a molecular understanding of the diverse invasion pathways for *P. falciparum* and other *Plasmodium* sp. Although other parasite proteins on the merozoite surface and in apical organelles have been proposed as receptors, there is no direct evidence so far. Because invasion is such a complex series of events from RBC binding, to apical reorientation, to entry, that it seems likely that multiple proteins are involved for efficient invasion. For example, evidence has been presented that invasion requires cleavage of a RBC surface protein by a parasite serine protease. This parasite enzyme has yet to be identified. Thus, the molecular and cellular events surrounding each step in invasion still remain to be elucidated. Understanding these pathways will give insight into parasite virulence and will facilitate rational vaccine design against merozoite invasion.

ANCHORING OF INFECTED RBC'S TO THE VASCULAR ENDOTHELIAL CELLS

An important difference between *P. falciparum* and other human malarias is the way that *P. falciparum* modifies the surface of the RBC for adherence of both asexual parasites and gametocytes to the endothelium and asexual parasites within placenta. As a result, only ring forms of *P. falciparum* are found within the circulating blood. The surface of *P. falciparum* trophozoite- and schizont-infected RBC is covered with knob-like excrescences that are the contact points with host cells. The adherence protects the parasite from destruction, as non-adherent mature parasitized RBCs are rapidly cleared within the spleen. Trying to decipher the highly complex and pathogenic adhesion process emphasizes how much we have learned and how little we understand. To answer whether and how sequestration can lead to pathogenesis, we should first look at how the parasite sequesters. The *P. falciparum* adhesion process is comparable to adhesion of leukocytes, where most parasites first tether, then roll, before becoming firmly adherent. Most host receptors are involved with tethering and rolling but are unable to support firm adhesion under flow on their own. Binding to these host receptors is important, as it significantly increases adhesion that may allow the parasite to efficiently bind to endothelium of various organs. Only two receptors, CD36 and chondroitin sulfate A (CSA), provide stable stationary adherence.

Parasites sequester in various organs including heart, lung, brain, liver, kidney, subcutaneous tissues, and placenta. The various endothelial cells in these organs and syncytiotrophoblasts in placenta express different and variable amounts of host receptors. To successfully adhere to these cells, the parasite binds to a large number of receptors. The adhesion phenotype is not homogenous, and different parasites can bind to variable numbers and combinations of host receptors. This variability is believed to affect the tissue distribution and pathogenesis of parasites. Amazingly, a single parasite protein, the *P. falciparum* erythrocyte membrane protein 1 (PfEMP1) expressed at the infected erythrocyte surface, mediates its binding to the various receptors. PfEMP1 is encoded by the large and diverse *var* gene family that is involved in clonal antigenic variation and plays a central role in *P. falciparum* pathogenesis. The multiple adhesion domains located at the extracellular region of PfEMP1 can simultaneously recognize several host receptors. These domains contain five different DBL domains, so named for the homology to the DBL domains involved in RBC invasion and 1-2 cysteine-rich interdomain regions (CIDR). The binding domains for several host receptors were recently mapped to various DBL and CIDR domains. The diversity within this gene family is extensive, and numerous *var* genes appear in the parasite population. Although each parasite expresses a single *var* gene, this can change at a rate of up to 2% per generation.

In most cases, the binding to host endothelium does not lead to pathogenesis, as most infections result in malaria that is devoid of complications. What leads to the transition from uncomplicated to a serious infection such as cerebral malaria is unclear at present. An intriguing possibility is that expression of particular binding properties will lead to distinct patterns of sequestration and to pathogenic consequences. One example is the sequestration of infected RBC within the placenta that causes premature delivery, low birth weight, and increased mortality in the newborn and anemia in the mother. Parasitized RBCs isolated from placentas have a unique adhesion property different from parasites collected from non-pregnant individuals. These parasites bound to CSA and failed to adhere to CD36, the critical host receptor for sequestration in microvasculature. The apparent dichotomy in adhesion to these receptors was selected to allow the parasite to sequester not to endothelium but in placenta, perhaps a site of reduced immunity. Indeed, CSA-binding parasites express PfEMP1 with a DBL domain that binds CSA and a non-CD36-binding CIDR1. In contrast, CD36-adherent parasites express a PfEMP1 with a CD36-binding CIDR1.

How adhesion progresses to pathology is a major question that remains unresolved. Several mechanisms that might cause damage to host endothelium and organs have been proposed, including obstruction of blood flow and systemic or local production and deposition of proinflammatory cytokines. Parasite adhesion can also affect the endothelium by inducing or blocking signal transduction mediated by host receptors such as CD36. The recent advances in adhesion research will hopefully provide leads for the mechanism of adhesion related pathogenesis.

Immune Responses Against the Malarial Parasite

Antibodies and the proinflammatory response protect against the asexual blood stages of some rodent malarias and probably also human malaria. The protection mediated by the proinflammatory response may relate to the cytokines TNF- and IFN- and the release of mediators such as nitric oxide (NO). Clark proposed that mediators, especially NO, are also central to disease. It is perfectly logical that these are involved in bone marrow suppression and cerebral malaria, but the data are lacking to prove this role. Furthermore, no model exists for the study of cerebral malaria. One hypothesis suggests that TNF- induces endothelial cells from brain to express ICAM-1 as vessels in the brain have increased expression of ICAM-1 in cerebral malaria. Although NO has been proposed as the cause of cerebral malaria, NO is at higher levels systemically in uncomplicated malaria than in cerebral malaria. Coma could be caused by local increases in NO in the brain and not increased levels in blood, but this has not been measured. Indeed, total nitrate plus nitrite levels in the CSF of children with cerebral malaria are low, and it has been suggested that this may exacerbate n-methyl-D-aspartate-mediated neurotoxicity due to excitotoxins such as quinolinic acid.

Data suggesting that a toxin of malarial origin drives the proinflammatory response are interesting, but the physiologic significance is unproven at present. The evidence that a particular molecule is involved in induction of the proinflammatory response was developed by an assay for the release of TNF- by macrophages in vitro. Isolation of subcellular components from the parasite and the in vitro assay led to the identification of the GPI anchor from parasite proteins MSP1 and MSP2 as an inducer of proinflammatory cytokines. Antibodies to the GPI anchor were associated with lack of disease in adults, but proof that this is causally related is lacking. Modifications in the immune response to malaria that may not be malaria specific have been identified. Infection with *P. falciparum* causes apoptosis of mononuclear cells in infected humans. In an animal model, infection with a rodent malaria to which they had previously been exposed led to apoptosis of T cells immune to malaria and not those immune to ova, a malaria-unrelated antigen. The cells that were eliminated were proinflammatory T cells, producing IFN- and IL-2, but not IL-4.

COMPLICATIONS IN MALARIAL INFECTIONS

Malaria is one disease which complicates itself so much that common modes of treatment and prophylaxis cannot be drawn on a single level basis. Instead, a case-by-case approach must be undertaken. This might not be practically feasible as of now, though some progress has been made in deciphering the common mechanisms leading to these intricate pathological manifestations. Two such factors which significantly affect the occurrence and severity of the disease are Recurrence and Resistance.

Recurrence

Recurrence is a problem which keeps the disease alive in a community and makes its control quite difficult. Absence of effective immune response is one of the many reasons for the recurrence phenomenon. Acquired immunity develops after several attacks of malaria over several years. This immunity is stage specific, species specific and 'strain' specific. It does not have any sterilizing effect on the parasitemia and immune adults are still re-infected. However, the clinical signs and symptoms are reduced with development of clinical immunity. various explanations have been offered for these observations. Generalized immunosuppression by the parasite, presence of T-cell independent antigens which fail to induce immune response, inhibition of B-cell proliferation, and extreme polymorphism or clonal variation of immunologically relevant antigens could be the causes for the poor immune response in malaria.

Secondly, exposure to repeated mosquito bites and re-infection is the most profiled cause for recurrence of malaria. The patient is exposed to fresh mosquito bites soon after completing the anti malarial treatment. There is no immunity from the past infection and to worsen the situation, the antimalarials do not prevent establishment of the fresh infection. Therefore, unless the patient observes stringent anti mosquito measures, re-infection is inevitable in an endemic area.

Non compliance to the treatment regimen combined with incomplete and improper treatment methods will make the patient pay heavily. All blood schizonticidal drugs suppress the erythrocytic schizogony and give symptomatic relief. The patient may stop the drugs due to various reasons like vomiting, ignorance and financial constraints. This results in recrudescence within a short period. Also, if the patient does not take the complete course of primaquine, relapses can occur from reactivation of hypnozoites in the liver. Proper patient education regarding the complete course of anti malarials is very important. In cases of *P. vivax* and P. ovale infections, recurrent attacks could be due to re-activation of hypnozoites in the liver. This can occur any time after 30-180 days from the primary attack. The relapses have the characteristic symptoms of malaria. Splenomegaly may be a prominent feature in these patients. Such long-term relapses commonly occur in patients who have either not taken primaquine or taken incomplete treatment.

Finally, in *P. falciparum* and P. malariae infections, the parasites can remain in the blood for months or even years and cause recurrent symptoms from time to time. In falciparum malaria, such recrudescence can occur within 28 days of the primary attack and may indicate partial resistance to chloroquine. However, treating every case of recurrent *P. falciparum* as resistant malaria is unjustified. One should consider the possibility of re-infection in most of these cases.

Resistance

Resistance to antimalarial drugs is proving to be a challenging problem in malaria control in most parts of the world. Since early 1960s the sensitivity of the parasites to chloroquine, the best and most widely used drug for treating malaria, has been on the decline. Newer antimalarials were discovered in an effort to tackle this problem, but all these drugs are either expensive or have undesirable side effects. Moreover after a variable length of time, the parasites, especially the falciparum species, have started showing resistance to these drugs also. The important factors that are associated with resistance are longer half-life, single mutation for resistance, poor compliance, host immunity, and number of people using these drugs. The characteristics of a drug that make it vulnerable to the development of resistance are a long terminal elimination half-life, a shallow concentration-effect relationship, and mutations that confer marked reduction in susceptibility. Drug resistance is most commonly seen in *P. falciparum*. Resistance to chloroquine is most prevalent, while resistances to most other antimalarials like pyrimethamine, quinine, mefloquine, artemesin and quinoline compounds have also been reported. These developments further justify the cause and urgency for formulating an effective vaccine against malaria.

Primary Requirements of Malarial Vaccines

From experience, it is learnt that different populations demand different types of malarial vaccines making use of the different arms of the natural immune response system The basic purpose of a vaccine is to reduce the incidence of severe malaria, and malaria-associated mortality in infants and children with heavy exposure to *Plasmodium falciparum*, such as those living in sub-Saharan Africa. This constitutes a type 1 vaccine.

At the other extreme is the requirement to prevent all clinical manifestations of malaria in individuals from areas with no exposure who travel to regions where malaria is endemic, primarily malaria caused by *P. falciparum* and *P. vivax*. The vaccine fulfilling this extreme requirement is the type 2 vaccine. This extreme approach to *Malaria Vaccine Development* does not take into account specifically populations affected by malaria that fall between these extremes, such as individuals in endemic regions at high risk of *P. vivax* infections. In fact, as type 1 and type 2 vaccines are developed, they will need to be assessed in many different populations. The problem is complicated by the varied epidemiology of the disease for the type 1 vaccine which is designed to reduce mortality among children in sub-Saharan Africa. In areas with extremely intense transmission, it is primarily infants who are dying of malaria, with severe anemia as the major cause of death. In areas with less intense transmission, it appears to be 2 to 5 year olds who are at risk of dying with cerebral malaria. It is a definite possibility that different vaccines, tailored to the predominant pathophysiology of the parasite in a particular region, or different vaccination strategies, targeting the age groups at greatest risk may be the most effective response to this heterogenous epidemiology.

Similarly, the target populations are also varied for type 2 vaccine designed to prevent all clinical manifestations of malaria in non-immune travelers to malaria-endemic areas. It is a general conception that the major recipients for this type of vaccine would be travelers from highly developed malaria-free-countries, but there are hundreds of millions of people living in non-malarious areas of malaria endemic countries, who travel to malarious areas of their own country. Surprisingly, there is little mention in the malaria literature of the increasing number of non-immune individuals living in countries with endemic malaria, who must receive short-term protection against malaria by a vaccine. Because of their susceptibility to the rapidly developing severe disease, and because of their brief exposure to transmission, it is generally thought that these in-country travelers, and their children, would require a vaccine with the same protective profile as a vaccine for travelers from highly developed malaria-free countries.

Recently, a type 3 vaccine has also been developed for the sole purpose of blocking transmission. This type of a vaccine is not designed to protect the immunized individual but the entire community by reducing transmission intensity. Such a vaccine or its components can be combined with a type 1 or type 2 vaccine to lead to what will be called a 'multipurpose' vaccine. Such a vaccine unquestionably would be of great value on islands with malaria, and in areas with only modest transmission. It might also be useful during prolonged epidemics. This cocktail vaccine could be quite useful, particularly when combined with vaccines targeting other parasite stages, for preventing a selective process favoring the emergence of rapidly growing and therefore virulent parasites. Even if not able to impact overall transmission levels, a transmission blocking component included in a type 1 or 2 vaccine could block the escape resistant mutants, thus preserving vaccine efficacy in the community and also preventing the emergence of virulent parasite strains. Thus the general idea is to block transmission along with eliciting protection against the disease.

An ideal malaria vaccine would prevent all infection by priming the immune system to destroy all parasites, whether free swimming in the blood, while in the liver, or even, theoretically, while in red blood cells. This degree of protection would be extremely difficult to achieve and might not be technically feasible with current vaccinology art and science. Many vaccine developers have therefore focused their efforts on creating a vaccine that limits the ability of the parasite to successfully infect large numbers of red blood cells. This would not prevent infection but would limit the severity of the disease and help prevent malaria deaths.

An Ideal Malarial Vaccine

An ideal malarial vaccine will have a range of properties satisfying many conditions towards which future research efforts will be directed at. So it is necessary to define the characteristics of an ideal, virtual malarial vaccine. The ideal malarial vaccine will be highly effective in all age ranges, that is, it must elicit protective immunity in infants, children and adults. It has to be immunogenic and at the same time should confer safety and not have any undesirable side effects. In addition to being immunogenic, it should have the property of engendering long-term immunity, i.e; it should not require boosting to supplement itself. The ideal vaccine should go hand in hand with existing immunization programmes and schedules and ought to be easy to administer. It should be devoid of other complications such as interference with traditional childhood vaccines. Last, but not the least, the vaccine should be easy and inexpensive to manufacture and be affordable in low-resource settings.

Studies Relating to Whole Parasite Elicited Immunity

Children who survive to the age of 7-10 years rarely develop life-threatening P.falciparum infections and rarely die of malaria in areas of sub-Saharan Africa, which has the most intense malaria transmission rates as well as the highest rates of malaria associated mortality and morbidity. This acquired immunity occurs more rapidly, the more intense the transmission of P.falciparum. Older children and adults become infected frequently, but it is thought that their immune systems limit the infections, thereby preventing severe disease. A vaccine that duplicates naturally acquired immunity and turned infants and children into 15-year old with respect to protective immunity would essentially eliminate severe disease and death without eliminating infection or mild to moderate disease. It was found that mice immunized with radiation-attenuated rodent malaria sporozoites were protected against challenge. Based on these rodent studies, human trials were conducted subsequently and it was reported that exposure of humans to the bite of irradiated mosquitoes carrying P.falciparum sporozoites in their salivary glands protected these volunteers. These studies have since been repeated more systematically.

Among 14 volunteers exposed to greater than 1000 infected, irradiated mosquitoes and first challenged 2-10 weeks after the last exposure, 13 of the 14 were completely protected against infection. It was also proved that there is apparently little or no genetic restriction of the protective immunity elicited by this immunization approach. Six volunteers were challenged 23-42 weeks after the last boost and 5 of the 6 were protected. A total of seven challenges have been done with strains of *P. falciparum* different from the one used of for immunization, and there was protection in all the seven individuals. To combine all studies, among volunteers exposed to at least 1000 infective bites and challenged within one year after the last exposure, 33 of the 35 challenges were associated with complete protection. Thus, the irradiated sporozoites vaccine protects greater than 90% of recipients against experimental challenge for at least 10 months, and the protection is not strain-specific. A vaccine encompassing such properties will prove to be as good as both type 1 and type 2 vaccines.

CHALLENGES IN FORMULATING AN EFFECTIVE MALARIAL VACCINE

The development of a malarial vaccine requires more than understanding the molecular, pathogenic, parasitic and epidemiologic aspects of the plasmodium species. A successful vaccine strategy requires an appreciation of how the human host immune response interacts with the parasite. Such an understanding provides vaccine developers with clues on how best to design products that stimulate the proper effector arm of the immune system to achieve the desired goal. Despite the knowledge that our immune system can control malaria, there is currently no vaccine in the market against this dreaded disease. It is not possible to consider immunizing people by exposure to live parasites, which is what occurs in naturally acquired immunity, as the individuals would become ill. It has not been practical to consider immunization by the bite of irradiated, infected mosquitoes or by intravenous injection of live-radiation attenuated sporozoites to duplicate the immunity elicited by the irradiated sporozoites vaccine. The approach has been to try to determine the immune responses responsible for the protective immunity seen in these two models, and the parasite life cycle stages and proteins, against which this protective immunity is directed, and then to develop vaccine delivery systems that would induce the required responses against the identified targets.

Current and future advances in understanding human immunology and the biology of the malarial parasites, many of which will be dependent on the data from the human genome sequencing projects and the malaria genome projects, should allow the identification of key antigens associated with the protection and the formulation of vaccines effective in all recipients, regardless of their genetic background. The availability of the entire *P.falciparum* genome has provided a major boost in increasing the number of identified candidate antigens and has significantly brightened the prospects of developing an effective malarial vaccine.

PARASITIC COMPLEXITY

Malarial parasites are much more complex than other microbes such as viruses or bacteria which have been controlled extensively by vaccination. The complexity of the malarial parasites is reflected by their life cycle which has many stages, each of which is characterized by the expression of different and unique proteins. When sporozoites are inoculated into humans by Anopheles mosquitoes, they circulate extracellularly in the bloodstream for less than 30 minutes before entering the liver. Within the hepatocyte, a uninucleate sporozoite develops into a schizont with estimated 10000-40000 uninucleate merozoites.

These merozoites rupture from the hepatocyte and each can invade an erythrocyte, initiating the cycle of intraerythrocytic stage development, rupture and reinvasion that leads to a 10-20 fold increase in the number of parasites in the bloodstream every 48 hours. These asexual erythrocytic stage parasites are responsible for the clinical manifestations and pathology of malaria. Erythrocytic stage sexual parasites, called gametocytes are ingested by mosquitoes, in which they develop into sporozoites over a period of 14-21 days. The proteins expressed by each of these various stages are antigenically distinct. Thus, if a vaccine elicits high levels of anti-sporozoite antibodies, those antibodies will generally not recognize the asexual erythrocytic stages that follow. Furthermore, for many of these genes and proteins, allelic and antigenic variation has been demonstrated. A single individual can be infected simultaneously with at least eight different strains (Felger et al 1999), which may vary at critical B and T cell epitopes. This allelic heterogeneity is expanded by extensive antigenic variation present within a single strain.

For example, PfEMP1, a protein expressed on the surface of erythrocytes, is encoded by 50-100 different genes, each with some variation in its sequence. The parasite probably expresses only one at a time, with each new variant escaping from antibodies induced by the previous variant and therefore creating a new wave of parasitemia. PfEMP1 is thought to mediate cytoadherence of infected erythrocytes to endothelial cells in the microcirculation during maturation of the parasite, thereby preventing removal of the infected erythrocyte in the spleen during this vulnerable phase of the cycle. Cytoadherence is thought to be responsible for the microcirculatory obstruction important to the pathogenesis of severe disease. In summary, stage-specific expression of proteins, the presence of multiple antigenically distinct strains in nature, and within-strain antigenic variation are critical to the parasite's survival, unfavorable to the host, and greatly complicate the challenge for vaccine developers.

New strides in research have been undertaken to develop subunit vaccines that provide protective immunity comparable to that of the human models of naturally acquired immunity and radiation attenuated sporozoite immunization. However, no such vaccine has provided comparable protection.

There are many reasons for the lack of success in developing a subunit vaccine which duplicates naturally acquired immunity. One of the reasons is that exposure to the whole parasite elicits a more potent, protective immune response than the subunit vaccines tested so far. However, in the case of people protected by the irradiated sporozoite vaccine or by naturally acquired immunity, T-cell and antibody responses against our current candidate antigens or, in the case of antibody responses, against whole parasites are generally modest at best and in many instances lower than those achieved by subunit vaccination. It is more likely that immunization with only a few parasite proteins cannot duplicate the immunity elicited by the exposure to a parasite that has thousand of proteins: modest immune responses against tens, hundreds or thousands of parasite proteins may be additive or synergistic and may underlie the protection observed in these human models. In case of naturally acquired immunity, this "breadth" would be expanded by exposure to so many polymorphic strains of P.falciparum. In summary, whole-parasite induced immunity could be directed at many of the 5000-6000 malaria parasite proteins. Knowledge of all these potential targets and their variability at the epitope level has been documented a great deal after the publishing of the malarial parasite's genome and also the SNP (Single Nucleotide Polymorphisms) profiles of the genes coding for many of the potential targets.

Tasking the Field Trials

Clinical trials are primary manifestations of the scientific methodologies employed in medical pharmacology. Subjectal and anecdotal experiences have been replaced by scientific methods providing greater and greater objectivity, rigor and efficiency in assessing the impact of a vaccine. Currently, the task is to get enough potential malaria vaccines to and through the series of clinical trials needed to bring to the world a licensed product. Vaccine field trials are long-term studies aimed at assessing the safety, efficacy and immunogenicity of a new vaccine product. Sometimes trials also assess how well the product in question meshes with existing healthcare delivery systems, such as national immunization programmes. Field trials and their organization continue to be very critical factors involved in confirming vaccine efficacy and acceptability. Clinical trials are carried out in phases and each phase informs the developers about the next steps of testing and development. The full set of clinical trials for a successful candidate can take more than 10 to 12 years and may involve as many as 100,000 volunteers and may cost upto $500 million. In this regard, the onus will be to decide which outcome variables to measure in field trials and which populations to study. Primarily, trials and testing should not result in mortality and disease of any degree. There is a potential problem that the vaccine may be discarded as a result of initial studies because the proper outcome variables were not measure appropriately. It will be difficult to use severe disease and death as the primary outcome variables in initial studies because of the very large sample sizes required.

It is very important to identify the groups at the highest risk so that the sample sizes can be reduced. Current investigations seek to identify surrogates of severe disease and death. These surrogates can be of different forms like parasitological, hematological, biochemical and clinical manifestations that are predictive about the disease outcome. Several other areas of field research could provide data to aid vaccine development. The most important of these is the identification of target groups for vaccines in different areas and the exclusion of groups, like those with sickle-cell trait, who are at decreased risk, and do not need to be immunized. It is important to determine whether there are measurable outcome variables that have a high predictive value for severe disease and malaria-associated mortality.

As discussed before, ideal vaccines are just virtual benchmarks which will be used as references for optimization. While a less-than-ideal vaccine is expected to have some significant public health impacts, lack of some desired characters could affect how and where the vaccine is implemented. For example, if annual or biannual booster doses are necessary, there will be an increased burden on the healthcare system. Or, if the best product limits the severity of the infection and reduces morbidity and mortality but does not prevent all disease, governments and individuals will have more to consider in deciding whether, when, and how to use the vaccine. This is why carefully designed and executed vaccine trials are so important. They actually help us in understanding the strengths and weaknesses of each vaccine formulation, and guide the way to the best, if not the ideal vaccine.

The Overwhelming Need to Redefine Immunological Indicators/Variables of Protection

Most existing vaccines are thought to provide protection primarily by the induction of protective, neutralizing antibodies. The humoral response can easily be assessed. Malarial vaccines are thought to have multiple and complex mechanisms of protection, including antibodies and cell-mediated immunity. Malarial infection comes with biggest problem that it has a strong possibility of reactivation following a temporal period of relapse. So malarial vaccines must confer long-lasting immunity which must prevent infection and disease. At the same time, we must recognize that it may be unreasonable to expect the degree of protection with new vaccines that we have taken for granted in the current childhood vaccines.

All these arguments bring us to the point of realization of absolute truth, which is that we need to understand the mechanisms of immunity and the responses that are necessary to engender protection. This thrust for knowledge begins with identifying correlates of protection and the immunological measures and tests that appear to parallel protection. Ultimately, such correlates or variables that are firmly established will be assessed in clinical trials as surrogates for immunity which translate into laboratory tests that predict protection with high accuracy. Different immune responses may be required for different forms of the parasite. For example, there are antibodies which have been shown to prevent mosquito-derived sporozoites from infecting liver cells, those that kill the blood forms, and those that kill the gametocytes. There has been a lot evidence to show that there are specific cytotoxic T-cell Lymphocytes that kill infected liver cells. These could be assayed in vitro, but the most challenging part in vaccine efficacy evaluation is to decide and finalize a set of the above-mentioned correlates which will indicate protective immunity elicited by the vaccine. So, one of the major visions of malarial vaccine research is to employ the best methodology and technology available in clinical trials and in animal models to analyze those immune responses that correlate best with protection. These correlates and surrogate end points will accelerate the period of clinical testing, reduce costs, and allow more vaccine candidates to be studied and analyzed.

Immunopathological Basis of Vaccine Design

Design and formulation of vaccines are always preceded by a thorough investigation of the immunopathological states and infection modes of the parasite. Parasites have to survive in their vertebrate host during a sufficiently prolonged time in order to achieve their life cycle through successful transmission via insect vectors. In their vertebrate hosts, parasites are often confronted by vigorous effector immune responses that they must subvert somehow in order to survive and be transmitted successfully. The immune response comprises several components in terms of effector cells, antibodies, and signalling molecules such as cytokines. It is now well-recognized that not all components of the immune response triggered during the process of parasitism have anti-parasitic activities or properties. In this context, one of the strategies devised by many parasites has been to utilize some components of the host immune response to its own benefit. Therefore, an effective vaccine against intracellular pathogens should only induce effector mechanisms ultimately leading to the destruction of the parasites. The vaccine should abstain from triggering immune components of the immune response favoring the survival of the parasites.

Parasites have also devised a variety of ways by which to escape the effector components of the immune response that they have elicited in their mammalian hosts. Therefore, the balance between the components of the immune response with effector functions and those irrelevant for protection on the one hand, and the effector immune response and the escape processes induced by parasites on the other largely determine the outcome of the infection. Thus, elucidation of the mechanisms involved in the progression of parasitic diseases and definition of the relevant immune effector mechanisms are equally important for the identification of potential targets for beneficial intervention and subsequent vaccinisation. Indeed, the specific triggering of potent effector mechanisms and responses without activating the immune responses' components leading to pathology, together with the prevention of the escape mechanisms evolved by parasites, are the aims of vaccinisation.

The importance of immunoregulatory molecules like cytokines in the immunopathology of diseases is worthy enough to be mentioned. Their central role as antiparasite factors and as mediators of pathology has been reinforced by the description of two functionally different CD4+ T cell populations that can be distinguished on the basis of the patterns of cytokines which they produce. In both mice and humans, Th1 cells produce Interleukin-2 (IL-2) and Interferon gamma (IFN gamma), whereas Th2 cells produce IL-3, IL-4, IL-5, IL-10, and IL-13. Th1 cells are responsible for cell-mediated immune reactions, whereas Th2 cells are involved in humoral immunity. Resistance and susceptibility to several infections by many pathogens have been analyzed with respect to the Th1-Th2 paradigm. Resistance to intracellular pathogens is often associated with the development of a polarized Th1 response. Although resistance to extracellular parasites is now known to correlate with the generation of Th2 cells, the respective roles of Th1 or Th2 effector responses in protective immunity against many diseases like Schistosoma, an extracellular pathogen, are not yet fully understood. Furthermore, expression of immunity in some parasitic diseases such as malaria cannot simply be analyzed in view of the development of polarized Th1 or Th2 responses because infection with this parasite is a multifocal process.

There is very little doubt that immune responses against *Plasmodium falciparum* can protect against malaria, probably by destroying the infectious agent as such or the host cells in which they reside, and also by inhibiting a function of the infectious agent critical for its survival. In naturally acquired immunity, all the arms of the immune system are probably activated against all stages of the parasite cycle.

Humoral Responses Against Malarial Invasion

To generalize, three important responses are thought to be very critical in governing the progress of the initial infection. These are also marked as the three most important responses directed against the parasite. These include antibodies directed against parasite proteins expressed on the surface of erythrocytes that prevent sequestration in the microcirculation, antibodies directed against parasite proteins expressed on the surface of merozoites that prevent invasion of erythrocytes, and antibodies expressed against either type of parasite protein that are capable of mediating antibody dependent cellular inhibition, where biologically active molecules including cytokines, nitric oxide and free oxygen intermediates are released from the reticuloendothelial or other cells after activation through the Fc component of the bound antibody molecule. In addition, biologically active molecules such as cytokines, free oxygen radicals and nitric oxide molecules released from the CD4 T cells after an antigen-specific interaction may also contribute to this immunity. The pathogenesis of the disease may be mediated by these same host-derived biologically active molecules, perhaps elicited by putative malarial toxins released from the infected erythrocytes. Antibodies against these toxins may contribute to naturally acquired immunity. It seems likely that immune responses against sporozoites or infected hepatocytes that limit the number of parasites that emerge from the liver into the bloodstream also play an important role in the resistance to clinical disease demonstrated by individuals with naturally acquired immunity. The most persuasive human data regarding the importance of antibodies against asexual erythrocytic stage antigens come from passive transfer studies in humans.

Cell-Mediated Responses Against Malarial Invasion

T cell mediated immunity plays a very significant role in perpetrating the resistance against the malarial parasite's invasion. For irradiated sporozoite-induced immunity, the protection is thought to be mediated primarily by T cells directed against peptides from parasite proteins expressed in infected hepatocytes by function independent killing via elimination of infected host cells and also by antibodies that reduce sporozoite invasion of hepatocytes. Humans immunized with radiation-attenuated sporozoites and also humans naturally exposed to malaria have been shown to have CD8+ cytotoxic lymphocytes and CD8+ T cell derived interferon-gamma responses against pre-erythrocytic stage proteins. However data regarding the importance of T cells in the immunity elicited by the radiation attenuated sporozoites come virtually entirely from rodent experiments, in which T cell subsets were depleted or adoptively transferred. These data indicate that in rodent models, protection is always dependent on CD8+ T cells and Interferon gamma, and often dependent on Interleukin-12 and nitric oxide (Denise et al 2000 and Renia et al 1993). Nonetheless, adoptive transfer of antigen specific CD4+ T cells can also protect against sporozoite challenge (Denise et al 2000) and in some strains of mice, depletion of CD4+ T cells also eliminates protection.

Complexity of the Factors Governing Immune Responses and Disease Outcomes

The most well identified difficulty in vaccine research is the rapid alteration of the antigenic determinants. Another area requiring attention is the human genetic polymorphism which is associated with resistance to malaria as in the cases of a and b thalassemia, haemoglobin C, G6PD deficiency, haemoglobin S and haemoglobin E, ABO blood groups (Fy^a and Fy^b) etc.

Human host genetics, transmission dynamics of the parasite, and probably the age of the host contribute to the overwhelming complexity associated with the development of an effective vaccine against malaria. Although it is clear that sickle cell trait protects against severe disease and that other genetic traits may influence outcome, our understanding of the relationship between host genetics and the response to infection is very limited. The elucidation of the sequence of the human genome and the development of scientific tools have led us to a better understanding of the role of host genetic factors in determining the severity of disease associated with infection.

The age of the individual when first exposed to a parasite or a vaccine plays an important role in determining the immune response. A number of reports have suggested that, among non-immune children and non-immune adults, adults are actually more susceptible than children to developing severe disease after their first infection. However, adults acquire immunity faster than children. In addition, the human immune response is also dependent upon transmission dynamics. In areas in which transmission is most intense, infants are at the highest risk of developing severe and fatal malaria, whereas in areas with less intense transmission, older children have a higher incidence of severe and fatal disease than infants.

Current Trends and Developments in Malarial Vaccine Discovery

Accine developers around the world are trying to develop all three types of malaria vaccine: pre-erythrocytic, blood stage, and transmission blocking. All three types have been tested in people, and some have shown promise. As noted above, the optimal malaria vaccine will likely combine antigens from all three stages of the malaria parasite's life cycle. Getting there will involve complex studies in the laboratory and in the field to prove that the antigens and the immune responses do not interact in an undesirable manner. Many single-antigen malaria vaccine candidates are being readied for clinical trials, and combination studies are being planned. The deployment of an effective malaria vaccine will take several years, but it will happen.

1. Optimization of Immune responses elicited by Single Stage Targeted vaccines

As of now, malarial vaccine development is being pursued by three different methods. The most work has been done and progress achieved in attempts to maximize the magnitude and quality of immune responses to a single or a few key antigens, such as the Circumsporozoite protein (CSP), which is a very dominant antigen on the surface of sporozoites and Merozoite Surface Protein (MSP), by immunizing with synthetic peptides or recombinant proteins in an adjuvant. These vaccines are primarily designed to induce antibody and CD4+ responses, but there is also interest in eliciting CD8+ T cell responses.

A. *Vaccines targeting Pre-erythrocytic Schizogony*

Extensive work and studies have been performed on the Circumsporozoite protein based recombinant vaccine RTS, S/ ASO2. This vaccine is formulated with an oil-in-water emulsion and the immunostimulants monophosphoryl lipid A and the saponin derivative QS21. It is consistently found to protect 40-50% of the volunteers experimentally challenged 2-3 weeks after their last immunization. When five protected volunteers were challenged six months after the last immunization, only one of the five was protected. The very first field trials of this vaccine have been conducted in The Gambia by the Medical Research Council, UK. Vaccine efficacy was found to be 71% during the first 9 weeks of surveillance, but subsequently declined in the last 6 weeks. The first trial of RTS, S/AS02 in a pediatric population was also conducted in the same country. Efforts aimed at improving the vaccine are ongoing and these efforts primarily include the evaluation of alternative adjuvants as well as the combination of RTS, S with other pre-erythrocytic and erythrocytic stage antigens.

New technologies in vaccine science have brought about a huge revolution in new discoveries. One of the most intriguing developments in this field has been that of the Malarial Multiple Antigen Peptide vaccine. This vaccine contains CSP repeat epitopes, which is known to elicit high levels of parasite-specific antibodies and CD4+ T cells in volunteers with specific Human Leukocyte Antigen genotypes. It has also been demonstrated that a synthetic triepitope polyoxime malaria vaccine containing B cell epitopes and a universal T cell epitope of *Plasmodium falciparum* CSP has immunogenicity (Alonso et al 1994). In an open labeled phase 1 study, volunteers of diverse HLA types developed antirepeat antibodies and T cells specific for the universal T cell epitope. A carboxy terminal synthetic peptide of *Plasmodium falciparum* CSP has also been developed and is under clinical trials.

B. *Vaccines Targeting Erythrocytic Schizogony*

Vaccines which target the erythrocytic stages of the malarial parasite's lifecycle obstruct the asexual stage of the parasite.

SPf66 is one vaccine formulation developed as a polymer containing an 11-amino acid sequence from the N terminus of *Plasmodium falciparum* Merozoite Surface Protein, the 4-aminoacid repeat of *Plasmodium falciparum* Circumsporozoite protein, and 2 other short amino acid sequences thought to be from *Plasmodium falciparum*. Initial trials have demonstrated moderate efficacy in adults and children aged one to five years.

In yet another discovery, newer vaccines such as the one containing purified recombinant proteins based on three blood stage *Plasmodium falciparum* proteins: a fragment of Merozoite Surface Protein 1, Merozoite Surface Protein 2, and a portion of the Ring-infected Erythrocyte Surface Antigen, has been formulated in the adjuvant Montanide ISA 720. This vaccine has been shown to have high T cell and antibody induction rates (Graves et al 1988). Vaccines based on the sole *Plasmodium falciparum* apical membrane antigen-1 are also under developmental studies and assessment.

C. *Sexual Stage Vaccines*

Some of the merozoites in the blood transform into sexual forms, called as gametocytes. These appear in the peripheral blood after 7-10 days of the infection in *P. vivax* and 10-20 days in *P. falciparum* infection. When anopheles mosquito bites an infected individual, these gametocytes enter the mosquito and continue their sexual phase of development within the gut wall of the mosquito. This completes the asexual - sexual cycle of the malarial parasite. Vaccines targeting the sexual stages are usually transmission blocking vaccines based on antigens like Pfs25 and Pvs25.

Currently, there are three target antigens of transmission-blocking immunity: (i) prefertilization antigens expressed either completely or predominantly in gametocytes; (ii) postfertilization antigens expressed solely or predominantly on zygotes or ookinetes; and (iii) late-midgut-stage antigens such as parasite-produced chitinase required for the ookin.

8

Microbiology of the Genitourinary System

INTRODUCTION

In women, genital infections may cause a vaginal discharge, mucosal ulceration producing local discomfort and pain on intercourse, or pelvic inflammatory disease. Ongoing infection of the upper genital tract leads to infertility, ectopic pregnancies and chronic pelvic pain. In men, genital infection may cause urethral discharge, pain on voiding, and painful scrotal swellings. Genital ulcers are usually painful. Some diseases cause enlarged inguinal lymph nodes.

Etiology

Primary genitourinary infections are usually sexually transmitted; common pathogens include parasites (*Trichomonas vaginalis*), bacteria (*Treponema pallidum, Neisseria gonorrhoeae, Chlamydia trachomatis, Haemophilus ducreyi*), and viruses (herpes simplex virus, human papillomavirus, human immunodeficiency virus). Members of the normal flora, such as the fungus *Candida albicans*, may cause opportunistic infections.

Pathogenesis

Pathogens may enter the genital tract by local invasion or ascending infection. *Treponema pallidum, H. ducreyi*, herpes simplex virus, etc., locally invade the skin and mucous membranes. *T. pallidum* and Human Immunodeficiency Virus (HIV) disseminate via the bloodstream to distant sites. Other pathogens such as *N. gonorrhoeae* cause ascending infection through the urethra and cervix. Infants born through a genital tract infected with some of these pathogens may become infected.

Microbiologic Diagnosis

The organisms responsible for genital infections are generally fastidious and often difficult to culture. Specimens must be correctly collected and transported. Dark-field examination and serologic studies are necessary to diagnose syphilis; specialized tissue culture or antigen detection techniques are used for *C. trachomatis*, viral culture for herpes simplex virus, and specialized media for culturing *N. gonorrhoeae* and *H. ducreyi*.

Prevention and Treatment

Education to modify sexual behavior and use of condoms are essential. Screening asymptomatic individuals in some populations and case contact tracing are also effective measures. Effective drug therapies exist for all bacterial genital infections and for herpes simplex.

URINARY TRACT INFECTIONS

Clinical Manifestations

Urinary tract infections in adults may cause painful, frequent urination with a feeling of incomplete emptying of the bladder, perineal pain, fever, chills, and back pain. Most elderly patients are asymptomatic, and in small children, the symptoms are nonspecific.

Etiology

Most urinary infections are caused by bacteria from the intestinal flora. *Eschericia coli* causes about 70 per cent of all infections. *Staphylococcus saprophyticus* causes about 10 per cent of infections in young women. *Pseudomonas aeruginosa, Serratia marcescens, Enterococcus faecalis*, and *Staphylococcus epidermidis* are common hospital-acquired pathogens. Yeasts and, in some parts of the world, protozoa are occasional pathogens.

Pathogenesis

Organisms can ascend through the urethra to infect the bladder and renal pelvis. Occasionally, they may interfere with renal function or produce abscesses within renal tissue. Because of the shorter urethra, intercourse can facilitate urinary tract infections in women. Pyuria is almost always present. Hydrolysis of urea by bacteria (e.g., *Proteus mirabilis*) can cause the formation of struvite stones.

Microbiologic Diagnosis

Presumptive diagnosis can be made by demonstrating pyuria. Quantitative urine culture is essential for diagnosis. Specimens should be refrigerated until cultured to prevent bacterial replication. Properly submitted urine that contains >105 or 108 organisms/ml indicates significant infection. However, with acute cystitis, bacterial counts may be lower. Blood cultures may be positive in patients with pyelonephritis.

Prevention and Treatment

Antimicrobial agents cure most urinary tract infections. Recurrence is common, and may be prevented by prolonged therapy. Prolonged use of a urinary catheter greatly increases the likelihood of a urinary tract infection.

Infections

Genitourinary infections fall into two main categories: (1) primary infections due to sexually transmitted pathogenic microorganisms; and (2) infections due to members of the resident flora. Genital infections are uncommon in children and increase dramatically in sexually active adults, in whom sexually transmitted diseases are the second most prevalent group of reportable communicable illness in North America. Sexually transmitted pathogens include parasites (*Trichomonas vaginalis*), bacteria (*Treponema pallidum, Neisseria gonorrhoeae, Chlamydia trachomatis, Haemophilus ducreyi*), and viruses (Herpes simplex virus, human papilloma-virus, human immunodeficiency virus).

Genital infections due to the fungus *Candida albicans* or to members of the endogenous bacterial flora (*Bacteroides fragilis* and members of the family Enterobacteriaceae) are not known to be sexually transmitted. Bacterial vaginosis occurs when the balance of vaginal flora is upset.

The urinary tract and urine are normally sterile. Numerous mechanical and biologic processes ensure that microorganisms do not enter the urinary tract. Women are more susceptible to urinary infections because the female urethra is short and because the area around the urethral opening is colonized with potential pathogens (e.g. *E. coli* and *E. faecalis*).

URETHRITIS AND EPIDIDYMITIS

Clinical Manifestations

Urethritis (inflammatory disease of the urethra) is characterized by urethral discharge. The incubation time varies, averaging three days for gonococcal urethritis and seven days for nongonococcal urethritis. The clinical symptoms range from mild to severe. In both men and women, dysuria is common. Discharge and dysuria are seen in 70 per cent of patients with gonococcal urethritis, whereas patients with nongonococcal urethritis are more likely to have one or the other of these symptoms but not both. Other symptoms include itching, frequency, urgency, or a feeling of heaviness in the genitals. Polyarthralgia, involving large joints, characteristic rash, and low-grade fever are typically present in patients with disseminated gonococcal infection.

Orchitis and epididymitis are complications of both *N. gonorrhoeae* and *C. trachomatis* infections that present as a painful, swollen mass in the scrotum. Testicular atrophy follows in some patients with orchitis.

Etiology

Neisseria gonorrhoeae and *C. trachomatis* account for most cases of urethritis in men. *Chlamydia trachomatis* is responsible for 40 to 60 per cent of cases of nongonococcal urethritis. The etiology of *chlamydia*-negative nongonococcal urethritis is uncertain. *Ureaplasma urealyticum* can cause nongonococcal urethritis; however, the high incidence of this organism in the normal genital flora makes it difficult to interpret its role in nongonococcal urethritis. Less common agents isolated from nongonococcal urethritis include herpes simplex virus and *Trichomonas vaginalis*. Although gonococcal urethritis is a more acute disease than nongonococcal urethritis, overlap in the symptoms mandates laboratory confirmation. Patients often have multiple sexually transmitted pathogens. Approximately 1/3 of heterosexual men infected with *Neisseria gonorrhoeae* are concurrently infected with *Chlamydia trachomatis*. If only the gonococci are treated, these patients develop a nongonococcal urethritis called postgonococcal urethritis. Therefore, patients with gonorrhea should also be treated with agents that will effectively eradicate *C trachomatis*.

Pathogenesis

Neisseria gonorrhoeae and *C trachomatis* are transmitted by sexual intercourse . *Neisseria gonorrhoeae* attaches to mucosal cells via pili and other surface proteins. The organism then is phagocytosed and passes through the mucosal epithelium. Proliferation occurs with subsequent influx of polymorphonuclear neutrophils (PMN), which produce the exudate that is the hallmark of gonorrhea. *Neisseria gonorrhoeae* spreads to cause disseminated gonococcal infection in approximately 1 to 3 per cent of patients with gonorrhea. Disseminated gonococcal infection is more prevalent in women than in men. Up to 80 per cent of patients with disseminated gonococcal infection have had an asymptomatic local infection for 7 to 30 days prior to dissemination.

Neisseria gonorrhoeae

Diagnosis of gonorrhea is based on microscopic examination of exudate, culturing of the organism, and rapid methods such as antigen or nucleic acid detection. Urethral exudates should be examined by Gram stain for leukocytes and Gram-negative intracellular diplococci. The Gram stain has good sensitivity (90 per cent) and specificity (95 per cent) in males. Ideally, urethral exudate should be planted directly onto a split plate containing modified Thayer-Martin and chocolate agar. The

Thayer-Martin agar contains vancomycin, colistin, nalidixic acid and trimethoprim. Approximately 5 per cent of strains of *N. gonorrhoeae* are susceptible to vancomycin, thus necessitating the use of a non-inhibitory medium such as chocolate agar. The medium is incubated in 5 per cent CO_2 in a moist environment for 48 hours. *Neisseria gonorrhoeae* grows as translucent gray colonies that are oxidase-positive. The identity of the cultures is confirmed by carbohydrate utilization: glucose is fermented, but lactose, maltose and sucrose are negative. Fluorescent-antibody analysis using monoclonal antibodies may also be used to confirm the identity of cultures. Culture confirmation can also be performed using DNA probes that detect specific sequences of the rRNA of *N. gonorrhoeae*.

Chlamydia trachomatis

Diagnosis of *C. trachomatis* infection involves growing the organism in tissue culture or using direct bacterial antigen detection techniques. Since the organism is an intracellular parasite, infected urethral cells must be collected on the swab sample. The best transport media are 2-sucrose-phosphate or sucrose-glutamate-phosphate. If swab specimens are not processed immediately, they should be stored at -70 °C prior to culturing. The swabs are then used to inoculate cell culture lines that have been treated with cyclohexamide. After 48 to 72 hours, the monolayer is fixed and, after staining, is examined for chlamydial inclusion bodies. Because of the labor intensiveness of tissue culture, direct antigen detection methods have been developed for *C. trachomatis*. These include either direct visualization of the organism using fluorescein-conjugated antibodies or enzyme-like immunosorbent assay (ELISA) methods which detect solubilized chlamydial LPS. Serologic tests based on either complement fixation or microimmuno-fluorescence are available in specialized laboratories. Nucleic acid detection systems using amplification steps are now commercially available.

Prevention and Treatment

No vaccines exist for *N. gonorrhoeae* or *Chlamydia trachomatis*. Control requires modification of sexual behaviour and cure of the patient and their contacts.

For gonorrhea, ceftriaxone is the drug of choice. Resistance to penicillin due to β-lactamase has been increasing; therefore, all isolates of *N. gonorrhoeae* should be tested for β-lactamase production and susceptibility testing performed if the strain is β-lactamase positive. Gonorrhea is a reportable disease, and contact tracing is one strategy to contain the spread of infection. As mentioned previously, all patients being treated for gonorrhea should be concomittantly treated for the agents of nongonococcal urethritis such as *C. trachomatis*. Thus, ceftriaxone combined with tetracycline is an optimal regime. Recently azithromycin given as a single oral dose has been recommended for treatment of *C. trachomatis*. This approach leads to better compliance.

Clinical Presentation

Endometritis and pelvic inflammatory disease usually result from ascending vaginal or cervical infections. Vaginal infections seldom have systemic manifestations; they present as an abnormal vaginal discharge that may have an unusual odor. Pruritus may also be present. The consistency of the discharge often reflects the nature of the disease. A thin watery discharge that sticks to the anterior and lateral vaginal walls is seen in bacterial or non-specific vaginosis; the vaginal walls appear normal. In candidiasis the vaginal walls are erythematous, and in trichomoniasis they have a strawberry appearance and the vaginal discharge is green and frothy. A yellow, purulent discharge suggests cervicitis or other forms of vaginitis. In prepubertal girls, gonorrhea causes an inflammatory response in the vagina, whereas following puberty, the infection is primarily a cervicitis. Mucosal ulceration of the vagina results in local discomfort and pain on intercourse. Abdominal discomfort is rare in vaginitis, and is more suggestive of cystitis or pelvic inflammatory disease.

Etiology

About one-half of the cases of vaginitis are due to *Candida albicans* or *Trichomonas vaginalis*. The rest are classified as bacterial vaginosis. Bacterial vaginosis involves an upset in the distribution of the normal flora that is associated with an increase in the numbers of *Gardnerella vaginalis* mobilencus sp.

and anaerobes of the *Bacteroides* group. Since 40 to 50 per cent of normal individuals may carry *Gardnerella vaginalis,* isolation of the organism does not reliably predict bacterial vaginosis. However, the absence of this organism almost rules out bacterial vaginosis.

Major causes of Vaginitis

Neisseria gonorrhoeae and *C. trachomatis* are responsible for the majority of cervical infections. Sexually transmitted infections with more than one pathogen are common. Due to the overlap in clinical features, accurate diagnosis requires laboratory confirmation. About two-thirds of women infected with *N. gonorrhoeae* or *C. trachomatis* do not exhibit purulent cervical discharge. Therefore, for both gonococcal and chlamydial cervicitis, physical examination is not adequate to exclude these infections. Herpes simplex is an occasional cause of cervicitis in women and can be isolated from approximately 90 per cent of women with primary herpes simplex virus infection.

Pathogenesis

Vaginitis due to *T vaginalis* and *C albicans* remains localized, producing vaginal discharge and itching. Yeasts are part of the normal flora in 50 per cent of adult women of child-bearing age. Antibiotics such as tetracyclines disturb the balance of the flora and cause overgrowth by *C. albicans,* with resulting vulvovaginal candidiasis.

Trichomonas vaginalis infection is superficial; penetration of the vaginal epithelial cells has not been described. Inflammation of the vaginal walls and exocervix includes erythema, punctate hemorrhages, and small ulcerations. The pH of the vaginal discharge is often greater than 4.5.

Ascending infection may take the form of salpingo-oophoritis or pelvic inflammatory disease. The onset of ascending infection frequently coincides with menses. Ascending genital infection occurs in approximately 10 to 20 per cent of women with *Neisseria gonorrhoeae* with endocervical infection.

Gonococcal ophthalmia neonatorum occurs as a result of the passage of the newborn through the birth canal of infected mothers.

The organism spreads by ascending infection from the vagina and endocervix to the endometrium, fallopian tubes and other contiguous structures. Pelvic inflammatory disease can be an acute or a chronic complication of endocervitis. Infection results in scarring of the fallopian tubes; this accounts for the ten-fold increase in risk of ectopic pregnancies in women with a history of pelvic inflammatory disease. Each episode of pelvic inflammatory disease also increases the incidence of sterility.

Microbiologic Diagnosis

A wet mount is the optimal method for detecting *T vaginalis* or *C albicans* in patients with vaginitis. However, the wet mount is negative in 30 per cent of symptomatic women with trichomoniasis and therefore does not rule out this infection. Active vaginal candidiasis is characterized by many yeast cells with active budding. Low numbers of *Gardnerella vaginalis* are often present in women who do not have nonspecific vaginitis. Gram-stained smears that show no lactobacilli but many curved, Gram-negative rods are very suggestive of nonspecific vaginitis. According to current recommendations, a diagnosis of nonspecific vaginitis should be based on a positive Gram-stained smear in conjunction with a vaginal pH greater than 4.5 and a positive "whiff test".

Microbiologic diagnosis of *N gonorrhoeae* involves examining Gram-stained cervical exudate, as well as culturing the organism on selected media such as modified Thayer-Martin agar. The sensitivity of the Gram stain is substantially lower for exudates from women than from men: it is positive in only about 80 per cent of women with cervical gonorrhea. If pelvic inflammatory disease or pelvic abscesses are suspected, material should, if possible, be aspirated from the infected site, smeared, and cultured.

Microbiologic diagnosis for *C trachomatis* is performed by either tissue culture or antigen detection techniques. Cervical mucus should be cleared, and then a second sample taken by vigorously rubbing the cervical orifice to ensure that cervical cells are sampled, since *C. trachomatis* is an intracellular parasite. The methods used for culturing and antigen detection are described above.

Prevention and Treatment

There are no vaccines for any of these sexually transmitted diseases. Preventive measures are directed at education with emphasis on safe sexual behavior. Barrier methods such as condoms are essential to decreasing the spread of genital infections. Contact tracing of the reportable infections has also been invaluable. *Trichomonas* infection is treated with metronidazole either as a single oral dose of 2 g or as 250 mg orally three times a day for 7 days. Treatment of candidal infection requires local application of an antifungal agent. The imadiazoles (e.g. clotrimazole or miconazole) are usually more effective than the polyenes (e.g. nystatin). The usual length of treatment is 3 days. Women who have frequent recurrences may be left on longer courses of systemic or local therapy.

Clinical Manifestations

Genital ulcers are transmitted by sexual intercourse and can be caused by a variety of microorganisms. However, some clinical features are found more commonly with a particular etiologic agent. Up to one-third of the episodes of genital ulceration have a clinical diagnosis that did not agree with the microbiologic diagnosis. This indicates the importance of microbiologic confirmation of diagnosis for genital ulcers. In developed countries, the most common genital ulcer diseases are herpes simplex, followed by syphilis. In developing countries, the most common causes of genital ulceration are chancroid, followed by syphilis, lymphogranuloma venereum and granuloma inguinale. The reason for this difference in prevalence between different geographical locations is not understood. The variable incubation period for genital ulcers and the fact that initial lesions are often overlooked are two factors that lead to the increased dissemination of these diseases. Genital ulcers increase the risk of heterosexual transmission of AIDS.

The incubation period for chancroid ranges from 3 to 10 days. The ulcers begin as small, inflammatory papules that develop into ulcers that have an undermined edge, contain purulent exudate and bleed easily. Chancroid is a sexually transmitted disease that is more prevalent in males than females, with a ratio of approximately 8:1. In men, the ulcer is located primarily on the prepuce and around the coronal sulcus. In women, the forchette, labia and perianal area can be involved. Multiple "kissing" ulcers (ulcers in direct opposition to each other) are common. Approximately one-third of the patients with chancroid also have enlarged inguinal lymph nodes that are extremely tender. These lymph nodes may coalesce and rupture and drain, forming buboes.

Syphilis usually presents as a small papule that develops into a painless, eroded, indurated ulcer. The mean incubation period is 21 days. If untreated, the genital ulcer disappears and, after a variable length of time, the patient may develop secondary syphilis with widespread, protean symptoms usually involving the skin with disseminated diffuse papules. The final stage of the disease, tertiary syphilis, can remain latent or appear as late syphilis consisting of neurosyphilis, cardiovascular syphilis, or gummatous syphilis.

Lymphogranuloma venereum, a disease due to restricted types of *C. trachomatis*, usually begins as a painless papule that frequently goes unnoticed. The second stage of the disease involves enlargement of regional lymph nodes and the third stage manifests as rectal strictures and fibrosis.

Granuloma inguinale also begins as a painless papule that ultimately develops into a painless, raised, beefy-red lesion.

The lesions of herpes simplex initially begin as small papules that develop into extremely painful vesicles or ulcers.

Etiology

Haemophilus ducreyi is the etiologic agent of chancroid. This organism is a fastidious, Gram-negative rod that requires hemin. The incidence of chancroid has been increasing in the United States. *Treponema pallidum*, a spirochete, is the agent of syphilis.

Pathogenesis

Treponema pallidum invades intact mucosa and, after entering the lymphatics, can disseminate throughout the body to almost any organ. Obliterative endarteritis is the pathologic hallmark of syphilis and is found in all stages of the disease. *Treponema pallidum* can infect the fetus of a syphilitic mother, producing congenital syphilis.

The pathogenesis of chancroid is poorly understood, but the organism is thought to gain access through minute breaks in the mucosal epithelium. The organism is drained to the regional lymph nodes but does not disseminate further in the body. The organisms remain localized in the superficial layers of the ulcer.

Chlamydia trachomatis serovars L1, L2 and L3 and *Calmatobacterium granulomatis* both remain localized at the site of ulceration but sometimes may show contiguous spread.

Microbiologic Diagnosis

Because the clinical symptoms of the genital ulcer diseases overlap, and because two or more pathogens may be present simultaneously, culture is critical to confirming the diagnosis. Chancroid is diagnosed by culturing either ulcer or bubo exudate. The organism is fastidious but can be grown in 48 hours by culturing on Mueller-Hinton or GC medium enriched with IsoVitaleX, fetal bovine serum, and vancomycin. The cultures grow best in a water saturated environment at 37°C with 5 per cent CO_2. Even under optimal culture conditions, the isolation rates are between 50 and 80 per cent. The organism is identified by hemin requirement, alkaline phosphatase production, ability to reduce nitrate and a positive oxidase test.

Treponema pallidum cannot be grown in vitro. Diagnosis is made by dark-field examination of ulcer material for spirochetes and by serologic detection of an antibody response. Herpes simplex is diagnosed by submitting appropriate vesicular fluid for a viral culture or antigen detection. Lymphogranuloma venereum is usually diagnosed by culturing *C. trachomatis* and examination for inclusion bodies in the inoculated cell line. Antigen detection methods using fluorescein-conjugated antibody have also proved useful. *Calmatobacterium granulomatis* is usually detected by staining histologic sections with Warthin-Starry silver stain and observing Donovan bodies within the host cells.

Prevention and Treatemnt

As with other sexually transmitted diseases, rapid diagnosis, treatment and contact tracing help contain the spread of the disease. Use of condoms and modification of sexual behavior are important preventitive measures. Effective treatment is available for all the genital ulcer diseases. Chancroid is treated with a seven day course of erythromycin. Other useful antibiotics include ceftriaxone, trimethoprim, either with or without sulfonamides, and ciprofloxacin. Syphilis is treated with penicillin. If the patient is allergic to penicillin, tetracycline is an effective alternative. Early treatment of pregnant women with syphilis is crucial to prevent congenital syphilis. The susceptibility profiles of Lymphogranuloma venereum strains are similar to those of other *C. trachomatis* serovars. Tetracyclines, erythromycin and sulfonamides are all effective. Granuloma inguinale has been successfully treated with trimethoprim-sulfamethoxazole, tetracycline and erythromycin. Treatment should be continued for 3 weeks.

Clinical Manifestations

Acute cystitis is a superficial inflammation of the bladder and urethra which leads to urinary frequency, painful urination, a feeling of fullness following voiding, and suprapubic discomfort. Acute pyelonephritis is due to bacterial invasion of the renal tissue with inflammation and swelling, leading to fever, back pain, and sometimes renal dysfunction. Acute cystitis occurs together with acute pyelonephritis in about one-third of patients. Acute prostatitis occurs when bacteria invade the prostate, causing perineal pain and fever.

Infection can spread within the urinary tract and patients often have recurrences of cystitis, sometimes interspersed with episodes of pyelonephritis. Symptoms that persist and recur are often referred to as chronic cystitis, chronic pyelonephritis or chronic prostatitis. However, these chronic conditions are much more difficult to define. Recurring kidney infection in childhood sometimes leads to renal damage and ultimate kidney failure. Hypertension is also an occasional outcome of chronic renal infection.

Asymptomatic infections of the urinary tractasymptomatic bacteriuriaare common. In childhood, about one per cent of girls have asymptomatic bacteriuria. The prevalence increases to 3 to 5 per cent among adult women and 10 to 50 per cent in elderly men and women. Occasionally, individuals do have symptoms such as incontinence or ongoing malaise that are not recognized as due to bacteriuria until it is diagnosed and treated.

Some patients have what are called "complicated urinary tract infections." This includes individuals who have congenital or acquired anatomic abnormalities of the urinary tract. Obstruction of the urinary tract as a result of either a stone or a malfunctioning bladder secondary to a neural injury also predisposes to infection and makes infections more difficult to treat. Kidney and bladder stones can be the consequence of infection, and management of the infection is usually only successful if the stone is also removed. Many individuals cared for by urologists have underlying abnormalities of the urinary tract that make infections complicated and difficult to cure without surgical restoration of normal urine flow. Urinary catheters, used to drain the urinary tract in cases of obstruction or incontinence, bypass normal host defenses, and individuals with indwelling catheters are very prone to infections. Nosocomial urinary infections due to catheterization account for almost one-half of all infections acquired in hospital and can lead to invasive, life-threatening sepsis.

Urinary infections are the commonest type of bacterial infection that causes women to seek medical care. In a given year, about 1 in 20 women have acute cystitis. Acute pyelonephritis is one of the most common infections that require hospital admission for intravenous antibacterial therapy.

Urinary infections are recurrent in about 5 per cent of women, and the recurring cystitis and pyelonephritis cause substantial morbidity. Recurrent urinary infection in women can be due to a number of underlying causes. Sexual intercourse, the syndrome referred to as "honeymoon cystitis", is responsible for about one-half of urinary infections in sexually active adult women. These infections are not acquired from the sexual partner but rather are due to the mechanical irritation associated with intercourse. Unfortunately, women who acquire frequent infections that are associated with intercourse often have difficulties developing healthy, normal sexual relations and this may require special attention. The use of a diaphragm for contraception is also a major risk factor, increasing the risk of cystitis threefold.

Etiology

Organisms normally present in the intestinal tract cause most urinary tract infections. The commonest of these by far is *Escherichia coli*, which is responsible for 80 per cent of infections that are acquired outside of hospitals . Other Gram-negative rods such as *Klebsiella*, *Enterobacter*, and *Proteus* spp are relatively common, each accounting for 3 to 5 per cent of infections. Within the hospital environment, *Pseudomonas aeruginosa*, *Serratia marscesens*, and other, more resistant, hospital-associated pathogens account for many infections.

Major Causes of Urinary Tract Infections

Gram-positive organisms, particularly coagulase-negative staphylococci and enterococci, cause some infections. *Staphylococcus saprophyticus* causes about 10 per cent of urinary tract infections in young women. *Candida albicans* is also a frequent pathogen in hospitalized patients, particularly if diabetes is present.

Anaerobes and fastidious organisms rarely cause urinary infections. A number of viruses, particularly mumps virus, cytomegalovirus, and coxsackieviruses, can be present in the kidneys and urine, but rarely cause symptoms or any consequences.

A number of sexually transmitted pathogens (e.g., *Neisseria gonorrhoeae*) may invade the urethra. *Chlamydia trachomatis* and herpes simplex can present with symptoms that mimic acute cystitis in both men and women.

Pathogenesis

Bacteria invade the urinary tract by ascending or hematogenous routes. The ascending route is the most common, with hematogenous spread causing kidney abscesses.

Pathogenesis of Urinary Tract Infections

Escherichia coli serogroups 01, 02, 04, 06, 07 and 075 are the most common agents of urinary tract infections. The most important virulence factor for these bacteria is the enhanced ability to adhere to uroepithelial cells. This attachment is mediated by specific pilus adhesins on the surface of *E coli*. The mucosal epithelial cells of women and children with recurrent urinary tract infections have been shown to have an increased avidity for attachment of *E. coli*. However, phasic variation occurs after the organism ascends to the kidney or pelvis, and pili are no longer produced. Motility has been shown to facilitate ascending infection and bacterial endotoxins can decrease urethral peristalsis.

Phasic Variation of *E. coli* in Urinary Tract Infections

Alterations of urine flow by scarring, obstruction due to stones, or catheterization greatly enhances the risk of acquiring a urinary tract infection.

Microbiologic Diagnosis

The diagnosis of a urinary tract infection is confirmed by culturing the organism from urine. Most bacteria that cause urinary infection grow readily, and the clinical diagnosis of urinary tract infection is usually confirmed within 24 hours.

Because urine is an excellent culture media for a variety of microorganisms, considerable effort must be made to ensure that a urine sample is not contaminated during collection and that organisms are not permitted to grow before the urine is cultured. Patients suspected of urinary infection are usually asked to collect a mid-stream sample after cleaning the perineum or glans penis with soap and water. An early-morning collection is best because the concentration of bacteria in the urine is greatest prior to the morning voiding. The urine is then refrigerated or taken to the laboratory for immediate culture. Urine can be stored in a refrigerator for up to 24 hours without any loss of bacterial viability.

In the laboratory, a quantitative loop that samples 0.001 ml is usually used to inoculate both a nonselective medium (blood agar) and a selective medium (MacConkey agar). The cultures are incubated at 37°C. By the following day, the organism can be identified and quantitated. Cultures that represent true infection rather than specimen contamination are identified quantitatively. Approximately 65 per cent of patients with acute cystitis have >105 organisms/ml of urine and almost 90 per cent of patients with acute pyelonephritis and asymptomatic bacteriuria also have counts in excess of 105 organisms/ml. Unless contaminated or overgrown, most negative urines have <104 organisms/ml. Antibacterial susceptibility profiles of the pathogens are also analyzed. Examination of urine to demonstrate the presence of pus cells is an important part of diagnosing urinary infection. Most infections of the urinary tract are associated with an inflammatory response. Thus, quantitative urine culture and the presence of pyuria are straightforward, reliable means of confirming the clinical diagnosis of urinary tract infection.

Prevention and Treatment

Most antimicrobial agents are excreted in the urine and, therefore many different treatment regimens can be used to cure urinary infections. The most commonly prescribed agents for *acute cystitis* are oral regimens of nitrofurantoin, a sulfonamide-trimethoprim combination, amoxicillin, cephalexin, and ciprofloxacin or other quinolones. Each of these regimens cure 90 to 95 per cent of females with acute cystitis. Amoxacillin which previously was the drug of choice now fails in 10 to 20 per cent of patients due to widespread resistance among *E. coli.* Long courses are not necessary, and many studies have shown that single dose therapy or therapy prescribed for 3 days is as effective as longer courses. Intravenous antimicrobials are usually prescribed for patients acutely ill with *acute pyelonephritis* or *acute prostatitis*. Aminoglycosides and cephalosporins are frequently chosen. Longer courses of oral antibacterial agents are useful to prevent recurring infections in women who are susceptible to frequent reinfections; women need not live in fear of their next infection. If they wish to not take continuous preventive therapy, the next treatment regimens should be carried for self-initiation with the onset of acute symptoms.

9

Vector (Organisms)

INTRODUCTION

In epidemiology, a vector is an organism that does not cause disease itself but which transmits infection by conveying pathogens from one host to another.

A classic example is the anopheles mosquito which acts as a vector for the disease malaria by transmitting the malarial parasite plasmodium to humans. In this case plasmodium is harmless to the mosquito (its intermediate host) but causes the disease malaria in humans (its definitive host).

In molecular biology and genetic engineering a **vector** is a vehicle for transferring genetic material into a cell.

A viral vector is a virus which has been modified to transduct specific genetic material into a cell, e.g. for gene therapy.

A plasmid vector is made by splicing a DNA construct into a plasmid. Various techniques are then used to transfect the plasmid into the cell.

Epidemiology

There are two types of vector that convey infectious organisms to a host: mechanical and biological. Microbes do not multiply within mechanical vectors - mechanical vectors only physically transport microbes from host to host. In contrast, microbes must propagate within a biological vector before the biological vector can transmit the microbes.

- mosquito (malaria, St. Louis encephalitis, dengue fever, yellow fever, West Nile virus)
- flea (bubonic plague)
- tick (Lyme disease, rocky mountain spotted fever, tick-borne encephalitis)
- deer mouse (hantavirus)
- kissing bug (Triatominae) (Chagas Disease)
- bat (Rabies)

Molecular Biology

Cell Transformation and Gene Therapy

- adenovirus
- adeno-associated virus
- tobacco mosaic virus (plants)
- cytomegalovirus
- bacteriophage (bacteria)
- viral vector

DNA

- SV40 (Simian virus 40)
- Plasmid
- Yeast artificial chromosome (Chromosome walking, Positional cloning)
- Bacterial artificial chromosome (Shotgun sequencing)

MOSQUITO

Mosquitoes are insects in the family Culicidae. They have a pair of scaled wings, a pair of halteres, a slender body, and long legs. The females of most mosquito species suck blood (hematophagy) from other animals, which has made them the most deadly disease vector known, killing millions of people over thousands of years and continuing to kill millions per year by the spread of infectious diseases.

Length varies but is rarely greater than 16 mm (0.6 inch) and weight up to 2.5 mg (0.04 grain). A mosquito can fly for 1 to 4 hours continuously at up to 1–2 km/h travelling up to 10 km in a night. Most species are nocturnal or crepuscular (dawn or dusk) feeders. During the heat of the day most mosquitoes rest in a cool place and wait for the evenings. They may still bite if disturbed. Mosquitos are adept at infiltration and have been known to find their way into residences via deactivated air conditioning units.

Feeding Habits

Both male and female mosquitoes are nectar feeders, but the females of many species are also capable of hematophagy (drinking blood]). Females do not require blood for their own survival, but they do need supplemental substances (like protein and iron) to develop eggs. Prior to and during blood feeding, they inject saliva into the bodies of their source(s) of blood. Female mosquitoes hunt their blood host by detecting carbon dioxide (CO_2) and 1-Octen-3-ol from a distance.

Mosquitoes of the genus *Toxorhynchites* never drink blood. This genus includes the largest extant mosquitoes, the larvae of which prey on the larvae of other mosquitoes. These mosquito eaters have been used in the past as mosquito control agents, with varying success.

Mosquito Saliva

In order for the mosquito to obtain a blood meal it must surmount the vertebrate physiological responses. The mosquito, as with all blood-feeding arthropods, has evolved mechanisms to effectively block the hemostasis system with their saliva which contains a complex mixture of secreted proteins. Mosquito saliva affects vascular constriction, blood clotting, platelet aggregation, inflammation, immunity, and angiogenesis Universally, hematophagous arthropod saliva contains at least one anticlotting, one anti-platelet, and one vasodilatory substance.

Mosquito saliva also contains enzymes that aid in sugar feeding and antimicrobial agents to control bacterial growth in the sugar meal. The composition of mosquito saliva is relatively simple as it usually contains fewer than 20 dominant proteins. Despite the great strides in knowledge of these molecules and their role in bloodfeeding achieved recently, scientists still cannot ascribe functions to more than half of the molecules found in arthropod saliva.

It is now well recognized that the feeding ticks, sandflies, and, more recently, mosquitoes have an ability to modulate the immune response of the animals (hosts) they feed on. The presence of this activity in vector saliva is a reflection of the inherent overlapping and interconnected nature of the host hemostatic and inflammatory/immunological responses and the intrinsic need to prevent these host defenses from disrupting successful feeding. The mechanism for mosquito saliva-induced alteration of the host immune response is unclear, but the data has become increasingly convincing that such an effect occurs. Early work described a factor in saliva that directly suppresses TNF-a release, but not antigen-induced histamine secretion, from activated mast cells. Experiments demonstrated that the inclusion of *Ae. aegypti* mosquito saliva into naïve cultures led to a suppression of interleukin (IL)-2 and IFN-? production, while the cytokines IL-4 and IL-5 are unaffected by mosquito saliva. Cellular proliferation in response to IL-2 is clearly reduced by prior treatment of cells with SGE. Correspondingly, activated splenocytes isolated from mice fed upon by either *Ae. aegypti* or *Cx. pipiens* mosquitoes produce markedly higher levels of IL-4 and IL-10 concurrent with suppressed IFN-? production. Unexpectedly, this shift in cytokine expression is observed in splenocytes up to 10 days after mosquito exposure, suggesting that natural feeding of mosquitoes can have a profound, enduring, and systemic effect on the immune response.

T cell populations are decidedly susceptible to the suppressive effect of mosquito saliva, showing enhanced mortality and decreased division rates. The T- and B-cell proliferation was inhibited in a dose dependent manner with concentrations as low as 1/7th of the saliva in a single mosquito

Depinay et al. (2005) observed a suppression of antibody-specific T cell responses mediated by mosquito saliva and dependent on mast cells and IL-10 expression. A recent study suggests that mosquito saliva can also decrease expression of interferon-α/ß during early mosquito-borne virus infection. The contribution of type I interferons (IFN) in recovery from infection with viruses has been demonstrated *in vivo* by the therapeutic and prophylactic effects of administration of IFN-inducers or IFN, and recent research suggests that mosquito saliva exacerbates West Nile virus infection, as well as other mosquito-transmitted viruses.

Mosquitoes and Health

Mosquitoes are a vector agent that carries disease-causing viruses and parasites from person to person without catching the disease themselves. Female mosquitoes suck blood from people and other animals as part of their eating and breeding habits. When a mosquito bites, she also injects saliva and anti-coagulants into the blood which may also contain disease-causing viruses or other parasites. This cycle can be interrupted by killing the mosquitoes, isolating infected people from all mosquitoes while they are infectious or vaccinating the exposed population. All three techniques have been used, often in combination, to control mosquito transmitted diseases. Window screens, introduced in the 1880s, were called "the most humane contribution the 19th century made to the preservation of sanity and good temper."

Mosquitoes are estimated to transmit disease to more than 700 million people annually in Africa, South America, Central America, Mexico and much of Asia with millions of resulting deaths. In Europe, Russia, Greenland, Canada, the United States, Australia, New Zealand, Japan and other temperate and developed countries, mosquito bites are now mostly an irritating nuisance; but still cause some deaths each year. Historically, before mosquito transmitted diseases were brought under control, they caused tens of thousands of deaths in these countries and hundreds of thousands of infections. Mosquitoes were shown to be the method by which yellow fever and malaria were transmitted from person to person by Walter Reed,

William C. Gorgas and associates in the U.S. Army Medical Corps first in Cuba and then around the Panama Canal in the early 1900s. Since then other diseases have been shown to be transmitted the same way.

The mosquito genus *Anopheles* carries the malaria parasite. Worldwide, malaria is a leading cause of premature mortality, particularly in children under the age of five, with around 5.3 million deaths annually, according to the Centers for Disease Control. Some species of mosquito can carry the filariasis worm, a parasite that causes a disfiguring condition (often referred to as elephantiasis) characterized by a great swelling of several parts of the body; worldwide, around 40 million people are living with a filariasis disability. The viral diseases yellow fever and dengue fever are transmitted mostly by *Aedes aegypti* mosquitoes. Other viral diseases like epidemic polyarthritis, Rift Valley fever, Ross River Fever, St. Louis encephalitis, West Nile virus (WNV), Japanese encephalitis, La Crosse encephalitis and several other encephalitis type diseases are carried by several different mosquitoes. Eastern equine encephalitis (EEE) and Western equine encephalitis (WEE) occurs in the United States where it causes disease in humans, horses, and some bird species. Because of the high mortality rate, EEE and WEE are regarded as two of the most serious mosquito-borne diseases in the United States. Symptoms range from mild flu-like illness to encephalitis, coma and death Viruses carried by arthropods such as mosquitoes or ticks are known collectively as arboviruses. West Nile virus was accidentally introduced into the United States in 1999 and by 2003 had spread to almost every state with over 3,000 cases in 2006.

A mosquito's period of feeding is often undetected; the bite only becomes apparent because of the immune reaction it provokes. When a mosquito bites a human, she injects saliva and anti-coagulants. For any given individual, with the initial bite there is no reaction but with subsequent bites the body's immune system develops antibodies and a bite becomes inflamed and itchy within 24 hours. This is the usual reaction in young children. With more bites, the sensitivity of the human immune system increases, and an itchy red hive appears in minutes where the immune response has broken capillary blood vessels and fluid has collected under the skin. This type of reaction is common in older children and adults. Some adults can become desensitized to mosquitoes and have little or no reaction to their bites, while others can become hyper-sensitive with bites causing blistering, bruising, and large inflammatory reactions, a response known as Skeeter Syndrome.

There are many methods used for mosquito control. Some target the larval stage, while others are used to kill or repel adults. Much of modern mosquito control is no longer dependent on pesticides but specialized organisms that eat mosquitoes, or infect them with a disease that kills them. Such methods can even be used in Conservation Areas, like the "Forsyth refuge", where some major mosquito control is performed and monitored using "killifish" and juvenile eels. The success is documented with most advanced underwater microscopes like the ecoSCOPE. However, outbreaks of human mosquito-borne diseases may still result in fogging with products that are less toxic than those used in the past.

A few varieties of the natural soil bacteria *Bacillus thuringiensis*, especially *Bt israelensis* (Bti), are used to interfere in the digestion systems of larvae. It can be dispersed by hand or dropped by helicopter in large areas. Unfortunately Bti is no longer effective after the larvae turn into pupae, because they stop eating. At this point larviciding oils, such as Golden Bear, can be used which increase the water tension until the pupae and larvae cannot break the surface to obtain air and therefore drown. A chemical commonly used in the United States is methoprene, considered slightly toxic to larger animals, which mimics and interferes with natural growth hormones in mosquito larvae, preventing development. Methoprene is frequently distributed in time-release briquette form in breeding areas. Malathion has also been sprayed in metropolitan areas like New York City to decrease the mosquito population and prevent the spread of West Nile Virus.

Dragonflies, also known as mosquito hawks, are excellent control agents. Dragonfly naiads consume mosquito larvae in the breeding waters, and adult dragonflies eat adult mosquitoes, particularly the day-flying Asian tiger mosquitoes. Fogging for adult mosquitoes can backfire and increase long-term populations if it removes dragonflies and other natural controls. Lizards are also useful predators which eat mosquitoes indoors.

Mosquito repellents generally contain one of the following active ingredients DEET, Catnip oil extract, nepetalactone, citronella, or eucalyptus oil extract. Often the best "repellent" is a fan or gentle breeze as mosquitoes do not like moving air.

The most effective solutions for malaria control efforts in the third world are: mosquito nets (klamboe), insecticide-laced mosquito nets, and DDT. Plain mosquito nets are cheap, they are completely effective in protecting humans within the net, they do not adversely affect the health of natural predators such as dragonflies, and do not require sophisticated public health capacity on the part of the government. The role of DDT in combating mosquitoes has been the subject of considerable controversy. While some argue that DDT deeply damages biodiversity, others argue that DDT is the most effective weapon in combating mosquitoes and hence malaria. While some of this disagreement is based on differences in the extent to which disease control is valued as opposed to the value of biodiversity, there is also genuine disagreement amongst experts about the costs and benefits of using DDT. Moreover, DDT-resistant mosquitoes have started to increase in numbers, especially in tropics due to mutations, reducing the effectiveness of this chemical.

Other popular methods of household mosquito control are the use of small electrical mats plugged into a socket, mosquito repellent vapour and mosquito coil all having a form of allethrin—a chemical commonly used to combat mosquitos and other pests in general. Mosquito repellent candles containing Citronella oil is another method to keep mosquitoes at bay. Some more lesser known methods use the cultivation of plants like wormwood or sagewort, lemon balm, lemon grass, lemon thyme and the mosquito plant (Pelargonium) which act against mosquitoes. However scientists have added that these plants are effective only when the leaves are crushed and used.

A newer approach to killing mosquitoes in a non-toxic way is to use a device that burns propane, thus generating carbon dioxide, warmth, and water vapor. These three elements, often coupled with a chemical attractant heated in this process, draws the mosquitoes toward the propane flame, where they are then sucked into a net or holder where they collect. Given that the typical mosquito's lifespan ranges from days to weeks, simply trapping them long enough allows them to die without any further effort.

One of the unconventional methods of mosquito control is the use of electromagnetic, ultrasound devices designed to confuse mosquitoes. It has found use in a variety of devices including a downloadable software which is claimed to thwart the insects using PC speakers. However the effectiveness is questionable since computer speakers aren't designed for high frequency sounds (15-20 kHz range).

Bats are an extremely effective form of natural mosquito control. One brown bat can consume 1200 mosquitoes in an hour. It's easy to build a bat box to encourage bats to live nearby. One averaged size bat box can provide a home for dozens of bats. Care must be taken, however, to ensure no humans are bitten by the bats, as bats are the number-one vector for rabies, a high fatality disease in the absence of immediate treatment. The purple martin swallow (*Progne subis*) is not, however, a prodigious consumer of mosquitoes as is so often claimed by companies that manufacture martin housing.

One of the main, non-chemical ways to prevent mosquito bites is the mosquito net. Mosquito netting if properly used and maintained (no holes), provides the maximum possible personal protection against biting insects. In many areas of the world, mosquitoes are not only a nuisance, but also pose a serious health threat. Sleeping under a bednet is highly recommended by the World Health Organization (WHO) and the U.S. Center for Disease Control (CDC) if staying in these areas.

One of the most popular chemical skin treatments is *N*, *N*-diethyl-*meta*-toluamide, commonly known as DEET. It has been used widely since its invention by the U.S. Department of

Agriculture in 1945. DEET products have been widely used for many years but these products have occasionally been associated with some minor to moderate adverse reactions. DEET concentrations in repellents range from 5% up to 100%.

Other less commonly used mosquito repellents include: catnip oil extract, nepetalactone (no known credible tests), citronella 10% solution (84% effective for about 1 hour), or eucalyptus oil extract. A soybean oil-based product worked for about 1.5 hours and a lemon eucalyptus-based solution worked for about three hours.

Picaridin, first used in Europe in 2001, has been reported to be effective by Consumer Reports (7% solution) and the Australian Army (20% solution) Consumer Report retests in 2006 show that a 7% solution of picaridin now has a protection time of about 0 minutes and a 15% solution was only good for about one hour. So far DEET is the champion effective repellent against mosquitoes, especially when worn in conjunction with light coloured clothing, long sleeved pants and shirts and a hat.

Mosquitoes use carbon dioxide (CO_2) and 1-octen-3-ol from human and animal breath and sweat as odor cues and DEET inhibits the detection of the latter in insects Other potent body and breath odor cues include lactic acid, dimethyldisulfide,and acetone.

Other commercial products offered for household mosquito "control" include small electrical mats, mosquito repellent vapor, DEET-impregnated wrist bands, and mosquito coils containing a form of the chemical allethrin. Mosquito-repellent candles containing citronella oil are sold widely in the U.S. All of these have been used with mixed reports of success and failure. Some claim that plants like wormwood or sagewort, lemon balm, lemon grass, lemon thyme and the mosquito plant (Pelargonium) will act against mosquitoes. However, scientists have determined that these plants are "effective" for a limited time only when the leaves are crushed and applied directly to the skin.

There are several, widespread, unproven theories about mosquito control such as the assertion that Vitamin B, in particular B1 Thiamine, garlic, ultrasonic devices, incense, can be used to repel or control mosquitoes. Moreover, some manufacturers of "mosquito repelling" ultrasonic devices have been found to be fraudulent and their devices were deemed "useless" in tests by the UK Consumer magazine *Which?* Application of other organic materials directly to the skin — aloe vera, lime juice, and peppermint oil, for example — is touted as somewhat effective, though the results have not been scientifically evaluated. One explanation is that such materials, with their strong odors, help mask the natural skin and sweat odors that initially attract mosquitos.

Bug zappers kill a wide range of flying insects including many beneficial insects that eat mosquitoes as well as some mosquitoes. Bug zappers have not been proven effective at controlling overall mosquito population.

Some newer mosquito traps or known mosquito attractants emit a plume of carbon dioxide together with other mosquito attractants such as sugary scents, lactic acid, octenol, warmth, water vapor and sounds. By mimicking a mammal's scent and outputs, female mosquitoes are drawn toward the trap, where they are typically sucked into a net or holder by an electric fan where they are collected. According to the American Mosquito Control Association, "these devices will, indeed, trap and kill measurable numbers of mosquitoes," but their effectiveness in any particular case will depend on a number of factors such as the size and species of the mosquito population and the type and location of the breeding habitat. They are useful in specimen collection studies to determine the types of mosquitoes prevalent in an area but are typically far too inefficient to be useful in reducing mosquito populations.

Natural Predators

Dragonflies are natural predators of mosquitoes.

The dragonfly eats mosquitoes at all stages of development and is quite effective in controlling populations. Although bats and Purple Martins can be prodigious consumers of insects, many of which are pests, less than one per cent of their diet typically consists of mosquitoes. Neither bats nor Purple Martins are known to control or even significantly reduce mosquito populations. In the shape of a larva, the toxorhynchites (mosquito hawks) are known as natural predators of the culicidae species. Each larva can eat an average of 10 to 20 mosquitoes larvae per day. During its entire development, a toxorhynchites can consume an equivalent of 5,000 larvae of the first stage (L1) or 300 larvae stage 4 (L4). However, it can consume all types of prey, of organic debris (Steffan & Evenhuis, 1981) or even exhibit cannibalistic behaviour.

Treatment of Mosquito Bites

Visible, irritating bites are due to an immune response from the binding of IgG and IgE antibodies to antigens in the mosquito's saliva. Some of the sensitizing antigens are common to all mosquito species, whereas others are specific to certain species. There are both immediate hypersensitivity reactions (Types I & III) and delayed hypersensitivity reactions (Type IV) to mosquito bites. There are several commercially available anti-itch medications. These are usually orally or topically applied antihistamines and, for more severe cases, corticosteroids such as hydrocortisone and triamcinolone. Many home remedies and recipes exist, most of which are effective against itching, including calamine lotion, baking soda, salt, rubbing alcohol, vinegar, and toothpaste. Also rubbing nail polish (preferably clear) on the bite will stop it from itching most of the time. Ammonia has been clinically demonstrated to be an effective treatment.

Cold or heat treatments, such as using running water, may be effective in reducing the itching sensation but bring relief mainly during their application. Scratching a mosquito bite may also provide temporary relief but will usually serve to irritate and inflame the area further and increase the risk of infection and scarring.

According to the "Mosquitoes" chapter in *Kwaidan: Stories and Studies of Strange Things*, by Lafcadio Hearn, mosquitoes are seen as reincarnations of the dead, condemned by the errors of their former lives to the condition of *Jiki-ketsu-gaki*, or "blood-drinking pretas".

The Babylonian Talmud asserts that the Roman Emperor Titus was punished by God for having destroyed the Temple in Jerusalem by having a mosquito fly into Titus' nose, picking at his brain, ceaselessly buzzing, driving him crazy and eventually causing his death. No such account appears in any Roman source. Titus died prematurely from unclear causes after only two years in power.

FLEA

Scientific Classification

Domain	:	Eukaryota
Kingdom	:	Animalia
Phylum	:	Arthropoda
Class	:	Insecta
Subclass	:	Pterygota
Infraclass	:	Neoptera
Superorder	:	Endopterygota
Order	:	Siphonaptera

Latreille, 1825

Infraorders

Ceratophyllomorpha

Hystrichopsyllomorpha

Pulicomorpha

Pygiopsyllomorpha

Synonyms

Aphaniptera

Flea is the common name for any of the small wingless insects of the order Siphonaptera (some authorities use the name Aphaniptera because it is older, but names above family rank need not follow the ICZN rules of priority, so most taxonomists use the more familiar name). Fleas are external parasites, living by hematophagy off the blood of mammals and birds. Genetic and morphological evidence indicates that they are descendants of the Scorpionfly family Boreidae, which are also flightless;

accordingly it is possible that they will eventually be reclassified as a suborder within the Mecoptera. In the past, however, it was most commonly supposed that fleas had evolved from the flies (Diptera), based on similarities of the larvae. In any case, all these groups seem to represent a clade of closely related insect lineages, for which the names Mecopteroidea and Antliophora have been proposed.

Some well-known flea species include:

- Cat flea (*Ctenocephalides felis*),
- Dog flea (*Ctenocephalides canis*),
- Human flea (*Pulex irritans*),
- Northern rat flea (*Nosopsyllus fasciatus*),
- Oriental rat flea (*Xenopsylla cheopis*).

Morphology and Behaviour

Fleas are small (1/16 to 1/8-inch (1.5 to 3.3 mm) long), agile, usually dark coloured (for example, the reddish-brown of the cat flea), wingless insects with tube-like mouthparts adapted to feeding on the blood of their hosts. Their bodies are laterally compressed (human anatomical terms), permitting easy movement through the hairs or feathers on the host's body (or in the case of humans, under clothes). Their legs are long, the hind pair well adapted for jumping (vertically up to seven inches (18 cm); horizontally thirteen inches (33 cm) - around 200 times their own body length, making the flea one of the best jumpers of all known animals (in comparison to body size), second only to the froghopper. The flea body is hard, polished, and covered with many hairs and short spines directed backward, which also assists its movements on the host. Its tough body is able to withstand great pressure, likely an adaptation to survive scratching etc. Even hard squeezing between the fingers is normally insufficient to kill the flea; it may be necessary to capture them with adhesive tape, crush them between the fingernails, roll them between the fingers, or put them in a fire safe area and burn them with match or lighter. They can also be drowned.

Fleas lay tiny white oval shaped eggs. Their larvae are small and pale with bristles covering their worm-like body. They are without eyes, and have mouthparts adapted to chewing. While the adult flea's diet consists solely of blood, the larvae feed on various organic matter, including the feces of mature fleas In the pupal phase the larvae are enclosed in a silken, debris-covered cocoon.

Fleas are holometabolous insects, going through the three life cycle stages of larva, pupa and imago (adult). The flea life cycle begins when the female lays after feeding. Adult fleas must feed on blood before they can become capable of reproduction. Eggs are laid in batches of up to 20 or so, usually on the host itself, which easily roll onto the ground. As such, areas where the host rests and sleeps become one of the primary habitats of eggs and developing fleas. The eggs take around two days to two weeks to hatch.

Flea larvae emerge from the eggs to feed on any available organic material such as dead insects, feces and vegetable matter. They are blind and avoid sunlight, keeping to dark places like sand, cracks and crevices, and bedding. Given an adequate supply of food, larvae should pupate and weave a silken cocoon within 1-2 weeks after 3 larval stages. After another week or two the adult flea is fully developed and ready to emerge from the cocoon. They may however remain resting during this period until they receive a signal that a host is near - vibrations (including sound), heat and carbon dioxide are all stimuli indicating the probable presence of a host Fleas are known to overwinter in the larval or pupal stages.

Once the flea reaches adulthood its primary goal is to find blood - adult fleas must feed on blood in order to reproduce Adult fleas only have around a week to find food once they emerge, though they can survive two months to a year between meals. A flea population is unevenly distributed, with 50 percent eggs, 35 percent larvae, 10 percent pupae and 5 percent adults. heir total life cycle can take as little as two weeks, but may be lengthened to many months if conditions are favorable. Female fleas can lay 500 or more eggs over their life, allowing for phenomenal growth rates.

Evolution and Classification

Fleas are apparently related to scorpionflies , winged insects with good eyesight. The flightless snow flea with its rudimentary wings seems to be close to the common ancestor of the 2000 or so currently known varieties of flea, which split off in many directions around 160 million years ago. Their evolution continued to produce adaptations for their specialized parasitic niche, such that they now have no wings and their eyes are covered over. The large number of flea species may be attributed to the wide variety of host species they feed on, which provides so many specific ecological niches to adapt to.

Flea systematics is not entirely fixed. While, compared to many other insect groups, fleas have been studied and classified fairly thoroughly, details still remain to be learned about the evolutionary relationships among the different flea lineages.

Infraorder Pulicomorpha

- Superfamily Pulicoidea
- Family Hectopsyllidae – sticktight and chigoe fleas ("chiggers" of Latin America)
- Family Pulicidae – common fleas
- Superfamily Malacopsylloidea
- Family Malacopsyllidae
- Family Rhopalopsyllidae – hosts: marsupials
- Superfamily Vermipsylloidea
- Family Vermipsyllidae – hosts: carnivores
- Superfamily Coptopsylloidea
- Family Coptopsyllidae
- Superfamily Ancistropsylloidea
- Family Ancistropsyllidae

Infraorder Pygiopsyllomorpha

- Superfamily Pygiopsylloidea
- Family Lycopsyllidae

- Family Pygiopsyllidae
- Family Stivaliidae

Infraorder Hystrichopsyllomorpha

- Superfamily Hystrichopsylloidea
- Family Hystrichopsyllidae – hosts: rats and mice. Includes Ctenopsyllidae, Amphipsyllidae
- Family Chimaeropsyllidae
- Superfamily Macropsylloidea
- Family Macropsyllidae
- Superfamily Stephanocircidoidea
- Family Stephanocircidae - hosts: rodents

Infraorder Ceratophyllomorpha

- Superfamily Ceratophylloidea
- Family Ceratophyllidae - hosts: rodents and birds. Includes Dolichopsyllidae
- Family Leptopsyllidae – hosts: mice and rats
- Family Ischnopsyllidae – hosts: bats
- Family Xiphiopsyllidae

Relationship with Host

Fleas attack a wide variety of warm-blooded vertebrates including dogs, cats, humans, chickens, rabbits, squirrels, rats, ferrets, and mice. Fleas are a nuisance to their hosts, causing an itching sensation which in turn may result in the host attempting to remove the pest by biting, pecking, scratching etc the vicinity of the parasite. Fleas are not simply a source of annoyance, however. Some people and animals suffer allergic reactions to flea saliva resulting in rashes. Flea bites generally result in the formation of a slightly-raised swollen itching spot with a single puncture point at the center. The bites often appear in clusters or lines of two bites, and can remain itchy and inflamed for up to several weeks afterwards. Fleas can also lead to hair loss as a result of frequent scratching and biting by the animal, and can cause anemia in extreme cases.

Besides the problems posed by the creature itself, fleas can also act as a vector for disease. For example, fleas transmitted the bubonic plague between rodents and humans by carrying *Yersinia pestis* bacteria. Murine typhus (endemic typhus) fever, and in some cases *Hymenolepiasis* (tapeworm) can also be transmitted by fleas.

Flea Treatments

The fleas, their larvae, or their eggs can be controlled with insecticides. Lufenuron is a veterinary preparation (Programme) that attacks the larval flea's ability to produce chitin but does not kill fleas. Flea medicines need to be used with care as many, especially the acetylcholinesterase inhibitors, also affect mammals. Popular brands of topicals that do not contain cholinesterase inhibitors include Advantage, Advantix, and Frontline and Frontline PLUS.

For the Home

Combating a flea infestation in the home takes patience as for every flea found on an animal there are many more developing in the home. A spot-on insecticide, such as Advantage, Frontline or Revolution will kill the fleas on the pet and in turn the pet itself will be a roving flea trap and mop up newly hatched fleas. The environment should be treated with a fogger or spray insecticide containing an insect growth regulator, such as pyriproxyfen or methoprene to kill eggs and pupae, which are quite resistant against insecticides. Frequent vacuuming is also helpful, but you must immediately dispose of the vacuum bag afterwards.

Diatomaceous earth can also be used as an effective home flea treatment in lieu of acetylcholinesterase inhibitory treatments or insecticides which carry with them a risk of poisoning for both humans and animals. Diatomaceous earth absorbs lipids from the cuticle, the waxy outer layer of insects' exoskeletons, causing them to dehydrate. Purchasable from most gardening suppliers or online retailers, it can be evenly distributed around the house (especially in corners and near furniture) with any type of shaker (salt shaker, spice shaker, etc.)

and then vacuumed away after about 7 days. Diatomaceous earth also has the added benefit of killing many other types of insects that might be residing in your house.

Using dehumidifiers with air conditioning and vacuuming all may interrupt the flea life cycle. Humidity is critical to flea survival. Eggs need relative humidity of at least 70-75 percent to hatch, and larvae need at least 50 percent humidity to survive. In humid areas, about 20 percent of the eggs survive to adulthood; in arid areas, less than five percent complete the cycle. Fleas thrive at higher temperatures, but need 70° to 90°F to survive. Lower temperatures slow down or completely interrupt the flea lifecycle. A laboratory study done at the University of California showed that vacuuming catches about 96 percent of adult fleas. A combination of controlled humidity, temperature and vacuuming should eliminate fleas from an environment, and altering even one of these environmental factors may be enough to drastically lower and eliminate an infestation.

TICK

Tick is the common name for the small arachnids in superfamily Ixodoidea that, along with other mites, constitute the Acarina. Ticks are ectoparasites (external parasites), living by hematophagy on the blood of mammals, birds, and occasionally reptiles and amphibians. Ticks are important vectors of a number of diseases, including Lyme disease and Tick-borne meningoencephalitis. According to Pliny the Elder, ticks are "the foulest and nastiest creatures that be."

Young ticks have six legs, and mature ticks have eight legs. They are about the size of a sesame seed, and males are black; females have a brick-red abdomen with a black shield-like plate close to their head.

Habitats and Behaviour

Ticks are blood-feeding parasites that are often found in tall grass and shrubs where they will wait to attach to a passing host. Physical contact is the only method of transportation for ticks. Ticks do not jump or fly, although they may drop from their perch and fall onto a host. Some species actively stalk the host by foot.

Changes in temperature and day length are some of the factors signaling a tick to seek a host. Ticks can detect heat emitted or carbon dioxide respired from a nearby host. They will generally drop off the animal when full, but this may take several days. In some cases, ticks will live for some time on the blood of an animal.

Ticks can be found in most wooded or forested areas throughout the world. They are especially common in areas where there are deer trails or horse paths.

Some of the more common diseases that can be contracted from a tick bite include (listed alphabetically): Babesiosis, Ehrlichiosis, Lyme disease, Rocky Mountain spotted fever, Southern tick-associated rash illness, Tick-borne relapsing fever, and Tularemia.

The blacklegged or deer tick (*Ixodes scapularis*) is dependent on the white-tailed deer for successful reproduction. Larval and nymph stages (immature ticks that cannot reproduce) of the deer tick feed on birds and small mammals. The adult female tick needs a large 3 day blood meal from the deer before she can reproduce and lay her 2000 or more eggs. Deer are the primary host for the adult deer tick and are key to the reproductive success of the tick See the Connecticut Agricultural Experiment Station and Connecticut Department of Public Health joint publication "Tick Management Handbook" for more details of the tick's life cycle and dependence on deer.

Numerous studies have shown that abundance and distribution of deer ticks are correlated with deer densities.

For example, when the deer population was reduced by 74% at a 248-acre (100 ha) study site in Bridgeport, Connecticut, the number of nymphal ticks collected at the site decreased by 92%. Furthermore, the relationship between deer abundance, tick abundance, and human cases of Lyme disease was well documented in the Mumford Cove Community in Groton, Connecticut, from 1996 to 2004. The deer population in Mumford Cove was reduced from about 77 deer per square mile to about 10 deer per square mile (4 deer per 30 square kilometers) after 2 years of controlled hunting. After the initial reduction, the deer population was maintained at low levels. Reducing deer densities to 10 deer per square mile (4 deer per square kilometer) was adequate to reduce by more than 90% the risk of humans contracting Lyme disease in Mumford Cove. Deer population management must serve as the main tool in any long-term strategy to reduce human incidences of Lyme disease.

Damminix

Damminix is a method of reducing deer tick (*Ixodes scapularis/dammini*) populations It consists of biodegradable cardboard tubes stuffed with permethrin-treated cotton and works in the following way: Mice collect the cotton for lining their nests. The pesticide on the cotton kills any immature ticks that are feeding on the mice. It is important to put the tubes where mice will find them, such as in dense, dark brush or at the base of a log; mice are unlikely to gather the cotton from an open lawn. Best results are obtained with regular applications early in the spring and again in late summer. The more neighbors who also use Damminix, the better. Damminix appears to help control tick populations, particularly in the year following initial use. Note that it is not effective on the West Coast of America.

Fipronil

A potential alternative to Damminix's permethrin is fipronil. It is used in the Maxforce Tick Management system, in which fipronil is painted onto rodents visiting the plastic baitboxes This system is no longer generally available for sale by Bayer. In 2005, there were selective reports of grey squirrels "chewing" into some Maxforce TMS boxes in areas of the northeastern United States, compromising the child resistant box. Due to this problem, the Environmental Protection Agency (EPA) asked that all similarly designed TMS boxes applied in 2006 be covered with a protective shroud capable of preventing squirrel damage. The Maxforce TMS system remains registered by the federal EPA for its continued use. A metal shroud has been developed and is reportedly in use to eliminate any potential squirrel damage to the plastic box. This shroud reportedly satisfies the EPA's mandate to protect the boxes from such damage and is recommended by Bayer Environmental Science. Availability outside of Connecticut, New York, New Jersey, and Rhode Island might be limited, however.

Other Control Measures

1. Also, the Centers for Disease Control and Prevention offers advice on reducing ticks around your home.
2. The parasitic Ichneumon wasp *Ixodiphagus hookeri* has long been investigated for its potential to control tick populations. It lays its eggs into ticks; the hatching wasps kill its host.
3. Another "natural" form of control for ticks is the Guineafowl. They consume mass quantities of ticks. Just 2 birds can clear 2 acres (8,100 m2) in a single year.
4. Topical (drops/dust) flea/tick medicines need to be used with care. Phenothrin (85.7%) in combination with Methopren was a popular topical flea/tick therapy for felines. Phenothrin kills adult fleas and ticks. Methoprene is an insect growth regulator that interrupts the insect's life cycle by killing the eggs. However, the EPA has made at least one manufacturer of these products withdraw some products and include strong cautionary statements on others, warning of adverse reactions

Example Species

Engorged deer tick attached to back of toddler's head. Adult thumb shown for scale.

- *Dermacentor variabilis*, the American dog tick, is perhaps the most well-known of the North American hard ticks. This tick does not carry Lyme disease, but can carry Rocky Mountain spotted fever.
- *Ixodes scapularis* (formerly *Ixodes dammini*), known as the black-legged tick or deer tick, is common to the eastern part of North America and is known for spreading Lyme disease.
- *Ixodes pacificus*, the Western black-legged tick, lives in the western part of North America and is responsible for spreading Lyme disease and Rocky Mountain spotted fever. It tends to prefer livestock as its adult host.

Ixodes Hexagonus

- Australia tick fauna consists of approximately 75 species, the majority of which fall into the *Ixodidae*, hard tick, family. The most medically important tick is the Paralysis tick, *Ixodes holocyclus*. It is found in a 20-kilometre band that follows the eastern coastline of Australia. As this is where much of the human population resides in New South Wales, encounters with these parasites are relatively common. Although most cases of tick bite are uneventful, some can result in life threatening illnesses including paralysis, tick typhus and severe allergic reactions.
- The southern cattle tick, Boophilus microplus (Canestrini), causes annual economic losses in the hundreds of millions of dollars to cattle producers throughout the world, and ranks as the most economically important tick from a global perspective. This tick also attacks sheep, horses, goats and a few related species.
- The Lone star tick, Amblyomma americanum, is part of the Ioxdidae family, classifying it as a hard tick. The adult females are distinguished by a white dot or "lone star" on its back. The adult males can also be seen with dots and white streaks on the edge of their bodies. This tick has been associated with transmission of Southern Tick Associated Rash Illness (STARI) in humans, which is a disease caused by a Borrelia sp. related to the agent that causes Lyme Disease.

TRIATOMINAE

The members of Triatominae, a subfamily of Reduviidae, are also known as conenose bugs, kissing bugs, assassin bugs or triatomines. Most of the 130 or more species of this subfamily are haematophagous, i.e. feed on vertebrate blood; a very few species feed on other invertebrates. They are mainly found and widespread in the Americas, with a few species present in Asia, Africa and Australia. These bugs usually share shelter with nesting vertebrates, from which they suck blood. In areas where Chagas disease occurs (from the southern United States to southern Argentina), all triatomine species are potential vectors of the Chagas disease parasite *Trypanosoma cruzi*, but only those species (such as *Triatoma infestans* and *Rhodnius prolixus*) that are well adapted to live with humans are considered *important* vectors.

At the beginning of the 19th century Charles Darwin made one of the first reports of the existence of triatomines in America in his *Journal and Remarks*, commonly known as *The Voyage of the Beagle*. The following is an extract of what he wrote on 25 March 1835:

There has been considerable medical speculation as to whether or not Darwin's contact with triatomines in Argentina was related to his later bouts of long term illness.

Discovery of Triatomines Relation with Chagas Disease

In 1909 the Brazilian doctor Carlos Chagas discovered that these insects were responsible for the transmission of *T. cruzi* to many of his patients in Lassance, a village located on the banks of the São Francisco River in Minas Gerais (Brazil). Poor people living there complained of some insects they called barbeiros that bite during the night. Carlos Chagas put his first observations in words:

Another Brazilian, Herman Lent, former student of Carlos Chagas, became devoted to the research of the triatomines and together with Peter Wygodzinsky made a revision of the Triatominae, a summary of 40 years of studies on the triatomines up to 1989.

Biological Aspects

Life Cycle

Triatomines undergo incomplete metamorphosis. A wingless first instar nymph hatches from an egg. About the sise of the tip of a fork. It passes successively through 2nd, 3rd, 4th and 5th instars. Finally, the fifth instar turns into an adult, acquiring two pair of wings.

Ecology

All triatomine nymph instars and adults are haematophagous and require the stability of a sheltered environment where they aggregate. Most species are associated with wild nesting vertebrates and are named "sylvatic" triatomines. These live in ground burrows with rodents or armadillos, or in tree-dwellings with bats, birds, sloths or opossums. Few species (5%) live in human dwellings or in the surroundings of human houses (peridomicile) in the shelters of domestic animals, these are named "domestic" species. Many sylvatic species are in process of domiciliation ("semidomestic").

Most triatomines aggregate in refuges during day and search for blood during night when the host is asleep and the air is cooler. Odours as well as heat guide these insects to the host. Carbon dioxide emanating from breath, as well as ammonia, short chain amines and carboxylic acids from skin, hair and exocrine glands from vertebrate animals, are among the volatiles that attract triatomines. Vision also serves triatomines for orientation. During night, adults of diverse species fly to houses attracted by light.

Adults produce a pungent odour (isobutyric acid) when disturbed, and are also capable to produce a particular sound by rubbing the rostrum over a stridulatory sulcus under the head (stridulation).

Epidemiology

Domestic and sylvatic species can carry the Chagas parasite to humans and wild mammals; birds are immune to the parasite. *T. cruzi* transmission is carried mainly from human to human by domestic kissing bugs; from the vertebrate to the bug by blood, and from the bug to the vertebrate by the insect's feces and not by its saliva as occurs in most bloodsucking arthropod vectors such as Malaria mosquitoes.

Triatomine infestation especially affects unkempt dwellings. One can recognize the presence of triatomines in a house by its feces, exuviae, eggs and individuals themselves. Triatomines characteristically leave two kinds of feces like strikes on walls of infected houses; one is white with uric acid, the other is dark (black) containing haem. Whitish or pinkish eggs can be seen in wall crevices. After having had a blood meal the insects sometimes show a limited mobility and can be identified easily.

10

Tissue Nematodes

INTRODUCTION

Trichinella spiralis is in fact a complex of three closely related worm species. They are morphologically identical, but differ in their host specificity and their biochemical characteristics. *T. spiralis spiralis* occurs in moderate regions and infects mainly pigs. *T. spiralis nativa* occurs in the polar regions (polar bear, walrus). These parasites are resistant to freezing which is important for meat storage. *T. spiralis nelsoni* occurs in Africa and southern Europe with a reservoir in wild carnivores and wild pigs. *T. britovi* and *T. pseudospiralis* rarely cause infections. *T. pseudospiralis* can also infect some birds as well as mammals, unlike the other *Trichinella* species.

In 1835 a man died of tuberculosis in St Bartholomew's Hospital, London. Dr Paget, a first-year student, carried out the autopsy and observed fine hard white inclusions in the muscles. Similar inclusions had been observed by doctors from time to time in the past, but were attributed to commonplace muscle calcification, which quickly blunted the dissecting scalpel. Dr Paget inspected the lesions with a hand lens and quickly recognised their worm-like structure. The name "*Trichina spiralis*" was suggested. This name *Trichina* had already been given to a certain fly, however, and the name was later changed to "*Trichinella*". The discovery of the parasite was published by the famous biologist and palaeontologist Richard Owen, at that time assistant conservator of the museum of the Royal College of Surgeons. In 1859 Rudolph Virchow carried out transmission experiments in which infected human muscle was fed to a healthy dog. After only 3 to 4 days adult *Trichinella* worms were found in the dog's duodenum and jejunum.

More than 100 species of mammals are susceptible to the infection. Infections with *Trichinella spiralis* affect chiefly carnivores and omnivores, although infection of horses has also been described. People become infected with this nematode by eating raw or insufficiently cooked infected meat, often pork or wild boar. The larvae of *Trichinella spiralis* which are in the meat develop in a few days into adult worms (2-4 mm) in the wall of the small intestine. There they lay larvae (100 m m). These spread via the bloodstream to various muscles, including the heart, where they undergo encapsulation [*Trichinella pseudospiralis* does not form a capsule. The larvae cannot continue to survive in the heart. The larvae are localised within the cells of the muscles, which is unique for a worm. After penetrating the muscle cell, a larva excretes a number of signal molecules and proteins, which convert the cell to what is called a nurse cell. In the cell the behaviour of the worm is rather similar to that of a virus. Many of its proteins are glycosylated and often carry an unusual sugar (tyvelose). These proteins are excreted from a special organ in the larva (the stichosome). Various muscle proteins such as actin and myosin change or disappear, nuclear division is stimulated and mitochondria are damaged. Local angiogenesis is stimulated by excretion of a blood vessel growth factor and new blood vessels, originating from nearby venules, develop and form a network around the infected cell. The metabolism of the nurse cell and the parasite is essentially anaerobic. After 1 to 4 months the adult worms die. The larvae in the muscles sometimes survive for years and can remain viable for a long time even in rotting flesh. *Trichinella* is unique among worms in that all development stages take place in the same host. There is never a free stage outside the mammalian body.

Infection may be asymptomatic. In typical cases there is diarrhoea, abdominal pain, vomiting and fever a few days after eating infected meat. After 10 days the fever increases, the patient is very ill and debilitated, there are muscle pains and a typical peri-orbital oedema (differential diagnosis acute trypanosomiasis and nephrosis). This oedema is caused by invasion of the small muscles around the eye. There may be signs of myocarditis, encephalitis, urticaria and asthma. There is often very significant eosinophilia. The myositis causes an increase in the muscle enzymes (creatine phosphokinase, CK). After a few months the symptoms are reduced or disappear. Mild infections are self-limiting.

The clinical picture is of a patient with acute fever and myalgia, pronounced asthenia, possibly diarrhoea and a swollen face. Cardiopulmonary, neurological or renal complications may be fatal. The consumption of insufficiently cooked or raw meat can often be found in the patient's history, and this is often game that the patient has hunted or which has been shot by a friend (e.g. wild boar). Sometimes the infection can be traced to infected horsemeat. There is leukocytosis with eosinophilia. Muscle biopsy should be performed. The larvae can be seen coiled inside myocytes. There are various serological techniques (e.g. Western blotting) for subtyping *Trichinella* species. Remember that there will be no eggs in the faeces.

TISSUE NEMATODES, *Trichinella Spiralis*, DIFFERENTIAL DIAGNOSIS

Not many nematodes are found in muscle tissue. Occasionally a migrating third stage larva of *Ancylostoma, Toxocara* or *Gnathostoma* may be found (visceral larva migrans). *Dracuncula medinensis* may also be found in muscle tissue. Another, less common nematode which may be found here is *Haycocknema perplexum* (Tasmania).

TISSUE NEMATODES, *Trichinella Spiralis*, THERAPY

In the early stage albendazole or mebendazole at high doses can eradicate adult worms in the intestine. Mebendazole is used in combination with corticoids. Albendazole 800 mg daily for 10 days may be used, in combination with high-dose prednisone for the first three days. With treatment the duration of the disease may be reduced to one or two weeks.

TISSUE NEMATODES, *Trichinella Spiralis*, PREVENTION

- Meat should be well boiled or roasted through.
- Importance of meat inspection. The diaphragm of a slaughtered animal is inspected (the piece of muscle is flattened between two glass slides and examined using transillumination). This technique (trichinoscopy) is not so good for *Trichinella pseudospiralis* because it is not surrounded by a capsule and is easily missed.
- Pig food (which may include infected rats) should be boiled for 30 minutes.
- To store pork for 10 days at -25° C is generally impractical in developing countries. In the West meat is sometimes irradiated with high doses of gamma rays, which will kill any larvae. *Trichinella spiralis nativa* is cold-hardy.

11

Diffrerent Parasites

INTRODUCTION

A parasite is regarded as an organism that derives nourishment by feeding on or within another animal. The most noted parasites in dogs and cats are 'worms' and that is because the majority of all puppies and kittens acquire intestinal worms either prior to or shortly after birth. Worms are only part of the parasite picture, however, as many non-worm parasites exist as well. Common parasites include fleas, flies, ticks, lice, and mites as well as worms and other intestinal parasites.

All parasites of concern can result in damage to an animal's health. Similarly, some can be transferred from the dog or cat to other household animals including humans. No dog or cat that is parasitized is considered healthy.

What are parasites?

You have heard of stowaways on ships. They slyly sneak on board, find a secret place where they can live, steal food, and then eventually jump ship. Parasites are much like stowaways. They get on or in a host, move to where they want to be, gain nourishment, warmth, and other amenities, and then they or their offspring leave the host to find another. In a broad sense, a *parasitic* relationship is defined as one in which one organism (the parasite) lives on or within the other (host), and may cause the host harm. Before we go on, let us take a step back and look at how this relationship differs from others in which different organisms live together.

How do different species relate in nature?

In nature, we are familiar with all types of relationships between different species. Some help each other; others harm or even kill the other.

MUTUALISM

In a relationship called *mutualism,* both organisms benefit. It is a win-win situation. Examples include the tickbird in Africa which rides on the back of elephants and eats the flies or ticks that are there. The tickbird gets a good meal, and the elephant gets rid of those pesky flies and ticks. Lichens are another example. Lichens are really very close relationships between fungi and algae. They need to be together in order to live.

Commensalism: Another type of relationship is called *commensalism*. This is a relationship in which one organism benefits, and the other neither benefits nor is harmed. Think of a hitchhiker. An example in nature would be the relationship between a remora and a shark. The remora attaches itself to the underside of the shark. This does not hurt or benefit the shark, but the remora gets free meals by eating the scraps of food left over from the shark's dinner. When you think about it, another benefit is that when you are attached to the shark, you can hardly become its dinner.

Predator-prey: Now we get to the win-lose relationships. In a *predator-prey* relationship, one organism quickly (or in the case of a cat with a mouse, not so quickly) kills the other. This is a win-lose relationship. Examples would include a cat and mouse, the fisherman and the trout, or a spider and its captured flies.

Parasite: The definition of *parasite* depends on whom you talk to. As we stated above, the broad definition of a parasite is any organism that is dependent on another (the host) for room and board, and does not necessarily cause the host any harm. Some scientists and veterinarians prefer to use the term *parasite* to mean a close relationship in which one organism harms the other while obtaining what it needs to live - basically a win-lose situation that takes more time to develop. In the following discussion, that is the definition we will be using.

Although a parasite may harm a host, it does not usually kill the host or it would eventually run out of a place to live. Parasites generally gain food from the host, but they also need a way to reproduce and get from one host to another. So the next topics we need to talk about are life cycles and transmission of parasites.

LIFE CYCLES AND TRANSMISSION OF PARASITES

Basically, a life cycle describes how an organism develops from the immature stage to the adult. Some animals produce live young and others produce eggs. The same is true of parasites. In addition, there are some one-celled parasites that reproduce by dividing into two identical parts.

Direct Life Cycle: There are two general types of life cycles. In a *direct life cycle*, the immature form of the parasite can infect the same host it came from. For instance, the adult parasite lives in the host's intestine, lays eggs which are passed in the stool, and the eggs can infect the same or similar host. Roundworms have a direct life cycle.

Indirect Life Cycle: In an *indirect life cycle*, the immature form must pass through a different type of host before it can re-enter and infect the host it came from. An example would be heartworms. The adult worm lives in the dog or cat. The immature form, laid by the adult heartworm, is taken up by the mosquito. The immature form develops within the mosquito, and is then reintroduced into another dog or cat where it develops into the mature adult and the cycle repeats itself. The host in which the immature form of the parasite lives is called the *intermediate host*, in this case, the mosquito. The host in which the adult form lives is called the *definitive host*.

Transport Hosts: Some life cycles incorporate what is called a *transport host*. It is a special kind of intermediate host in which no development of the immature parasite occurs. The transport host is really a way for the immature parasite to get from one mammalian host to another. The parasite does not develop within the transport host, but is just transferred from one host to another. Rodents can be transport hosts for the roundworms of dogs and cats.

Many parasites have life cycles that include a phase of migrating through the body, often from the digestive system to the lungs or other organs such as roundworms. Others, including hookworms and heartworms migrate from their entrance through the skin to other organs.

Aberrant Parasites: Most parasites are host-specific, which means they only infect and live in certain animals. If they enter the wrong animal, or host, they may not survive or they may migrate abnormally. When a parasite enters the wrong host it is said to be *aberrant*. Often, aberrant parasites will cause an over-reaction in the body of this wrong host and serious disease can result.

Zoonoses: Infections that can be passed from animals to humans are called zoonotic diseases, or *zoonoses*. There are many parasites that fit this category. For some parasitic zoonoses, humans will have the same symptoms as a dog or cat. In others, because the parasite is aberrant, the symptoms may be very different because the parasite affects different organs or the human body reacts differently. Roundworms, hookworms, and *Toxoplasma* are all zoonoses.

Prepatent Period: There is one more term related to life cycles that we would like you to be familiar with. That is the *prepatent period*. This is the time interval between when the parasite enters the host and the subsequent form of the parasite can be recovered from the host. For example, the prepatent period for heartworms is 6 months. It takes 6 months from the time the immature forms enter the body through a mosquito bite, and the presence of heartworms in the heart. For many parasites, the prepatent period is close to the time between the point when the animal became infected and when we can diagnose the infection. The prepatent period for whipworms is three months, i.e., it takes three months from the ingestion of the eggs until the adult worms are in the intestine (and soon laying their own eggs).

You may have heard of a time interval called the *incubation period*. This represents the time from when the parasite enters the host and the development of signs or symptoms of disease. The incubation period is usually longer than the prepatent period. For instance, the prepatent period for heartworms is 6 months, but infected animals may not become ill for a year or more after that fateful mosquito bite.

Parasites can get on a host and remain 'on deck.' These are called *ectoparasites* (ecto=outside). Examples of ectoparasites are fleas and ticks. Other parasites move to the inner cabins of the host and are called *endoparasites* (endo=in). Roundworms, heartworms, and tapeworms are examples of endoparasites.

Obligatory Parasites: By definition, a parasite must live on a host sometime during its life or it would not be a parasite. Parasites differ, however, in how much of their lives they spend on their hosts. *Obligatory* parasites live on a host all the time. They cannot live and reproduce free in the environment. Heartworms are obligatory parasites – they either have to be in a mammal or a mosquito to live. Most parasites of dogs and cats are obligatory parasites. The reproductive forms, e.g., eggs of obligatory parasites can sometimes live for long periods of time outside of a host, as in the case of roundworms. But these reproductive forms are dormant, and can do nothing until they get into a new host.

Periodic Parasites: Other parasites are called *periodic* parasites. They live part of their lives on a host, and part of it off. These guys keep jumping on and off ships throughout their lives. Ticks are a good example of periodic parasites. They get on an animal to eat, but then they detach themselves when they are done eating – they 'eat and run (detach, really).'

Facultative Parasites: There are other parasites that can actually eat, sleep, and lay eggs while off of the host. These are *facultative* parasites. When they are not on a host we call them 'free-living.' When a host comes around, they will take advantage of a change of scenery and live on the host a while. *Pelodera strongyloides* is an example of a facultative parasite. It normally lives in the soil, being especially fond of moist, decaying organic matter such as bedding. When a dog lies down on the bedding, *P. strongyloides* invades the upper layers of skin and can cause a severe inflammation.

CLASSIFYING PARASITES

Now that we have possibly overwhelmed you with all of the different ways parasites can be classified, we will add one more. This classification really takes all the characteristics we described above, as well as anatomic features and uses them to organize the parasites by their similarities. This classification system is also used for plants and larger animals. You probably remember it from biology class. It is called the Linnaean classification scheme.

'Kingdom' is the most general category, and the categories get more specific until we reach 'Species' (there is actually a more specific classification after that called 'Variety'). The classifications of some more well known organisms.

We can see that of those organisms listed, the dog hookworms and the roundworms are most closely related to each other. They have the same kingdom, phylum, and class. *Giardia canis* is the most different from the rest – it is not even in the same kingdom as the others.

It is customary to place the *genus* and *species* in italics or quote marks (" "). Once the genus has been specified in a text, it is often only indicated by its first letter in later text. For instance, *Toxocara canis* is referred to as *T. canis*.

MAJOR CLASSES OF PARASITES

Helminths: The term 'helminths' is a kind of generic word for 'worm.' It comes from the Greek 'helmins' which means 'worm.' The term is used to group certain parasites together and includes the Nematodes, which are long, cylindrical worms, tapeworms, and flukes. You have maybe heard of medications to treat infestations with worms called 'antihelmintics.' This group of drugs is literally 'against helminths.' Let us take a look at the various helminths.

Nematodes: In general, Nematodes are round in cross-section, are longer than they are wide, and are unsegmented. They come in many sizes, from microscopic to a yard in length. Nematodes are a significant cause of disease in dogs and cats. For every organ system in the body, there is probably a nematode that lives there, or at least passes through. Though they are in the same class, Nematodes have extremely varied life cycles. Some require intermediate hosts and some are facultative parasites. Some lay eggs and others bear live larvae.

The class 'Nematodes' is sometimes referred to as 'Roundworms.' This can be a bit confusing since we often use the term 'roundworm' when we are talking about the spaghetti-like intestinal worms of dogs and cats. The dog and cat roundworms are 'Roundworms' but not all 'Roundworms' are dog and cat roundworms. As a matter of fact, there are hundreds of 'Roundworms' or Nematodes.

Tapeworms: Tapeworms are flat worms that are segmented. They consist of a head, neck, and then a number of segments. The head usually has suckers or muscular grooves that enable it to attach itself to the animal's intestine.

Each tapeworm segment has its own reproductive organs. New segments are continually formed in the neck region while those at the end of the tapeworm are cast off as they mature. These mature segments are really egg packets. The segments may often be seen near the anus of the dog or cat. These segments may move if recently passed, or if dried, they look like grains of uncooked rice or cucumber seeds. Tapeworm infections are usually diagnosed by finding these segments on the animal.

Tapeworms of dogs and cats all have life cycles that include an intermediate host. These hosts include fleas, fish, and domestic animals such as sheep and pigs. All of these tapeworms live in the dog's or cat's digestive system. It is interesting that tapeworms have no digestive systems themselves, but absorb nutrients through their skin.

Flukes: Flukes are flat, leaf-shaped, unsegmented worms that look similar to leeches. Flukes have suckers, hooks, or clamp-like appendages with which they attach themselves to the host's organs. Flukes that infest dogs and cats vary in size from ½ millimeters (less than 2/100 of an inch) to almost ½ inch. Fluke eggs have a unique characteristic - the shell around the egg has a trap door called an operculum.

The flukes that infect dogs and cats have indirect life cycles. The intermediate hosts differ quite a bit, from lizards, to fish, to snails. In general, flukes do not cause serious disease in dogs and cats unless they are present in very high numbers.

Arthropods: The term *arthropod* means joint-foot and refers to the fact that all members of this phylum have jointed legs. The two classes that include parasites of dogs and cats are Insects and Arachnids. Other classes include the Crustaceans with members such as crayfish and lobsters, and the class Myriapoda to which millipedes and centipedes belong. The phylum of Arthropods also includes a group of organisms that nobody seems to be able to categorize. These are the pentasomes, one of which is a parasite of dogs and cats. Let us take a closer look at the parasitic arthropods.

Insects: Insects make up 70% of all known species of animals of all kinds, so it comes as no surprise that some of them are parasites. When we think of insects, we tend to think of flies and mosquitoes – pests. But insects can be more than just pests; they can be the cause of severe disease since the class of Insects also includes lice and fleas.

Insects can be a threat to the health of animals through a number of different mechanisms. Take fleas for example. They are parasites. They can serve as intermediate hosts for other parasites (the fish tapeworm). They can also serve as vectors (carriers) of diseases like bubonic plague. Still other insects have poisonous bites such as bees and wasps.

Insects have antennae, compound eyes, and a body composed of head, thorax, and abdomen. Many insects have wings, though in some insects these wings are so small they are more like stabilizers. Fleas are actually wingless insects, though they do have a mustache.

Arachnids: When we think of arachnids we often first think of spiders. But spiders have some pretty nasty cousins including ticks and mites. As a Class, Arachnids are carnivorous animals.

Some, such as various species of lice feed on the tissue fluids of other animals through a sucking apparatus. Some mites eat portions of other animals through the use of their front legs that may have suckers or hooks. And as we remember from biology class, arachnids have eight legs as adults, not six like the insects.

Protozoa: Now we come to the last large group of parasites. These are the one-celled organisms called Protozoa. They are microscopic and were first discovered by the man who actually invented the microscope, Anton van Leeuwenhoek. There are over 45,000 species of Protozoa. They cover the globe and are responsible for millions of cases of disease in both humans and animals.

Protozoa have two main parts – the nucleus and the cytoplasm. They are surrounded by a non-rigid membrane and have various means of locomotion. Some Protozoa, such as *Giardia canis* and *Giardia cati,* move about with the assistance of flagella. Flagella are long, hair-like structures that can whip back and forth rapidly, propelling the organism. Other Protozoa move about through the use of cilia. Cilia are much shorter, hair-like structures that often cover the organism. *Balantidium coli* has numerous cilia with which it moves. Some Protozoa, like *Toxoplasma gondii,* move about through gliding motions without the aid of appendages.

ARACHNID

Arachnids are a class (Arachnida) of joint-legged invertebrate animals in the subphylum Chelicerata. The term arachnid is from the Greek word or *arachne,* meaning spider, and also referring to the mythological figure Arachne.

Arachnids are chiefly terrestrial arthropods, but are also found in freshwater and, with the exception of the pelagic zone, in all marine environments. They comprise over 100,000 named species, including spiders, scorpions, harvestmen, ticks, and mites.

It is commonly understood that arachnids have four pairs of legs, and that arachnids may be easily distinguished from insects by this fact (insects have six legs or three pairs). Arachnids generally have a total of 6 pairs of appendages — two pairs of which have become adapted for feeding, defense, and sensory perception. The first pair of appendages, the chelicerae, serve in feeding and defense. The next pair of appendages, the pedipalps have been adapted for feeding, locomotion, and/or reproductive functions. In Solifugae, the palpi are quite leg-like and make Solifugae appear to have ten legs. The larvae of mites (and Ricinulei) have only six legs; the fourth pair appears when they moult into nymphs. However, there are also adult mites with six, or even four legs.

Arachnids are further distinguished by the fact they have no antennae and no wings. Their body is organised into two tagma called the prosoma, or cephalothorax, and the opisthosoma, or abdomen. The cephalothorax (prosoma) is derived from the fusion of the cephalon (head) and the thorax. The abdomen (opisthosoma) can be further divided into the preabdomen and postabdomen in many taxa, although in some orders such as the Acari the abdominal sections are fused.

There are some important modifications that are particularly important for the terrestrial lifestyle of an arachnid, such as internal respiratory surfaces in the form of trachea, or modification of the book gill into a book lung, an internal series of vascular lamellae used for gas exchange with the air. Further adaptations are appendages modified for more efficient locomotion on land, internal fertilisation, special sensory organs, and water conservation enhanced by more efficient excretory structures (coxal glands and Malpighian tubules) as well as a waxy layer covering the cuticle.

Arachnids are mostly carnivorous, feeding on the pre-digested bodies of insects and other small animals. Only in the harvestmen and among mites, such as the house dust mite, is there ingestion of solid food particles and thus exposure to internal parasites althougth it is not unusual for spiders to eat their own silk. Several groups are largely venomous — they secrete venom from specialized glands to kill prey or enemies. Several mites are parasites, some of which are carriers of disease. Arachnids usually lay eggs, which hatch into immatures that resemble adults, but scorpions bear live young.

It is true that all arthropods have exoskeletons, and they also have an internal structure of cartilage like tissue called the endosternite, where certain muscle groups are attached. Calcification in the endosternite has been found in some Opiliones.

Arachnids have two kinds of eyes, the lateral and median ocelli. The lateral ocelli evolved from compound eyes and may have a tapetum, which enhances the efficiency of photon capture. The median ocelli develop from a transverse fold of the ectoderm. The ancestors of modern arachnids probably had both types, but modern ones often lack one type or the other.

ACARINA

Acarina or Acari are a taxon of arachnids that contains mites and ticks. Its fossil history goes back to the Devonian era, although there is also a questionable Ordovician record. The Devonian era was the time frame in which certain species of animals developed legs. In most modern treatments, the Acari is considered a subclass of Arachnida and is composed of 2–3 orders or superorders: Acariformes, Parasitiformes, and Opilioacariformes. Most acarines are minute to small (e.g. 0.080–1.00 mm), but the giants of the Acari (some ticks and red velvet mites) may reach lengths of 10–20 mm. It is estimated that over 50,000 species have been described (as of 1999) and that a million or more species are currently living. The study of mites and ticks is called acarology.

Only the faintest traces of primary segmentation remain in mites, the prosoma and opisthosoma being insensibly fused, and a region of flexible cuticle (the cirumcapitular furrow) separates the chelicerae and pedipalps from the rest of the body. This anterior body region is called the capitulum or gnathosoma and is also found in the Ricinulei. The remainder of the body is called the idiosoma and is unique to mites. Most adult mites have four pairs of legs, like other arachnids, but some have fewer. For example, gall mites like *Phyllocoptes variabilis* (superfamily Eriophyioidea) have a wormlike body with only two pairs of legs; some parasitic mites have only one or three pairs of legs in the adult stage. Larval and prelarval stages have a maximum of three pairs of legs; adult mites with only three pairs of legs may be called 'larviform'.

Acarine ontogeny consists of an egg, a prelarval stage (often absent), a larval stage (hexapod except in Eriophyoidea, which have only 2 pairs of legs), and a series of nymphal stages. Larvae (and prelarvae) have a maximum of 3 pairs of legs (legs are often reduced to stubs or absent in prelarvae); legs IV are added at the first nymphal stage.

Acarines live in practically every habitat, and include aquatic (freshwater and sea water) and terrestrial species. They outnumber other arthropods in the soil organic matter and detritus. Many are parasitic, and they affect both vertebrates and invertebrates. Most parasitic forms are external parasites, while the free living forms are generally predaceous and may even be used to control undesirable arthropods. Others are detritivores that help to break down forest litter and dead organic matter such as skin cells. Others still are plant feeders and may damage crops. Damage to crops is perhaps the most costly economic effect of mites, especially by the spider mites and their relatives (Tetranychoidea), earth mites (Penthaleidae), thread-footed mites (Tarsonemidae) and the gall and rust mites (Eriophyoidea). Some parasitic forms affect humans and other mammals, causing damage by their feeding, and can even be vectors of diseases such as scrub typhus and rickettsial pox. A well-known effect of mites on humans is their role as an allergen and the stimulation of asthma in people affected by the respiratory disease. The use of predatory mites (e.g. Phytoseiidae) in pest control and herbivorous mites that attack weeds are also of importance. An unquantified, but major positive contribution of the Acari is their normal functioning in ecosystems, especially their roles in the decomposer subsystem.

Amblypygi

Amblypygids are also known as tailless whip scorpions or cave spiders. Approximately 5 families, 17 genera and 136 species have been described. They are found in tropical and subtropical regions worldwide. Some species are subterranean; many are nocturnal. During the day, they may hide under logs, bark, stones, or leaves. They prefer a humid environment. Amblypygids may range from 5 to 40 mm. Their bodies are broad and highly flattened and the first pair of legs (the first walking legs in most arachnid orders) are modified to act as sensory organs. (Compare solifugids, uropygids, and schizomids.) These very thin modified legs can extend several times the length of body. They have no silk glands or venomous fangs, but can have prominent pincer-like pedipalps. Amblypygids often move about sideways on their six walking legs, with one "whip" pointed in the direction of travel while the other probes on either side of them. Prey are located with these "whips", captured with pedipalps, then torn to pieces with chelicerae. Fossilised amblypygids have been found dating back to the Carboniferous period.

Amblypygids, particularly the species *Phrynus marginemaculatus* and *Damon diadema*, are thought to be one of the few species of arachnids that show signs of social behavior. Research conducted at Cornell University by entomologists suggests that mother amblypygids comfort their young by gently caressing the offspring with her feelers. Further, when two or more siblings were placed in an unfamiliar environment, such as a cage, they would seek each other out and gather back in a group.

Araneae

Spiders are the most familiar of the arachnids, and the most numerous, if only described species are counted. All spiders produce silk, a thin, strong protein strand extruded by the spider from spinnerets most commonly found on the end of the abdomen. Many species use it to trap insects in webs, although there are many species that hunt freely. Silk can be used to aid in climbing, form smooth walls for burrows, build egg sacs, wrap prey, temporarily hold sperm, and even fly, among other applications.

All spiders except those in the families Uloboridae and Holarchaeidae, and in the suborder Mesothelae (together about 350 species) can inject venom to protect themselves or to kill and liquefy prey. Only about 200 species, however, have bites that can pose health problems to humans. Many larger species' bites may be painful, but will not produce lasting health concerns.

Spiders are found all over the world, from the tropics to the Arctic, with some extreme species even living underwater in silken domes they supply with air, and on the tops of the highest mountains.

Haptopoda is an extinct order known exclusively from a few specimens from the Upper Carboniferous of the United Kingdom. It is monotypic, i.e. has only one species: *Plesiosiro madeleyi* Pocock 1911. Relationships with other arachnids are obscure, but closest relatives may be the Amblypygi, Thelyphonida and Schizomida of the tetrapulmonate clade.

Opiliones (better known as "harvestmen" or "daddy longlegs") are arachnids that are harmless to people and are known for their exceptionally long walking legs, compared to their body size. As of 2005, over 6,300 species of Phalangids have been discovered worldwide. The order Opiliones can be divided in four suborders: Cyphophthalmi, Eupnoi, Dyspnoi and Laniatores. Well-preserved fossils have been found in the 400-million year old Rhynie cherts of Scotland, which look surpringly modern, indicating that the basic structure of the harvestmen hasn't changed much since then. Their closest relatives are probably the mites (Acari).

The difference between harvestmen and spiders is that in harvestmen the two main body sections (the abdomen with ten segments and cephalothorax, or *prosoma* and *opisthosoma*) are nearly joined, so that they appear to be one oval structure. In more advanced species, the first five abdominal segments are often fused into a dorsal shield called the *scutum*, which is normally fused with the *carapace*. Sometimes this shield is only present in males. The two most posterior abdominal segments can be reduced or separated in the middle on the surface to form two plates lying next to each other. The second pair of legs are longer than the others and works as antennae. They have a single pair of eyes in the middle of their heads, orientated sideways. They have a pair of prosomatic scent glands that secrete a peculiar smelling fluid when disturbed. Harvestmen do not have silk glands and do not possess poison glands, posing absolutely no danger to humans. They breathe through tracheae. Between the base of the fourth pair of legs and the abdomen a pair of spiracles are located, one opening on each side. In more active species, spiracles are also found upon the tibia of the legs. They have a gonopore on the ventral cephalothorax, and the copulation is direct as the male has a penis (while the female has an ovipositor).

Typical body length does not exceed 7 mm (about ¼ in) even in the largest species. However, leg span is much larger and can exceed 160 mm (over 6 in). Most species live for a year. Many species are omnivorous, eating primarily small insects and all kinds of plant material and fungi; some are scavengers of the decays of any dead animal, bird dung and other fecal material. They are mostly nocturnal and coloured in hues of brown, although there are a number of diurnal species that have vivid patterns in yellow, green and black with varied reddish and blackish mottling and reticulation.

PALPIGRADI

Palpigradi, commonly known as "microwhip scorpions", are tiny cousins of the uropygid, or whip scorpion, no more than 3 mm in length. They have a thin, pale, segmented carapace that terminates in a whip-like flagellum, made up of 15 segments. The carapace is divided into two plates between the third and fourth leg set. They have no eyes. Some species have three pairs of book lungs, while others have no lungs at all. Approximately 80 species of Palpigradi have been described worldwide, all in the family Eukoeneniidae, which contains four genera.

They are believed to be predators like their larger relatives, feeding on minuscule insects in their habitat. Their mating habits are unknown, except that they lay only a few relatively large eggs at a time. Microwhip scorpions need a damp environment to survive, and they always hide from light, so they are commonly found in the moist earth under buried stones and rocks. They can be found on every continent, except in Arctic and Antarctic regions.

PHALANGIOTARBIDA

Phalangiotarbi (Haase, 1890) is an extinct arachnid order known exclusively from the Palaeozoic (Devonian to Permian) of Europe and North America.

The affinities of phalangiotarbids are obscure, with most authors favouring affinities with Opiliones (harvestmen) and/ or Acari (mites and ticks). Phalangiotarbida has been recently proposed to be sister group to (Palpigradi+Tetrapulmonata): the taxon Megoperculata sensu Shultz (1990). (Pollitt et al., 2004).

PSEUDOSCORPIONS

Pseudoscorpions are small arthropods with a flat, pear-shaped body and pincers that resemble those of scorpions. They range from 2 to 8 mm (1/12 to 1/3 inch) in length. The opisthosoma is made up of twelve segments, each guarded by plate-like tergites above and sternites below. The abdomen is short and rounded at the rear, rather than extending into a segmented tail and stinger like true scorpions. The colour of the body can be yellowish-tan to dark-brown, with the paired claws often a contrasting colour. They may have two, four or no eyes. They have two very long *palpal chelae* (pedipalps or pincers) that strongly resemble the pincers found on a scorpion. The pedipalps generally consist of an immobile "hand" and "finger", with a separate movable finger controlled by an adductor muscle. A venom gland and duct are usually located in the mobile finger; the poison is used to capture and immobilise the pseudoscorpion's prey. During digestion, pseudoscorpions pour a mildly corrosive fluid over the prey, then ingest the liquefied remains. Pseudoscorpions spin silk from a gland in their jaws to make disk-shaped cocoons for mating, molting, or waiting out cold weather. Another trait they share with their closest relatives, the spiders, is breathing through spiracles. Most spiders have one pair of spiracles, and one of book lungs, but pseudoscorpions do not have book lungs.

There are more than 2,000 species of pseudoscorpions recorded. They range worldwide, even in temperate to cold regions, but have their most dense and diverse populations in the tropics and subtropics. The fossil record of pseudoscorpions dates back over 380 million years, to the Devonian period, near the time when the first land-animal fossils appear.

During the elaborate mating dance, the male of some pseudoscorpion species pulls a female over a spermatophore previously laid upon a surface. In other species, the male also pushes the sperm into the female genitals using the forelegs .The female carries the fertilised eggs in a brood pouch attached to her abdomen, and the young ride on the mother for a short time after they hatch. Up to two dozen young are hatched in a single brood; there may be more than one brood per year. The young go through three molts over the course of several years before reaching adulthood. Adult pseudoscorpions live 2 to 3 years. They are active in the warm months of the year, overwintering in silken coccoons when the weather grows cold.

Pseudoscorpions are generally beneficial to humans since they prey on clothes moth larvae, carpet beetle larvae, booklice, ants, mites, and small flies. They are small and inoffensive, and are rarely seen due to their size. They usually enter the home by "riding along" with larger insects (known as phoresy), or are brought in with firewood. They are often observed in bathrooms or laundry rooms, since they seek humidity. They may sometimes be found feeding on mites under the wing covers of certain beetles.

RICINULEI

Riniculei (*hooded tickspiders*) are 5–10 mm long. Their most notable feature is a "hood" that can be raised and lowered over the head; when lowered, it covers the mouth and the chelicerae. Ricinulei have no eyes. The pedipalps end in pincers that are small relative to their bodies, when compared to those of the related orders of scorpions and pseudoscorpions. The heavy-bodied abdomen forms a narrow pedicel, or waist, where it attaches to the prosoma. In males, the third pair of legs are modified to form copulatory organs. Malpighian tubules and a pair of coxal glands make up the excretory system. They have no lungs, as gas exchange takes place through the trachea.

Ricinulei are predators, feeding on other small arthropods. Little is known about their mating habits; the males have been observed using their modified third leg to transfer a spermatophore to the female. The eggs are carried under the mother's hood, until the young hatch into six-legged "larva", which later molt into their adult forms. Ricinulei require moisture to survive. Approximately 57 species of ricinuleids have been described worldwide, all in a single family that contains three genera.

SCHIZOMIDA

Schizomida is an order of arachnids that tend to live in the top layer of soils. Schizomids present the prosoma covered by a large protopeltidium and smaller, paired, mesopeltidia and metapeltidia. There are no eyes. The opisthosoma is a smooth oval of 12 recognisable somites. The first is reduced and forms the pedicel. The last three are much constricted, forming the pygidium. The last somite bears the flagellum, which in this order is short and consists of not more than four segments.

The name means "split or cleaved middle", referring to the way the cephalothorax is divided into two separate plates. Like the related orders Uropygi, Amblypygi, and Solpugida, the schizomids use only six legs for walking, having modified their first two legs to serve as sensory organs. They also have large well-developed pedipalps (pincers) just behind the sensory legs.

SCORPIONS

Scorpions are characterised by a metasoma (tail) comprising six segments, the last containing the scorpion's anus and bearing the telson (the sting). The telson, in turn, consists of the vesicle, which holds a pair of venom glands and the hypodermic aculeus, the venom-injecting barb. The abdomen's front half, the mesosoma, is made up of six segments. The first segment contains the sexual organs as well as a pair of vestigial and modified appendages forming a structure called the genital operculum. The second segment bears a pair of featherlike sensory organs known as the *pectines*; the final four segments each contain a pair of book lungs. The mesosoma is armored with chitinous plates, known as tergites on the upper surface and sternites on the lower surface.

The cuticle of scorpions is covered with hairs in some places that act like balance organs. An outer layer that makes them fluorescent green under ultraviolet light is called the hyaline layer. Newly molted scorpions do not glow until after their cuticle has hardened. The fluoresent hyaline layer can be intact in fossil rocks that are hundreds of millions of years old.

Scorpions are opportunistic predators of small arthropods and insects. They use their chela (pincers) to catch the prey initially. Depending on the toxicity of their venom and size of their claws, they will then either crush the prey or inject it with neurotoxic venom. The neurotoxins consist of a variety of small proteins as well as sodium and potassium cations, which serve to interfere with neurotransmission in the victim. Scorpions use their venom to kill or paralyze their prey so that it can be eaten; in general it is fast acting, allowing for effective prey capture. Scorpion venoms are optimised for action upon other arthropods and therefore most scorpions are relatively harmless to humans; stings produce only local effects (such as pain, numbness or swelling). A few scorpion species, however, mostly in the family Buthidae, can be dangerous to humans. The scorpion that is responsible for the most human deaths is the *Androctonus australis*, or fat-tailed scorpion of North Africa. The toxicity of *A. australis*'s venom is roughly half that of *L. quinquestriatus*, but since *A. australis* injects quite a bit more venom into its prey, it is the most deadly to humans. Human deaths normally occur in the young, elderly, or infirm; scorpions are generally unable to deliver enough venom to kill healthy adults. Some people, however may be allergic to the venom of some species, in which case the scorpion's sting can more likely kill. A primary symptom of a scorpion sting is numbing at the injection site, sometimes lasting for several days. It has been found that scorpions have two types of venom: a translucent, weaker venom designed to stun only, and an opaque, more potent venom designed to kill heavier threats.

Unlike the majority of Arachnida species, scorpions are viviparous. The young are born one by one, and the brood is carried about on its mother's back until the young have undergone at least one moult. The young generally resemble their parents, requiring between five and seven moults to reach maturity. Scorpions have quite variable lifespans and the lifespan of most species is not known. The age range appears to be approximately 4-25 years (25 years being the maximum reported life span in the species *H. arizonensis*). They are nocturnal and fossorial, finding shelter during the day in the relative cool of underground holes or undersides of rocks and coming out at night to hunt and feed. Scorpions prefer to live in areas where the temperatures range from 20°C to 37 °C (68°F to 99 °F), but may survive in the temperature range of 14 °C to 45 °C (57 °F to 113 °F.

Scorpions have been found in many fossil records, including coal deposits from the Carboniferous Period and in marine Silurian deposits. They are thought to have existed in some form since about 425–450 million years ago. They are believed to have an oceanic origin, with gills and a claw like appendage that enabled them to hold onto rocky shores or seaweed.

SOLIFUGAE

Solifugae is a group of 900 species of arachnids, commonly known as *camel spiders, wind scorpions,* and *sun spiders*. The name derives from Latin, and means *those that flee from the sun*. Most Solifugae live in tropical or semitropical regions where they inhabit warm and arid habitats, but some species have been known to live in grassland or forest habitats. The most distinctive feature of S Eremobatidae possess a flagellum on the basal article of the chelicera. Solifugae also have long pedipalps, which function as sense organs similar to insects' antennae and give the appearance of the two extra legs. Pedipalps terminate in eversible adhesive organs.

Solifugae are carnivorous or omnivorous, with most species feeding on termites, darkling beetles, and other small arthropods; however, solifugae have been videotaped consuming larger prey such as lizards. Prey is located with the pedipalps and killed and cut into pieces by the chelicerae. The prey is then liquefied and the liquid ingested through the pharynx. Reproduction can involve direct or indirect sperm transfer; when indirect, the male emits a spermatophore on the ground and then inserts it with his chelicerae in the female's genital pore.

TRIGONOTARBIDA

The Order Trigonotarbida is an extinct group of arachnids whose fossil record extends from the Silurian to the Lower Permian and are known from several localities in Europe, North America and Argentina. They superficially resemble spiders, to which they were clearly related.

These early arachnids seem to have been adapted to stalking prey on the ground. They have been found within the very structure of ground-dwellings plants, possibly where they hid to await their prey. Trigonotarbids are currently among the oldest known land arthropods. They lack silk glands on the opisthosoma and cheliceral poison glands, and most likely represented independent offshoots of the Arachnida.

UROPYGI

The Uropygi, commonly known as *whip scorpions*, range from 25 to 85 mm in length; the largest species, of the genus *Mastigoproctus*, reaches 85 mm. Like the related orders Schizomida, Amblypygi, and Solifugae, the uropygids use only six legs for walking, having modified their first two legs to serve as antennae-like sensory organs. Many species also have very large scorpion-like pedipalps (pincers). They have one pair of eyes at the front of the cephalothorax and three on each side of the head. Whip scorpions have no poison glands, but they do have glands near the rear of their abdomen that can spray a combination of acetic acid and octanoic acid when they are bothered. Other species spray formic acid or chlorine. As of 2006, over 100 species of uropygids have been described worldwide.

Whip scorpions are carnivorous, nocturnal hunters feeding mostly on insects but sometimes on worms and slugs. The prey is crushed between special teeth on the inside of the trochanters (the second segment of the leg) of the front legs. They are valuable in controlling the population of roaches and crickets.

Males secrete a sperm sac, which is transferred to the female. Up to 35 eggs are laid in a burrow, within a mucous membrane that preserves moisture. Mothers stay with the eggs and do not eat. The white young that hatch from the eggs climb onto their mother's back and attach themselves there with special suckers. After the first molt they look like miniature whip scorpions, and leave the burrow; the mother dies soon after. The young grow slowly, going through three molts in about three years before reaching adulthood.

Uropygids are found in tropical and subtropical areas worldwide, usually in underground burrows that they dig with their pedipalps. They may also burrow under logs, rotting wood, rocks, and other natural debris. They enjoy humid, dark places and avoid the light.

12

Parasitosis in Children

INTRODUCTION

Protein-energy malnutrition and intestinal parasitic infections are common problems in those populations characterized by low socioeconomic status and low level of public health sanitation. *Ascaris lumbricoides* infection is often associated with malnutrition, but it is difficult to clarify whether the relationship is causative or casual, since both are ubiquitous in such conditions of poverty and poor sanitation.

Several data suggest that parasite infections can affect the nutritional status of infected people, by modifying the key stages of food intake, digestion and absorption. Parasites can adversely affect the host food intake by decreasing, increasing or changing the preference for food, as in patients with pica. They can affect sensory, neural and hormonal factors that are considered to modulate food intake, and can cause anorexia1, or vomiting. It was found that trophozoites of *Giardia lamblia* may damage the brush borders of enterocytes and impair the activity of mucosal enzymes, particularly the disaccharidases, causing carbohydrate and fat malabsorption. Abnormalities were observed in the intestinal tract mucosa in *Ascaris lumbricoides*-infected children through jejunal biopsy, which disappeared rather rapidly after deworming treatment, accompanying by the improvement of the nitrogen retention, d-xylose absorption and steatorrhea. However, it is still controversial whether such alterations influence the nutritional status of children when tested in field studies. While some studies have shown a beneficial impact of antiparasitic treatment on the nutritional status and growth of children, others have not achieved the same results. It was observed that periodically deworming *Ascaris lumbricoides*-infected children may improve their nutritional status, and that a single course of antiparasitic treatment increased arm skinfold and improved growth. A significant negative correlation between the burden of *Ascaris* and nutritional status, but exclusively in the population submitted to low nutritional intake and living in conditions of poor health care facilities. Moreover, periodic treatment of *Giardia lamblia* improved the weight gain of treated children. No impact on anthropometric indices after ascariasis treatment, Geengberg et al showed that a single dose of piperazine was an unsuccessful method to promoting growth, not found any effect on nutritional status after deworming *Ascaris lumbricoides*-infected children for one year, and Kightlinger et al observed that children with the heaviest worm burdens had growth scores very similar to the lightly and non-infected ones. Thus, it is not yet clear whether parasites can influence the nutritional status of children. A major difficulty in interpreting these results is the fact that several parasites and nutritional deficiencies can coexist and influence each other. For instance, hypovitaminosis A, a problem of public health among young children living in areas of poverty that can led to blindness and death, can be caused by impairment of vitamin A absorption due to *Ascaris lumbricoides* or *Giardia lamblia* infections, while iron-deficiency anemia has been associated to infection by *Ancylostomidae, Trichuris trichiura* and *Schistosoma mansoni*.

In conditions of poverty and low level of sanitation when multiple deficiencies coexist, the consequences of interactions between multiple nutritional deficiencies and multiple intestinal parasites are not clear, and these associations have not yet been assessed in the same population. This work aimed to evaluate the relationship between protein-energy malnutrition, hypovitaminosis A and intestinal parasitic infections in children living in poor social conditions in Brasilia.

STUDY GROUPS AND METHODS

All the 124 children, younger than 6-year old, of both sexes, living in Varjão, a slum area in Brasilia, Brazil, were evaluated for their nutritional status and presence of parasites in their stool in a cohort study performed in 1983. In this small community, the children were submitted to the same social, cultural, economic and environmental influences. The family incomes were similar, and in the area they lived there was no supply of treated water or public sanitation.

All the children were evaluated by a clinical examination. The weight, height and head circumference were measured using standard anthropometric measurement by the same observer (MIM-J). The nutritional status was evaluated by the standard deviation score (Z-score), percentile and Waterlow classification41. The 50th percentile of the growth charts of the National Center for Health Statistic (NCHS), USA, was used as normal standard. Sixty-eight out of 124 children were younger than three years old and their head circumference was analyzed using the 50th percentile from the NCHS chart. The food intake was estimated for energy, protein, retinol and iron by the 24 hour-recall method for 104 children using the IBGE (Brazil) nutrient composition table, and the FAO/WHO criteria for daily recommended intake. Dietary intake of carotenoid precursors and preformed vitamin A were computed together and expressed as retinol equivalent intake. Sixteen breast-fed babies receiving human milk together with supplementary food were excluded from the analysis. Therefore only the results of the intake of 88 children were considered.

The intestinal parasites were detected in the stools of 102 children using four different tests: sedimentation test of Hoffmann, Pons and Janer, Baermann test for larvae, Faust test for protozoa cysts, and Kato-Kats test. The latter was also used for calculating the burden of *Ascaris lumbricoides*. All stool samples were submitted to the four tests. The 24-hour samples of stools collected in a plastic bag were weighed. The number of *Ascaris lumbricoides* infecting each child was estimated by the number of eggs counted in 1g of stool (detected by the Kato-Kats method), multiplied by the weight of the stools collected during 24 hours; divided by 200,000 (number of eggs expelled by each female *Ascaris lumbricoides*), multiplied by 2 (proportion between male and female of *Ascaris lumbricoides*), according to the equation proposed by WHO45: number of parasites = [(number of eggs per gram of stools X weight of stools from 24h)/200,000] $\times$ 2.

The presence of 5 or less parasites was considered as light infection, from 6 to 25 as moderate and over 25 worms as heavy infection.

Samples of 2 to 5ml of peripheral venous blood were obtained and sera were kept at -20°C until used. Levels of vitamin A in serum from 122 children were evaluated in duplicate for individual sample by the colorimetric method employing the Carr Price reaction using trifluoroacetic acid (TCA) as a chromogen, and were expressed as mg of retinol per 100ml. Hemoglobin was detected in duplicate samples of blood immediately after collection from 121 children by the cyanmethemoglobin method, and was expressed as g per dL of blood.

The statements of the Helsinki Declaration and of the Health Ministry of Brazil for research in human subjects were strictly followed throughout this investigation. All children received 200,000 U vitamin A and their parasite infections were treated as soon as they were detected.

Statistical analysis was performed by one way ANOVA and subsequent Student-Newman-Keuls multiple comparison when the samples showed a normal distribution, or by Kruskall-Wallis test followed by Dunn's method of multiple comparisons to compare non-gaussian distributed samples. The Mann-Whitney test was performed to compare two non-gaussian distributed samples. Chi-square test was used to compare proportions. Correlation between variables was assessed by Spearman coefficient. All results with a p value < 0.05 were considered statistically significant. The SigmaStat Jandel's statistical software (Jandel Scientific, San Rafael/California, USA, 1992) was used for the analysis.

RESULTS

The mean weight-for-age and height-for-age Z-score of all children were skewed about one standard deviation to left in relation to NCHS reference standard, while the mean weight-for-height was not different from that of the NCHS reference standard. There was no statistical difference in the mean Z-score between ages.

The height-for-age showed the distribution skewed toward the lower percentiles, with 46% (57/124) of the children below the 10th percentile, and 22.6% (28/124) below the 3rd percentile. The weight-for-age was also skewed toward lower values, with 30.6% (38/124) of the children below the 10th percentile, and 12% (15/124) below the 3rd percentile . The weight-for-height showed a homogeneous arrangement with 7.3% (9/124) below the 10th percentile and 2.4% (3/124) below the 3rd percentile . The same skew toward the lower percentiles was observed in head circumference, with 61.8% (42/68) of the children below the 10th and 47% (32/68) below the 3rd percentile. Application of the Waterlow classification showed that 8.9% (11/124) of the children were stunted.

The predominant diet of these children was rice and beans. Sixty-eight per cent (60/88) of the children ingested less than 80% of daily recommended intake of energy, while 61% (54/88) of them had an intake of more than 100% daily recommended intake in protein.

Anemia (hemoglobin concentration below 11g/dL) was detected in 16.5% (20/121) of the children, all younger than 30 months of age. In 12.4% (15/121) of the children, hemoglobin concentration was between 10-11g/dL, and in 4.1% (5/121), it was between 7-10g/dL. The lowest hemoglobin concentration was found in children aged between 6 months and 1.5 years ($p<0.001$, ANOVA).

Fifty percent (10/20) of children with hemoglobin concentration below 11g/dL had *Ascaris lumbricoides*, 25% (5/20) *Giardia lamblia*, 15% (3/20) *Hymenolepis nana*, 20% (4/20) were polyparasitized, and 30% (6/20) had no intestinal parasites. Prevalence of parasitic infection in 27 children with the same age (below 30 months old) and with hemoglobin concentration ^{3}11g/dL were: 33.3% (9/27) for *Ascaris lumbricoides*-infected, 25.9% (7/27) for *Giardia lamblia*, 7.4% (2/27) for multiple parasites, while 48.15% (13/27) had no parasite. No difference was found in the mean concentration of serum retinol and the anthropometric indices in the groups with normal (<11g/dL) and low (<11g/dL) hemoglobin concentrations.

Iron intake was below 80% daily recommended intake in 68 out of 88 (77%) children. In 11 out of 12 (91%) children with hemoglobin concentration below 11g/dL and that received no human milk, the daily recommended intake of iron was lower than 60%.

Parasites were present in the stools of 75.5% (77/102) of the examined children *Ascaris lumbricoides* was the most prevalent parasite, being present in 47% (48/102) of the children. The estimated load of *Ascaris lumbricoides* varied from 2 to 114 worms, 56.3% (27/48) of the children showing a light burden, 27.1% (13/48) a moderate one, and 16.7% (8/48) a heavy burden of *Ascaris lumbricoides*. There was no difference in the mean ± SD of weight-for-age Z-score in children with light (-0.76 ± 0.98), moderate (-0.60 ± 0.82) or heavy (-0.74 ± 0.44) burden of *Ascaris lumbricoides* ($p > 0.05$, ANOVA), and no correlation was found between the age and the burden of *Ascaris lumbricoides* ($p > 0.05$, Spearman correlation). Eggs of *Ascaris lumbricoides* and *Hymenolepis nana* were detected in children from 9 months old onwards, and cysts of *Giardia lamblia* from 11 months old. The prevalence of intestinal parasites according to children's age . Cysts of *Giardia lamblia* were also highly prevalent, with 30.4% (31/102) of the children infected. In 29.4% (30/102) of the subjects more than one parasite were observed The percentage of parasitized children below -2 SD Z-score for weight-for-age.

Among the parasites detected, only *Giardia lamblia* influenced the weight-for-age and weight-for-height. Children infected exclusively with *Giardia lamblia* showed weight-for-age Z-score lower than that of children exclusively infected with *Ascaris lumbricoides* ($p < 0.048$, ANOVA), and the weight-for-height Z-score were lower than that of non-infected children or those exclusively infected with *Ascaris lumbricoides* or *Hymenolepis nana* ($p = 0.03$, ANOVA). Children coinfected with *Ascaris lumbricoides* and *Giardia lamblia* were in an intermediate situation. Parasitic infections caused no change of height-for-age Z- score ($p > 0.05$, ANOVA).

Only 36.9% (45/122) of the children showed normal serum retinol concentration (>20mg/100 ml), while 60.6% (74/122) presented levels between 10-20mg/100ml, and 2.45% (3/122) below 10mg/100ml. There was no statistical difference in retinol concentration in serum in the different age-groups . Sixty five out of 88 children (74%) showed retinol equivalent intake below 80% of daily recommended intake.

Sixty out of 122 children (49.2%) were suffering some mild infectious disease when evaluated, including skin infections, diarrhea, acute otitis or upper respiratory tract infections. Only three out of 124 children presented axillary temperature higher than 37.5°C. The retinol concentration in children with infections (18.3mg/100ml) were similar to that without infections (18.2mg/100ml) ($p>0.05$, Mann-Whitney test). Again, no difference in the serum retinol concentrations was detected among those infected with (17.5mg/100 ml) or without (18.5mg/100ml) concomitant malnutrition, and also between well-nourished children with (19.9mg/100ml) or without (17.4mg/100ml) infection ($p>0.05$, Kruskal-Wallis test).

Although the wasted children (weight-for-age Z-score < -2 SD) had lesser retinol in serum (median = 14.9mg/100ml) than the better nourished children (> -2SD) (median = 17.1mg/100ml; 19.5mg/100ml; 18.3mg/100ml) these differences were not statistically significant ($p>0.05$, Kruskal Wallis test) (A higher percentage of wasted children (75%; 9/12) showed retinol in serum below 20mg/100ml than the better nourished children (59%, 65/110), although also without statistical significance.

Children exclusively infected by *Hymenolepis nana* showed serum retinol levels higher than those infected with other parasites ($p=0.02$, Kruskal-Wallis test)). No one child infected with *Hymenolepis nana* had weight-for-age below -2 SD Z-score.

Both *Ascaris lumbricoides*-infected or non-infected wasted children (<-2 SD Z-score) showed low serum retinol concentrations . However, the wasted children (<-2 SD Z-score) infected with *Ascaris lumbricoides* had the lowest value of serum retinol concentration.

Discussion

The group of children studied showed a high prevalence of protein-energy malnutrition, hypovitaminosis A and intestinal parasitic infections. The head circumference and the height-for-age were the most altered anthropometric indices. However, these children showed a normal weight-for-height, suggesting an adaptation to the chronic nutritional deficit. Children under one year of age showed a higher deficit in weight-for-age and height-for-age than older children, with 20% and 40%, respectively, below - 2 SD Z-score.

Two major consequences may result from protein-energy malnutrition: deficient physical growth and intellectual performance. Wachs suggested that chronic, mild postnatal malnutrition might be associated with a variety of cognitive and behavioral deficits across the life span. However, malnutrition appears to be a necessary but not a sufficient condition for causing behavioural deficits. Waterlow considers that the consequences for intellectual development of the non-severe lower physical growth and the lower head circumference, related to the international growth charts of NCHS, as observed in our Brazilian children, are not yet clarified. However, it has been recognized that the risk of a child dying is increased when infection is associated to malnutrition, even a mild one.

Anemia detected by laboratory test was present in 17% of the children and was possibly due to the low iron intake. This occurred mainly in the age group between 6 months and 2.5 years old. This is when the predominance of cow's milk intake (poor in iron) in diet may led to low iron intake3. In fact, we detected a low iron intake in 91% of these anemic children. In 78% of the whole group, iron intake was deficient. The possibility that the iron stores of these children were depleted cannot be excluded.

Parasites were present in 75.5% of the children, and 29.4% of them were infected by multiple parasites. *Ascaris lumbricoides* and *Giardia lamblia* were the two most prevalent parasites observed in our study population. Eggs of *Ancilostomidae* were not observed and anemia was not a major problem in these children. However, it is possible that these parasites were not found because we studied only children under 6 years old, and *Ancylostomidae* are mostly prevalent in adult workers. Eggs of *Ascaris lumbricoides* and *Hymenolepis nana* were present in children as young as 9 months suggesting a low degree of sanitation and education in this population.

The pathologic consequences of multiple parasitic infections for the host and its metabolic cost are unknown. It has been suggested that the interactions between parasites in the host may have either antagonistic or synergistic effects, and can result in worsening of inflammatory reactions and clinical manifestations to the parasites. In our study, only *Giardia lamblia* infection was related to deleterious consequences to protein-energy nutritional status. *Giardia lamblia*-infected children had significantly decreased weight-for-age and weight-for-height, while these anthropometric indices were not negatively affected in children infected with *Ascaris lumbricoides* and *Hymenolepis nana*. Children coinfected by *Ascaris lumbricoides* and *Giardia lamblia* were in an intermediate situation between the children infected exclusively by *Giardia lamblia* or *Ascaris lumbricoides*, in relation to protein-energy nutrition. This finding suggests an antagonistic effect between these two parasites. Whether the infection by *Giardia lamblia* was acute or chronic may also have influenced the end result.

ASCARIS LUMBRICOIDES

Hymenolepis nana-infected children presented weight-for-age and height-for-weight higher than the non-infected. It is recognized that the level of adult helminth infection in an individual host is determined by the balance between establishment of the parasites (input) and their death (output). The input depends mainly on public health sanitation and educational level, while output depends on the factors associated to the parasite and/or host. For the worm intestinal expulsion to occur, an environment must be created that is too hostile for juvenile and adult worms to continue to develop, or maintain their position. Thus, it is a possibility that, in well-nourished children the abundance of food and the favourable microenvironment around the parasite in the intestinal environment facilitates maintenance of the established parasite for a longer time. Another possibility is that some specific nutrient may be necessary for parasite survival.

The children under study showed predominantly mild or moderate protein-energy malnutrition, and only 14.5% of them presented a heavy load of *Ascaris lumbricoides*. Malnutrition was not a problem in helminth-infected children; on the contrary, these children were better nourished. This fact may suggest a minor influence of infection by intestinal helminthes on the nutrition and growth of the children when they have a low burden of parasite and mild malnutrition. It is possible to conclude that light or moderate parasitism with *Ascaris lumbricoides* did not cause a major detrimental effect on the nutritional status of the children, but it is possible that a heavy burden of the parasite in children also with a deficit in food supply can do so. Furthermore, it is not possible to determine whether these better nourished children would have been heavier and taller if they had grown without parasitic infections. Neither helminth nor *Giardia lamblia* infection influenced the height-for-age. This fact suggests that parasites had only a short and temporary influence on the children's growth.

The group younger than 1-year old presented a low frequency of parasite infection but showed a higher percentage of protein-energy malnutrition. The reasons why these non parasite-infected children had low antrophometric indices and vitamin A serum levels were not clarified. It is possible that in the first year of the life the children may be more susceptible to other negative outside influences independent of parasite infections.

The concomitant infections by viruses and bacteria in the group investigated need to be analyzed. Most infections, including those responsible for mild diarrhea and respiratory diseases, provoke an acute-phase reaction which reduces the synthesis of retinol-binding protein in the liver, and so depresses circulating retinol. This fact does not imply reduced overall vitamin A stores, but may result in a temporary impairment of transport of Vitamin A to functional locations. Infectious diseases apparently were not the main cause of the lower values of retinol observed in these children. However, we cannot rule out the possibility that the level of retinol in such infected-children would be higher if they were non-infected.

Hypovitaminosis A was a major nutritional deficiency in this population under investigation. The main sources of vitamin A are milk, meat, liver, fish, eggs, green vegetables and some orange colored fruits and vegetables, besides, it is fat-soluble and depends on lipids for intestinal absorption, and these kinds of food are not cheap. Considering the low vitamin A intake, the absence of relation from retinol with parasitoses, and the absence of relationship between retinol and infectious diseases, it appears that the low food intake was the main cause of this deficiency. Besides, children below -2 SD weight-for-age Z-score also showed the lowest level of serum retinol. It is possible that in these children the low supply, and poor variety of food, with predominance of rice and beans, had affected both protein-energy nutritional status and vitamin A status. It is not clear why children infected by *Hymenolepis nana* showed values of retinol higher than the other groups.

Our data indicate that malnutrition is more importantly affected by socio- economical and cultural factors, capable of impairing food supply and intake, than by metabolic cost of parasitism and the impairment in digestion and absorption by intestinal parasitic infections, except for *Giardia lamblia*. This latter parasite apparently facilitated the development of protein-energy malnutrition. However, it is likely that helminth infection is not detrimental to nutritional state, provided that food intake is adequate. The association of both low food intake and parasite infections was detrimental.

Our data support the hypothesis that early treatment of *Giardia lamblia* infection will improve the growth of infected children. We need to treat helminth diseases to decrease the morbidity and mortality of related illnesses. However, treatment of helminthes alone would not be efficient as a measure to improve growth of children since these children were no more malnourished than non-parasitized children before treatment. Strategies to increase the supply and intake of food would probably be more effective in poor populations.

13

Parasitoid Wasp

INTRODUCTION

The term Parasitoid wasp refers to a large evolutionary grade of hymenopteran superfamilies, mainly in the Apocrita. They are primarily parasitoids of other animals, mostly other arthropods. Many of them, such as the family Braconidae, are considered beneficial because they control populations of agricultural pests. Some of these wasps help pest control in a rather sophisticated manner. Certain types of plants have compounds that work in part with the saliva of caterpillars. When the saliva of the caterpillar and the juices of the plant mix, a fragrance is emitted that certain parasitoid wasps are very attracted to. The parasitoid wasps then kill the caterpillars and often use the carcasses to lay eggs within. This is a form of mutualism between the plant and the wasp and works only when the fragrance from the plant and the saliva combine.

TAXONOMY AND SYSTEMATICS

Historically, the classification system of Hymenoptera included two divisions or infraorders within the suborder Apocrita: one of these, the "Parasitica" containing the parasitoid wasp. However, the use of the name Parasitica (or its alternative, "Terebrantia") has been phased out in recent years, as it is a paraphyletic grouping, and most modern classifications explicitly reject the use of any groups that are not monophyletic.

Presently, it is not clear what the eventual taxonomic fate of these groups will be. A number of clades seem to stand out in newer studies, and these may be treated as unranked taxa or at the ranks of infraorder and division.

Superfamilies

The traditional superfamilies united in the "Parasitica" are:

Superfamily Ceraphronoidea

Superfamily Chalcidoidea

Superfamily Cynipoidea

Superfamily Evanioidea

Superfamily Ichneumonoidea

Superfamily Megalyroidea

Superfamily Mymarommatoidea (sometimes included in Serphitoidea)

Superfamily Platygastroidea

Superfamily Proctotrupoidea

Superfamily Serphitoidea (fossil)

Superfamily Stephanoidea

Superfamily Trigonaloidea

Other than the "Parasitica", there are a few Apocrita that are also sometimes called "parasitic wasps": most of the members of the superfamily Chrysidoidea, as well as most of the families superfamily Vespoidea such as Bradynobaenidae, Mutillidae, Rhopalosomatidae, Sapygidae, Scoliidae, Sierolomorphidae, Tiphiidae, and a few species of Pompilidae. Most of these groups are ectoparasitoids. Among the sawflies, which are not Apocrita, there is only one small parasitic family, Orussidae. This is the Apocrita's closest living relative. It thus appears that the ancestors of bees and bumblebees were parasitic too.

SYSTEMATICS

According to recent cladistic studies, there are a number of basal lineages among the Apocrita, as well as a diverse group of parasitic wasps that seems to form a major clade. If the Apocrita are divided into infraorders, about 6 of these must be recognized, and several of these warrant further subdivision, with a number of families being moved out of the Proctotrupoidea:

- Superfamily Ichneumonoidea seems closer to the Aculeata than to other parasitic wasps. If the Aculeata are treated as a division, the Ichneumonoidea would form a basal superfamily in a new infraorder.
- Superfamily Stephanoidea forms a clade or infraorder of its own.
- Another clade or infraorder contains the following groups:
  - Superfamily Megalyroidea
  - Superfamily Trigonaloidea
  - a clade or division containing
  - Superfamily Ceraphronoidea
  - Superfamily Evanioidea.
- A clade or infraorder containing families formerly in the Proctotrupoidea:
  - Family Maamingidae
  - a clade, division or superfamily containing

    Family Austroniidae

    Family Diapriidae

    Family Monomachidae.

Another clade or infraorder of families formerly in the Proctotrupoidea:

Family Proctorenyxidae

Family Roproniidae

The bulk of the parasitic wasps, a clade or infraorder containing two very distinct groups:

One clade or division containing:

Superfamily Platygastroidea

Superfamily	Chalcidoidea
Superfamily	Mymarommatoidea (sometimes included in Serphitoidea)
Superfamily	Serphitoidea (fossil, tentatively placed here)

Another clade or division containing:

Superfamily	Cynipoidea
Superfamily	Proctotrupoidea *sensu stricto*

ARTHROPOD

Arthropods are animals belonging to the Phylum Arthropoda (from Greek *arthron*, "joint", and *podos* "foot", which together mean "jointed feet"), and include the insects, arachnids, crustaceans, and others. Arthropods are characterized by their jointed limbs and cuticles, which are mainly made of a-chitin; the cuticles of crustaceans are also biomineralized with calcium carbonate. The rigid cuticle inhibits growth, so arthropods replace it periodically by molting. The arthropod body plan consists of repeated segments, each with a pair of appendages. It is so versatile that they have been compared to Swiss Army knives, and it has enabled them to become the most species-rich members of all ecological guilds in most environments. They have over a million described species, making up more than 80% of all described living species, and are one of only two groups very successful in dry environments – the other is amniotes. They range in size from microscopic plankton up to forms a few metres long.

Arthropods have body cavities (coelomates); their main internal cavity is a hemocoel, which accommodates their internal organs and through which their blood circulates – they have open circulatory systems. Like their exteriors, the internal organs of arthropods are generally built of repeated segments. Their nervous system is "ladder-like", with paired ventral nerve cords running through all segments and forming paired ganglia in each segment. Their heads are formed by fusion of varying numbers of segments, and their brains are formed by fusion of the ganglia of these segments and encircle the esophagus. The respiratory and excretory systems of arthropods vary, depending as much on their environment as on the subphylum to which they belong.

Vision relies on various combinations of compound eyes and pigment-pit ocelli: in most species the ocelli can only detect the direction from which light is coming, and the compound eyes are the main source of information, but the main eyes of spiders are ocelli that can form images and, in a few cases, can swivel to track prey. Arthropods also have a wide range of chemical and mechanical sensors, mostly based on modifications of the many setae (bristles) that project through their cuticles. Methods of reproduction and development of arthropods are diverse – all terrestrial species use internal fertilization, but this is often by indirect transfer of the sperm via an appendage or the ground, rather by direct injection. Aquatic species use either internal or external fertilization. Almost all arthropods lay eggs, except for scorpions, who give birth to live young after the eggs have hatched inside the mother. Arthropod hatchlings vary from miniature adults to grubs and caterpillars that lack jointed limbs and eventually undergo a total metamorphosis to produce the adult form. The level of maternal care for hatchlings varies from zero to the prolonged care provided by scorpions.

The versatility of the arthropod modular body plan has made it difficult for zoologists and paleontologists to classify them and work out their evolutionary ancestry, which dates back to the Cambrian period. From the late 1950s to late 1970s, it was thought that arthropods were polyphyletic, that is, there was no single arthropod ancestor. Now they are generally regarded as monophyletic. Traditionally the closest evolutionary relatives of arthropods were considered to be annelid worms, as both groups have segmented bodies. It is now generally accepted that arthropods belong to the superphylum Ecdysozoa ("animals that molt"), while annelids belong to another superphylum, Lophotrochozoa. The relationships between various arthropod groups are still actively debated.

Although arthropods contribute to human food supply both directly as food and more importantly as pollinators of crops, they also spread some of the most severe diseases and do considerable damage to livestock and crops.

Description

Arthropods are invertebrates with segmented bodies and jointed limbs he limbs form part of an exoskeleton which is mainly made of a-chitin, a derivative of glucos One other group of animals, the tetrapods, has jointed limbs, but tetrapods are vertebrates and therefore have endoskeletons.

Diversity

Estimating the total number of living species is extremely difficult because it often depends on a series of assumptions in order to scale up from counts at specific locations to estimates for the whole world. A study in 1992 estimated that there were 500,000 species in Costa Rica alone, of which 365,000 were arthropods. Another estimate indicates that arthropods have over a million described species, and account for over 80% of all known living species They are important members of marine, freshwater, land and air ecosystems, and are one of only two major animal groups that have adapted to life in dry environments – the other is amniotes, whose living members are reptiles, birds and mammals One arthropod sub-group, insects, is the most species-rich member of all ecological guilds (ways of making a living) in land and fresh-water environments. The smallest insects weigh less than 25 micrograms (millionths of a gram), while the largest weigh over 25 grams (0.88 oz). Some living crustaceans are much larger, for example the legs of the Japanese spider crab may span up to 4 metres (13 ft).

Segmentation

The last common ancestor of living arthropods probably consisted of a series of undifferentiated segments, each with a pair of appendages that functioned as limbs. However all known living and fossil arthropods have grouped segments into tagmata in which segments and their limbs are specialized in various ways; The three-part appearance of many insect bodies and the two-part appearance of spiders is a result of this grouping; in fact there are no external signs of segmentation in mites.

Arthropods also have two body elements which are not part of this serially repeated pattern of segments, an acron at the front, ahead of the mouth, and a telson at the rear, behind the anus. The eyes are mounted on the acron.

In some segments of all known arthropods the appendages have been modified, for example to form gills, mouth-parts, antennae for collecting information, or claws for grasping – arthropods are "like Swiss Army knives, each equipped with a unique set of specialized tools." In many arthropods, appendages have vanished from some regions of the body, and it is particularly common for abdominal appendages to have disappeared or be highly modified.

The most conspicuous specialization of segments is in the head. The four major groups of arthropods - Chelicerata (includes spiders and scorpions), Crustacea (shrimps, lobsters, crabs, etc.), Tracheata (arthropods that breathe via channels into their bodies; includes insects and myriapods), and the extinct trilobites – have heads formed of various combinations of segments, with appendages that are missing or specialized in different ways. In addition some extinct arthropods, such as Marrella, belong to none of these groups, as their heads are formed by their own particular combinations of segments and specialized appendages Working out the evolutionary stages by which all these different combinations could have appeared is so difficult that it has long been known as "the Arthropod head problem". In 1960 R.E. Snodgrass even hoped it would not be solved, as trying to work out solutions was so much fun.

Exoskeleton

Arthropod exoskeletons are made of cuticle, a non-cellular material secreted by the epidermis. Their cuticles vary in the details of their structure, but generally consist of three main layers: the epicuticle, a thin outer waxy coat which moisture-proofs the other layers and gives them some protection; the exocuticle, which consists of chitin and chemically hardened proteins; and the endocuticle, which consists of chitin and unhardened proteins. The exocuticle and endocuticle together are known as the procuticle. Each body segment and limb section is encased in hardened cuticle The joints between body segments and between limb sections are covered by flexible cuticle.

The exoskeletons of most aquatic crustaceans are biomineralized with calcium carbonate extracted from the water. Some terrestrial crustaceans have developed means of storing the mineral, to deal with the unavailability of dissolved calcium carbonate Biomineralization generally affects the exocuticle and the outer part of the endocuticle. Two recent hypotheses about the evolution of biomineralization in arthropods and other groups of animals propose that it provides tougher defensive armor and that it allows animals to grow larger and stronger by providing more rigid skeletons nd in either case a mineral-organic composite exoskeleton is cheaper to build than an all-organic one of comparable strength.

The cuticle can have setae (bristles) growing from special cells in the epidermis. Setae are as varied in form and function as appendages. For example, they are often used as sensors to detect air or water currents, or contact with objects; aquatic arthropods use feather-like setae to increase the surface area of swimming appendages and to filter food particles out of water; aquatic insects, which are air-breathers, use thick felt-like coats of setae to trap air, extending the time they can spend under water; heavy, rigid setae serve as defensive spines.

Although all arthropods use muscles attached to the inside of the exoskeleton to flex their limbs, some still use hydraulic pressure to extend them, a system inherited from their pre-arthropod ancestors[– for example all spiders extend their legs hydraulically and can generate pressures up to eight times their resting level.

MOLTING

The exoskeleton cannot stretch and thus restricts growth. Arthropods therefore replace their exoskeletons by molting, or shedding the old exoskeleton after growing a new one which is not yet hardened. Molting cycles run nearly continuously until an arthropod reaches full size.

In the initial phase of molting, the animal stops feeding and its epidermis releases molting fluid, a mixture of enzymes that digests the endocuticle and thus detaches the old cuticle. This phase begins when the epidermis has secreted a new epicuticle to protect it from the enzymes, and the epidermis secretes the new exocuticle while the old cuticle is detaching. When this stage is complete, the animal makes its body swell by taking in a large quantity of water or air, and this makes the old cuticle split along predefined weaknesses where the old exocuticle was thinnest. It commonly takes several minutes for the animal to struggle out of the old cuticle. At this point the new one is wrinkled and so soft that the animal cannot support itself and finds it very difficult to move, and the new endocuticle has not yet formed. The animal continues to pump itself up to stretch the new cuticle as much as possible, then hardens the new exocuticle and eliminates the excess air or water. By the end of this phase the new endocuticle has formed. Many arthropods then eat the discarded cuticle to reclaim its materials.

Because arthropods are unprotected and nearly immobilized until the new cuticle has hardened, they are in danger both of being trapped in the old cuticle and of being attacked by predators. Molting may be responsible for 80 to 90% of all arthropod deaths.

Internal Organs

Arthropod bodies are also segmented internally, and the nervous, muscular, circulatory and excretory systems have repeated components. Arthopods come from a lineage of animals that have a coelom, a membrane-lined cavity between the gut and the body wall that accommodates the internal organs. The strong, segmented limbs of arthropods eliminate the need for one of the coelom's main ancestral functions, as a hydrostatic skeleton which muscles compress in order to change the animal's shape and thus enable it to move. Hence the coelom of the arthropod is reduced to small areas around the reproductive and excretory systems. Its place is largely taken by a hemocoel, a cavity that runs most of the length of the body and through which blood flows

Arthropods have open circulatory systems, although most have a few short, open-ended arteries. In chelicerates and crustaceans, the blood carries oxygen to the tissues, while hexapods use a separate system of tracheae. Many crustaceans, but few chelicerates and tracheates, use respiratory pigments to assist oxygen transport. The most common respiratory pigment in arthropods is copper-based hemocyanin; this is used by many crustaceans and a few centipedes. A few crustaceans and insects use iron-based hemoglobin, the respiratory pigment used by vertebrates. As with other invertebrates and unlike among vertebrates, the respiratory pigments of those arthropods that have them are generally dissolved in the blood and rarely enclosed in corpuscles.

The heart is typically a muscular tube that runs just under the back and for most of the length of the hemocoel. It contracts in ripples that run from rear to front, pushing blood forwards. Elastic ligaments, or small muscles, connect the heart to the body wall and expand sections that are not being squeezed by the heart muscle. Along the heart run a series of paired ostia, non-return valves that allow blood to enter the heart but prevent it from leaving before it reaches the front.

Arthropods have a wide variety of respiratory systems. Small species often do not have any, since their high ratio of surface area to volume enables simple diffusion through the body surface to supply enough oxygen. Crustacea usually have gills that are modified appendages. Many arachnids have book lungs. Tracheae, systems of branching tunnels that run from the openings in the body walls, deliver oxygen directly to individual cells in many insects, myriapods and arachnids.

Living arthropods have paired main nerve cords running along their bodies below the gut, and in each segment the cords form a pair of ganglia from which sensory and motor nerves run to other parts of the segment. Although the pairs of ganglia in each segment often appear physically fused, they are connected by commissures (relatively large bundles of nerves), which give arthropod nervous systems a characteristic "ladder-like" appearance. The brain is in the head, encircling and mainly above the esophagus. It consists of the fused ganglia of the acron and one or two of the foremost segments that form the head - a total of three pairs of ganglia in most arthropods, but only two in chelicerates, which do not have antennae or the ganglion connected to them. The ganglia of other head segments are often close to the brain and function as part of it. In insects these other head ganglia combine into a pair of subesophageal ganglia, under and behind the esophagus. Spiders take this process a step further, as all the segmental ganglia are incorporated into the subesophageal ganglia, which occupy most of the space in the cephalothorax (front "super-segment")

There are two different types of arthropod excretory systems. In aquatic arthropods, the end-product of biochemical reactions that metabolise nitrogen is ammonia, which is so toxic that it needs to be diluted as much as possible with water. The ammonia is then eliminated via any permeable membrane, mainly through the gills. All crustaceans use this system, and its high consumption of water may be responsible for the relative lack of success of crustaceans as land animals. Various groups of terrestrial arthropods have independently developed a different system: the end-product of nitrogen metabolism is uric acid, which can be excreted as dry material; Malphigian tubules filter the uric acid and other nitrogenous waste out of the blood in the hemocoel, and dump these materials into the hindgut, from which they are expelled as feces Most aquatic arthropods and some terrestrial ones also have organs called nephridia ("little kidneys"), which extract other wastes for excretion as urine.

The stiff cuticles of arthropods would block out information about the outside world, except that they are penetrated by many sensors or connections from sensors to the nervous system. In fact, arthropods have modified their cuticles into elaborate arrays of sensors. Various touch sensors, mostly setae, respond to different levels of force, from strong contact to very weak air currents. Chemical sensors provide equivalents of taste and smell, often by means of setae. Pressure sensors often take the form of membranes that function as eardrums, but are connected directly to nerves rather than to auditory ossicles. The antennae of most hexapods include sensor packages that monitor humidity, moisture and temperature.

Head of a wasp with three ocelli (centre), and compound eyes at the left and rightMost arthropods have sophisticated visual systems that include one or more usually both of compound eyes and pigment-cup ocelli ("little eyes"). In most cases ocelli are only capable of detecting the direction from which light is coming, using the shadow cast by the walls of the cup. However the main eyes of spiders are pigment-cup ocelli that are capable of forming images, and those of jumping spiders can rotate to track prey.

Compound eyes consist of fifteen to several thousand independent ommatidia, columns that are usually hexagonal in cross-section. Each ommatidium is an independent sensor, with its own light-sensitive cells and often with its own lens and cornea Compound eyes have a wide field of view, and can detect fast movement and, in some cases, the polarization of light. On the other hand the relatively large size of ommatidia makes the images rather coarse, and compound eyes are shorter-sighted than those of birds and mammals – although this is not a severe disadvantage, as objects and events within 20 centimetres (7.9 in) are most important to most arthropods. Several arthropods have color vision, and that of some insects has been studied in detail – for example, the ommatidia of bees contain receptors for both green and ultra-violet.

Most arthropods lack balance and acceleration sensors, and rely on their eyes to tell them which way is up. The self-righting behavior of cockroaches is triggered when pressure sensors on the underside of the feet report no pressure. However many malacostracan crustaceans have statocysts, which provide the same sort of information as the balance and motion sensors of the vertebrate inner ear.

The proprioceptors of arthropods, sensors which report the force exerted by muscles and the degree of bending in the body and joints, are well understood.

14

Human Intestinal Parasites Worms

INTRODUCTION

Human intestinal parasites worms infection air food water cause constipation, stomach bloating, disease health problems. Other symptoms include anemia, asthma, diarrhea, digestive disorders, fatigue, low immune system, nervousness, skin rash. Most will not face this reality or even want to think about this subject and will continue in their suffering.

There can be over 100 different types of parasites worms living in human bodies. Some are microscopic in size while others can be seen quite easily. These common organisms can be found everywhere in our environment, in the air we breath, in the water we drink, or in the food we eat.

Parasite is an organism that lives on or in other organisms from which it obtains nutrients to live and causes harm in the process. Its name comes from the Greek word para that means beside, and sitos, which means food.

Most parasites require some host to complete their life cycle. Animals can also serve as the host. The parasite will vary in size from one-thousandth of one micron to whale tapeworms one hundred feet long.

Parasites and worms can invade your bodies through food and water intake, through transmitting agents (like mosquito), sexual conduct or through the nose and skin. Once established, they will eat the same foods you eat or they will eat you.

People with intestinal parasite infections are usually undernourished and weak, infected with viral, fungal, or bacteria, and have various types of chemical and metal poisoning. Human intestinal parasites can be present in any disease, in any person, at any age.

They are responsible for many health problems because they secrete toxins and steal the vital nutrients from our bodies. They can irritate or exaggerate other health problems you may be experiencing. Everyone is at risk and under their mercy during parasitic infections.

We create the perfect living environment for parasites when the bowel becomes ineffective in the elimination of our waste products. The build-up of fecal material on the walls of the colon is attributed to constipation and the amounts of junk food, chemicals, bad fats and sweets we consume.

We poison ourselves from our own toxic waste and the waste from these creatures (auto intoxication) when this ideal habitat for is created. Testing for parasites are only available for about five percent of the known varieties with twenty-percent accuracy.

Cancer cases are afflicted with worms that often lump together and look like tumors. Female worms can release 3,000 to 200,000 eggs per day depending on their type. This is one topic that most people do not want to discuss, let alone think about, but now reality must be faced.

These topics are very important for detoxification and your well-being. Most doctors are not trained to recognize the symptoms of parasitic infections. The only way to avoid the problems associated with parasite infections is by educating yourself.

PARASITES, SOME DIFFERENT VARIETIES

There are 3200 varieties of parasites in the four major categories, Protozoa, Trematoda, Cestoda and Nematoda.

Roundworms look similar to an earthworm and can produce 200,000 eggs daily. Approximately 1,008 million people are infected, making it the most common worldwide. The most frequent symptom from roundworms is upper abdominal discomfort. Other symptoms are asthma, eye pain, insomnia, and rashes due to the secretions or waste products from the worms.

Large numbers can cause blockages in the intestinal tract, hemorrhage when penetrating the intestinal wall, appendicitis, peritonitis, abscesses in the liver, hemorrhagic pancreatitis, loss of appetite, and insufficient absorption of digested foods. Adults grow to 15 inches long.

Hookworm larvae penetrate the skin. When hookworms reach adulthood, they can sap the victim's strength, vitality and overall well-being. Young worms use their teeth to burrow through the intestinal wall and feed on your blood. Symptoms from hookworm are iron deficiency, abdominal pain, loss of appetite, craving to eat soil, protein deficiency, dry skin and hair, skin irritations, edema, distended abdomen, stunted growth, delayed puberty, mental dullness, cardiac failure and death (½ inch long)

Pinworms can infect one in five children. Symptoms are itching and irritation of the anus or vagina, digestive disorders, insomnia, irritability or nervousness. Female worms crawl out of the anus and lay about 15,000 eggs per day. Once airborne, the eggs can survive about two days anywhere in your living environment.

Worldwide, about 500 million are infected with pinworms. The worm is white and can grow to about half inch in length.

Infections from whipworms are estimated at several hundred million worldwide. Symptoms of whipworms are bloody stools, pain in the lower abdomen, weight loss, rectal prolapse, nausea and anemia. Hemorrhage can occur when worms penetrate the intestinal wall and bacterial infections usually follow. 1 to 2 inches length.

Amoebae are an irregular shaped microorganism that infects the end of the smaller intestine and colon. Amebiasis is the most common infection and caused by the species Entamoeba histolytica.

Amoebae also release an enzyme that causes ulcers or abscesses where they can enter the bloodstream. They can eventually reach other organs like the brain or liver. (25 micro meters in diameter)

Cryptosporidium is associated with water-borne outbreaks. The victim might experience diarrhea and abdominal pain lasting for about ten days.

Giardia is the most prevalent intestinal parasite in humans and found in drinking water. Giardia resides in the smaller intestine and at times in the gall bladder. Millions of these giardia organisms will coat the intestinal walls, prevents the absorption of nutrients and later causing illness. Symptoms are mild to moderate abdominal cramps, intestinal gas, light colored stools, bad absorption, weakness, chills, stomach bloating and diarrhea. (14 um x 10 um)

Trichomonas vaginalis are pathogens that resides in the vagina in females and the urethra, epididymis, and swelling in the prostate gland in males. In women there is some yellowish discharge accompanied by itching and burning.

Malaria, the most prevalent and debilitating disease among the protozoa type is caused by Plasmodium. About two million people die annually from Malaria.

Cestodes (Tapeworms); bladder worms, pork tapeworms, broad fish, dog tapeworms, dwarf and rat tapeworms. Broad fish tapeworms may grow to 35 feet long and live ten years inside the persons intestines. Some tapeworms can lay as many as one million eggs per day. Their bodies are in separate segments with hooks and suction cups on their skull.

Trematodes (Flukes); Flatworms, bladder, blood, liver, lung, kidney and intestinal flukes. Human infections of flukes (Schistosomes) are in excess of 250 million worldwide. They can cause severe disease of the gastrointestinal tract, bladder, liver and destroy blood cells. Size varies from 1 to 2.5 centimeters in length (½ to 3 inches long).

Spirochetes are very tiny organisms that are spiral-shaped, and multiply in the blood and lymphatic system. Spirochetes (largest), Saprospira, Cristispira, Treponema (smallest), and many more. The host or carrier is usually lice, ticks, fleas, mites, and flying insects, which is then transmitted to humans. Spirochetes are responsible for relapsing fever, infectious jaundice, Lymes disease, sores, ulcers, Vincent angina and Wyles disease.

Some parasites worms have the ability to fool bodies into thinking they are normal part of the tissue or organ and the immune system will not fight off the intruders. When these alien invaders are established in our bodies, they do several things:

They can make Swiss cheese out of your organs. Worm infections can cause physical trauma by perforating (burrowing) the intestines, the circulatory system, the lungs, the liver or the whole bodies.

They can erode, damage or block certain organs by lumping together in balls or tumors. They can be mistaken for cancer tumors, and travel into the brain, heart and lungs.

They rob us of our vital vitamin and mineral nutrients, and amino acids needed for digestion. Some become anemic (anemia) and are drowsy after meals.

They give off certain metabolic waste products (toxic waste) that poison our bodies. This particular condition is called verminous intoxification. Most have trouble disposing of the toxins that are re-absorbed through the intestines. Your bodies have to work twice as hard to remove these toxic waste products.

Depresses the immune system, which leads to further degeneration, fatigue and illness.

They can destroy cells faster than cells can be regenerated.

Some conditions that promote parasitic infections are excess mucus, an imbalance in the intestinal flora, chronic constipation, and toxic internal environment.

Nose is supposed to act as the natural airway for respiration and the main inlet for oxygen. It also acts as an air conditioner, by filtering, moistening and warming the air that is breathed. The hairs and mucus membranes help prevent dust from entering the rest of the respiratory tract. The nose is responsible for smell and gives your voice its own characteristic tone.

Problems associated with the nose are sinus (sinusitis, an inflammation), nasal polyp and tumors. These can cause restrictions in the nasal passage hinder the amount of oxygen needed.

Bones surrounding the nose contain honeycomb (air filled cavities between the outer and inner layers of the skull) known as the facial sinuses. These comprise of 2 frontal, one sphenoid, 2 ethmoidal and 2 maxillary sinuses. Each sinus drains mucus into the nasal passages through tiny ducts or channels.

Sinus inflammation or infections can be caused by an abscess in an upper tooth or from bacteria and viruses. Parasites or candida can also take up residence in all those little nooks and crannies, and they are the hardest to eliminate. After time, the sinuses can become encrusted in toxic matter like in the colon. Mycoplasmas infecting the sinus will cause drainage with bad nasal odors. Swabbing the inside of the nose with one drop of Oil of Oregano on an ear swab may help over time.

Polyp or tumours, which bulge out into the nasal passage may also be filled with parasites. It is important to clear the nasal passages so you can breathe in the Breath of Life, more oxygen. Self-examination of the nasal passages is possible with small flash light held in the front of the nose and looking in the mirror. The airway should clear almost to the throat. If you can only see in about an inch, problems may exist.

Cleaning if required, dip an ear swab into 3 percent H_2O_2 and swab inside the nose. It may be necessary to plug the other side and breathe in slightly to get the hydrogen peroxide past the obstructions. Let it sit until the sinuses open and then blow out the excess mucus. Repeated use will show where parasites may be dwelling under the tissue by the bubbling and oxidation effect of the H_2O_2. With the aid of tweezers, it is possible to pull out the parasites and waste matter for disposal.

Another test for parasites is using black walnut oil on the swab. One or two drops are sufficient to start. If there is burning and twitching of the toes or it feels like rocks inside or scaling may appear on the outside are indications that parasites may exist. Applying ozonated oil or vitamin E on the dry skin will help soften the tissue.

Another method is direct applications of the ozone in the ears and in the nose. Insert the hose into each nostril while closing eyes and holding breath during each treatment. Sneezing will occur and the sinuses will open. Do as tolerated.

Extreme skin reactions can occur when drinking black walnut oil in water for the elimination of worms. When they are exposed to the oil, they will eliminate their toxins to protect their living environment. The poisons are absorbed into the blood causing rashes on the skin. To avoid this condition, start out slow and increase dosage over longer periods.

Treatments can be followed up by adding the oils to your vitamins and supplements for daily maintenance.

Humans with worm infections may feel bloated, tired or hungry, allergies, asthma, gas, digestive disorders, unclear thinking or feel toxic. Damage and symptoms will vary on the type of parasite infection.

Some people may not have any symptoms from infection. About 25 percent may only have some aches and pains that they can ignore. The quality of life and health may be compromised in another 55 percent. Those who are disabled from parasites are about 5 percent. In the USA, about 85 percent is infected with parasites.

PARASITE SIGNS, ADULTS, CHILDREN

Allergies, Many allergies are caused by worm infections. Tissue becomes inflamed and reactions to foods are the result when eosinophils (white blood cells) are increased due to them. Extreme skin rashes with blisters and food allergies or sensitivities may result.

- *Anemia,* Worms leach nutrients from bodies causing anemia. When they are present in large numbers, they can create enough blood loss to cause anemia or iron deficiency in some people.
- *Constipation,* Some worms can obstruct certain organs like the colon causing constipation, liver and the bile duct.
- *Diarrhea,* Most of the time diarrhea is nature's way of removing toxins.
- *Fatigue,* Symptoms include tiredness, flue-like symptoms, apathy, depression and lack of concentration.
- *Gas and Stomach Bloating,* Some parasites live in the upper intestine, which can cause both gas and stomach bloating.
- *Immune Dysfunction,* Parasites depress the immune system by decreasing immunoglobulin.
- *Nervousness,* The waste products from parasites irritate the nervous system, resulting in anxiety and restlessness.

Other Signs of Parasites in Children

Blisters appear on the inside of the lower lip, wiping of the nose, restlessness and grinding of the teeth at night, dark circles under the eyes, hyperactive, bed wetting, headaches, sensitive to light, twitching eyelid, gum, rectum, or nose bleeding are signs they may have parasites.

There are many natural foods, herbal cleansing products, and essential oils that one can take to rid themselves of worms. When taking herbal combinations, it is best taking them on an empty stomach. The best way to treat parasitic infection is to detoxify using good nutritional rebuilding programmes that will restore balance and the immune system. Everyone infected with worms is deficient in the essential nutrients. All essential vitamin and mineral supplements are necessary.

If parasites are the problem, it is very important to take larger doses of plant-derived nutrients due to deficiencies. Some worms suck your vitamins and minerals directly out of the blood. Others absorb your nutrients through their outer skin layer. The nutrients need replacing daily.

High carbohydrate diet, low in protein, and high in alkaline has been found to make parasitic infections worse. Sugar should also be avoided because parasites thrive on it and it is possible you could have candida. This candida or yeast infections create an environment in the colon that equals the environment needed for them to thrive. Foods that lower pH from high alkaline conditions in the colon are apple cider vinegar and cranberry juice.

Pumpkin seeds and onions mixed with soy milk is another remedy for worms. Herbal combinations for blood flukes are milkweed, pennyroyal and black walnut. Herbal combinations for liver flukes are cloves, goldenrod and goldenseal root. Bitter melon is effective against pinworms. Fasting on raw pineapples for three days helps with tapeworms.

Another remedy for prevention is mixing one or two teaspoons of apple cider vinegar in one glass of water. Alternatively, you can take one tablespoon daily of 1 part apple cider vinegar, 2 parts apple juice, 1 part apple brandy.

Constipation problems can be helped with friendly bacteria, cascara sagrada bark, chamomile tea, or elder flowers. Licorice added to herbal teas has slight laxative action.

Liquid multi vitamin and mineral nutrients derived from plants like those found in Tropical Sunrise will help clean and replace your vital nutrients. The OXY-MEGA oxygen supplement is more effective against parasites and cleaning the intestinal tract than herbs. High doses of herbs may make them retreat to the colon but to kill and eliminate the parasites you need to flush them out by colon irrigation and ozone.

One can save money and create your own herb formulas by buying herbs in bulk, capsules, and capsule machine for filling the capsules. Mix the herbs equally and purchase high quality only. The book, The Breath of Life contains most all the herbs with anti-parasitic properties and the herbal combinations for mixing.

PREVENT, ELIMINATE PARASITES

Healthy immune system is the best defense against parasites and disease. Some of the things you can do to reduce the risk of parasitic infections are:

- Wash all fruits and vegetables. Scrape off the wax substance on the outer surface on any fruit or vegetable with knife before washing. Anything with nicks or recess can harbor just about anything and should be cut out. Avoid eating grapes with open splits. Washing in ozonated water, hydrogen peroxide (1 teaspoon per gallon of water), or bleach (add 1/2 teaspoon to each gallon and soak for 10 minutes) will kill parasites. Rinse well after to remove bleach residue. Some prefer to wash them in chlorinated water, but these things are organic in nature. Chlorine and organics do not go well together because of the carcinogenic compounds that are produced.
- Thoroughly cook meats and fish. Do not eat raw or uncooked meats or fish. Check for worms, especially on fish. Spray with hydrogen peroxide or wash in ozonated water before cooking. Keep all work surfaces clean.
- Drink pure water. Parasites are associated with many water-borne outbreaks and are highly resistant to conventional methods of disinfecting. Water that is properly purified with ozone is free of parasites.
- Practice good personal hygiene. Wash your hands before eating and after going to the bathroom, changing diapers, or handling pets. Keep your fingernails short and clean. Parasites can live for two months under the fingernails.
- Keep your living environment clean. Breathing the dust in your house can contain human skin, soil particles, or fecal material from dust mites and cockroaches. An easy test to determine if this is the problem is by looking across the room when the sunlight is shining through the window and checking for particles floating in the air. Then let the kids run around and recheck. The elimination of carpets reduces this problem considerably.

- Do not walk barefoot on warm, moist soil or while working in the garden. Parasites are abundant in soil and can absorb (penetrate) through skin cells. Fertilizers are added to garden soil and its the pets favorite place to go. Use gloves and shoes for protection.
- Swimming in rivers, lakes, ponds, or public swimming pools. Avoid swallowing or drinking the water while swimming anywhere. Avoid swimming if cuts or open sores are present.
- If pets are infested with parasites, de-worm and keep them outside. You are at higher risk in contracting worms when pets are allowed indoors. Dogs and cats are host to many parasites that humans can contract. Garlic added to their food will help control some parasites. Animals can spread 240 diseases to humans because of parasites.
- Overuse of antibiotics. Reducing the numbers of friendly bacteria in the colon allows for the proliferation of parasites.
- Global travel. Ten years ago, you might have been at higher risk for parasite infections when traveling to another country. Today, you may be at higher risk to infection by staying home.
- Use more cloves with every meal. Adding some cloves to foods will help kill the eggs from parasites in the intestinal tract. Cloves added to coffee or herbal teas adds better taste.
- Total annihilation of these invaders you have to get serious and declare all out war and fight back with the most powerful weapons in your arsenal. Your best defense is knowledge; knowing the enemy and the harm they cause. Then, attack with all the weapons that follow without letting up, and you will be the victor instead of the victim.

Most effective treatment or cleansing product for the elimination of parasites in the large intestine is to cleanse the colon with ozonated water and hydrogen peroxide by colonic irrigation. This method is extremely lethal to all types of bad bacteria, food pathogens, parasites and viruses. As the colon becomes cleaner, the ozone and oxygen will reach other organs where parasites may be problems. The least expensive treatment is OXY-MEGA colon cleanser.

Why does ozone work so well? Healthy cells and friendly bacteria are aerobic, which means they need oxygen to survive. Unhealthy cells, parasites, pathogens and viruses are anaerobic, they can only survive in non oxygenated environments. Change their living environment and you win the war.

No one knows the total number or types of parasites living in our environment. They hardly ever get full credit for the destruction they do to the human bodies. Only few get credit for the people they harm.

High infection rate in the USA is surprising to many, but most of these creatures have always been living within our bodies. When the immune system weakens, they can grow to numbers that cause physical harm.

People poison their bodies with chemicals, drugs, processed and over cooked foods, it starts the process that allows the parasites to take over our inner environment. When they take over, they are in control, whether you know it or not. When we make the wrong choices and do not take preventive measures, they win.

Are Parasites Having This Cocktail Party in Your Intestinal Tract?

Breath of Life describes detoxification in depth with self cleansing products, techniques and illustrations on the colon, parasites, and directions for making your own board for home colonics. It also describes how to keep in balance using ozone with other natural remedies and the risk factors we all face in our daily life.

Brief summary and contents of the New Revised 2007 Edition is available in The Breath of Life section where you can purchase by credit card for 20.00. This book could SAVE YOUR LIFE! To receive the book go to the book order in the contents.

We are proud to announce the first affordable ozonator, the AOS-1M. The AOS-1M is perhaps the smallest and most inexpensive type corona discharge ozonator on the market. This powerful little unit in white plastic enclosure comes standard with variable control for adjustable output. It can be used to purify your drinking water or any other useful application.

Index

A

A. astronyxis, 99
A. australis, 194
A. *culbertsoni*, 98
A. trachomatis, 133
Aberrant parasites, 179
Acanthamoeba rhysodes, 99
Acanthamoeba, 97, 98-100
AIDS, 1, 27, 104, 139
American Society for Microbiology News, 3
Antimicrobial chemotherapy, 73-96
    bacterial cytoplasmic membranes, 80-86
    biochemical basis of antimicrobial action, 76
    combinations of antimicrobial agents, 94-96
    inhibition of bacterial cell wall synthesis, 76-79
    introduction, 73-75
    resistance due to altered receptors, 87-94
Arachne, 184
Arthropod, 213-215
Arthurdendyus triangulates, 32
Ascaris lumbricoides, 1

B

Balamuthia mandrillaris, 98
Balantidium coli, 68, 184

C

Candida albicans, 133, 136
Candida, 94
Centers for Disease Control and Prevention, 168
Centers for Disease Control in Atlanta, 3
Chemotherapy, 73-96
Chlamydia, 84, 95
Chlamydia trachomatis, 132, 133, 144
Clostridium difficile, 96
Clostridium, 89
Commensalisms, 177
Cryptococcus, 94
Cryptococcus neoformans, 97
Cryptosporidium parvuym, 70
Cx. pipiens, 150

D

Damon diadema, 188
Darwin, Charles, 66
DDT, 154
Different parasites, 176-197
    acarina, 186-190
    arachnid, 184-186
    classifying parasites, 181
    introduction, 176-177

life cycles of parasites, 178-181
major classes of parasites, 181-184
mutualism, 177-178
palpigradi, 190
phalangiotarbida, 191
pseudoscorpions, 191-192
ricinulei, 192-193
schizomida, 193
scorpions, 193-195
solifugae, 195
transmission of parasites, 178-181
trigonotarbida, 196
uropygi, 196-197

E

Entamoeba, 100
Entamoeba coli, 1
Enterobacter aerogenes, 97
Enterococcus faecalis, 94, 133
Environmental Protection Agency (EPA), 167
Escherchia coli, 97, 131, 133, 145
Euhaplorchis californiensis, 13

F

Facultative parasites, 180
Free-living amoebae, 97-101
acanthamoeba, 98-100
rhizopoda, 100-101
free-living, 98-100
introduction, 97-98

G

Gardnerella vaginalis, 138
Genitourinary system, 130-146
Giardia canis, 184
Giardia cati, 184
Giardia lamblia, 67, 206, 208
Gibberella fujikuroi, 17

H

Haemophilus, 84, 93
Haemophilus ducreyi, 140
Health Ministry of Brazil, 201
Human Immunodeficiency Virus (HIV), 131
Human intestinal parasites worms, 222-234
introduction, 222-223
parasite signs, adults, children, 228-230
–, some different varieties, 224-228
prevent, eliminate parasites, 231-234
Hymenolepiasis, 164
Hymenolepis nana, 204, 208

I

Introduction, 1-6
Ixodes scapularis, 166

K

Kala-azar, 66
Klebsiella pneumoniae, 95

L

Legionella, 84
Leishmania donovani, 66

M

Malaria Vaccine Development, 114
Malaria, 102-129
Malarial Multiple Antigen Peptide vaccine, 128
Malarial parasite, 105-108
McConnell, 35, 36
Medical Research Council, 128

Microbiology of the genitourinary system, 130-146
clinical manifestations, 139-140
– presentation, 136
epididymitis, 133-136
etiology, 136-137
introduction, 130-132
microbiologic diagnosis, 138, 145
pathogenesis, 140-141
phasic variation of E. coli in urinary tract infections, 145
prevention and treatment, 139
urethritis, 133-136
urinary tract infections, 131-133, 145
Monogenea, 61-63
Mutualism, 177
Mycoplasma, 84

N

Naegleria fowleri, 97
Naegleria, 97
National Centre for Health Statistics, 200
Neisseria gonorrhoeae, 130, 137

O

Obligatory parasites, 180

P

P. falciparum, 103, 105
P. vivax, 113
P. yoelii, 106
Palpal chelae, 191
Palpigradi, 190
Parasites, 176-197
Parasites worms, 222-234
Parasitic protozoa, 64-72
giardia, 67
introduction, 64
leishmaniasis, 66-67
malaria, 71-72
sickle-cell anemia, 72
trichomonas vaginalis, 64
trypanosome, 64-66
Parasitic worm, 30-63
acanthocephalan, 48-54
cestoda, 54-55
digenea, 55-61
flatworm, 31-36
introduction, 30-31
leech, 42-48
monogenea, 61-63
nematode, 36-42
Parasitism, 7-29
adaptation, 12
ecology, 10-12
evolutionary aspects, 8-10
introduction, 7-8
parasitic fungi, 16-22
parasitic plants, 22-27
– protests, 27-29
parasitoid, 15-16
roles in ecosystems, 13-14
transmission, 12-13
types of parasitism, 8
Parasitoid wasp, 210-221
arthropod, 213-215
introduction, 210
molting, 217-218
systematics, 211-213
taxonomy and systematics, 210-211
Parasitosis in children, 198-209
Ascaris lumbricoides, 206-209
discussion, 205-206

introduction, 198-199
results, 202-205
study groups and methods, 200-202
Periodic parasites, 180
Phalangiotarbida, 191
Phoradendron pauciflorum, 26
Phyllocoptes variabilis, 186
Pilostyles thurberi, 26
Plasmodium brassicae, 18
Plasmodium falciparum, 124, 128, 129
Plasmodium vivax, 103, 105
Plasmodium, 7, 106
Pneumocystis carinii, 1
Progne subis, 155
Protection from malaria, 102-129
anchoring of infected RBC to the vascular endothelial cells, 108-111
challenges in formulating an effective malarial vaccine, 117-118
complications in malarial infections, 111
introduction, 102-105
parasitic complexity, 118-129
pathophysiology and lifecycle to the malarial parasite, 105-108
Proteus mirabilis, 132
Pseudomonas aeruginosa, 131
Pseudomonas, 90
Pseudoscorpions, 191-192
Pulex irritans, 160

R

Reuter, O.M., 14
Rhizopoda, 100-101
Ricinulei, 192-193

S

S. epidermidis, 92
Schistosoma mansoni, 199
Schistosoma, 61
Schizomida, 193
Scorpions, 193-195
Serratia marscesens, 144
Solifugae, 195
Staphyloccus aureus, 87, 89
Streptococcus pneumoniae, 87

T

T. canis, 181
T. cruzi, 66
T. deformans, 19
T. gambiense, 65
T. spiralis nelsoni, 172
Thompson, 35
Tissue nematodes, 172-175
introduction, 172-174
Toxoplasma gondii, 2, 69
Toxorhynchites, 149
Treponema pallidum, 130
Trichinella spiralis, 174, 175
Trichinella, 172
Trichomonas vaginalis, 64, 130, 225
Trichomonas, 139
Trigonotarbida, 196

U

United States, 3
Urinary tract infections, 131-133, 145
Uropygi, 196-197
US Army Medical Corps, 152
US Center for Disease Control, 155
US Department of Agriculture in 1945, 156

USA, 228

V

Vector, 147-171
biological aspects, 170-171
evolution and classification, 162-165
FLEA, 159-160
introduction, 147-148
morphology and behaviour, 160-161
mosquito, 148-149
mosquitoes and health, 151
natural predators, 157-158
tick, 165-167
treatment of mosquito bites, 158-159
triatominae, 169-170
Voyage of the Beagle, 170

W

West Nile Virus, 153
Wheeler, W.M., 14
World Health Organization (WHO), 27, 104, 155, 200

❑❑❑